Scripting Recipes for Second Life

Scripting Recipes for Second Life

by Jeff Heaton

Heaton Research, Inc.
St. Louis

Scripting Recipes for Second Life

First printing

Publisher: Heaton Research, Inc

Author: Jeff Heaton

Editor: Mark Biss

Cover Art: Carrie Spear

```
ISBN's for all Editions:
1-6043900-0-X, Softcover
1-6043900-1-8, Adobe PDF e-book
```

SOFTWARE LICENSE AGREEMENT: TERMS AND CONDITIONS

The media and/or any online materials accompanying this book that are available now or in the future contain programs and/or text files (the "Software") to be used in connection with the book. Heaton Research, Inc. hereby grants to you a license to use and distribute software programs that make use of the compiled binary form of this book's source code. You may not redistribute the source code contained in this book, without the written permission of Heaton Research, Inc. Your purchase, acceptance, or use of the Software will constitute your acceptance of such terms.

The Software compilation is the property of Heaton Research, Inc. unless otherwise indicated and is protected by copyright to Heaton Research, Inc. or other copyright owner(s) as indicated in the media files (the "Owner(s)"). You are hereby granted a license to use and distribute the Software for your personal, noncommercial use only. You may not reproduce, sell, distribute, publish, circulate, or commercially exploit the Software, or any portion thereof, without the written consent of Heaton Research, Inc. and the specific copyright owner(s) of any component software included on this media.

In the event that the Software or components include specific license requirements or end-user agreements, statements of condition, disclaimers, limitations or warranties ("End-User License"), those End-User Licenses supersede the terms and conditions herein as to that particular Software component. Your purchase, acceptance, or use of the Software will constitute your acceptance of such End-User Licenses.

By purchase, use or acceptance of the Software you further agree to comply with all export laws and regulations of the United States as such laws and regulations may exist from time to time.

SOFTWARE SUPPORT

Components of the supplemental Software and any offers associated with them may be supported by the specific Owner(s) of that material but they are not supported by Heaton Research, Inc.. Information regarding any available support may be obtained from the Owner(s) using the information provided in the appropriate README files or listed elsewhere on the media.

Should the manufacturer(s) or other Owner(s) cease to offer support or decline to honor any offer, Heaton Research, Inc. bears no responsibility. This notice concerning support for the Software is provided for your information only. Heaton Research, Inc. is not the agent or principal of the Owner(s), and Heaton Research, Inc. is in no way responsible for providing any support for the Software, nor is it liable or responsible for any support provided, or not provided, by the Owner(s).

WARRANTY

Heaton Research, Inc. warrants the enclosed media to be free of physical defects for a period of ninety (90) days after purchase. The Software is not available from Heaton Research, Inc. in any other form or media than that enclosed herein or posted to www.heatonresearch.com. If you discover a defect in the media during this warranty period, you may obtain a replacement of identical format at no charge by sending the defective media, postage prepaid, with proof of purchase to:

```
Heaton Research, Inc.
Customer Support Department
1734 Clarkson Rd #107
Chesterfield, MO 63017-4976

Web: www.heatonresearch.com
E-Mail: support@heatonresearch.com
```

After the 90-day period, you can obtain replacement media of identical format by sending us the defective disk, proof of purchase, and a check or money order for $10, payable to Heaton Research, Inc..

DISCLAIMER

Heaton Research, Inc. makes no warranty or representation, either expressed or implied, with respect to the Software or its contents, quality, performance, merchantability, or fitness for a particular purpose. In no event will Heaton Research, Inc., its distributors, or dealers be liable to you or any other party for direct, indirect, special, incidental, consequential, or other damages arising out of the use of or inability to use the Software or its contents even if advised of the possibility of such damage. In the event that the Software includes an online update feature, Heaton Research, Inc. further disclaims any obligation to provide this feature for any specific duration other than the initial posting.

The exclusion of implied warranties is not permitted by some states. Therefore, the above exclusion may not apply to you. This warranty provides you with specific legal rights; there may be other rights that you may have that vary from state to state. The pricing of the book with the Software by Heaton Research, Inc. reflects the allocation of risk and limitations on liability contained in this agreement of Terms and Conditions.

SHAREWARE DISTRIBUTION

This Software may contain various programs that are distributed as shareware. Copyright laws apply to both shareware and ordinary commercial software, and the copyright Owner(s) retains all rights. If you try a shareware program and continue using it, you are expected to register it. Individual programs differ on details of trial periods, registration, and payment. Please observe the requirements stated in appropriate files.

*This book is dedicated to
Encog Dod, for all his
help with this book.*

Acknowledgments

There are several people who I would like to acknowledge. First, I would like to thank the many people who have given me suggestions and comments on my Second Life scripts.

I would like to thank WordsRU.com for providing editing resources. I would like to thank Mark Biss for editing the book.

I would like to thank my sister Carrie Spear for layout and formatting suggestions.

Contents at a Glance

Introduction XXXI
Chapter 1: Introduction to LSL 35
Chapter 2: String Handling 49
Chapter 3: Components for Buildings 67
Chapter 4: Particle Effects 99
Chapter 5: Vehicles 123
Chapter 6: Scanners 177
Chapter 7: Miscellaneous Recipes 195
Chapter 8: Commerce 223
Chapter 9: Rental Property 269
Chapter 10: Weapons 289
Chapter 11: Wearable Objects 317
Appendix A: Downloading Examples 345
Appendix B: Built In Animations 347
Appendix C: Event Functions... 351

Contents

Introduction XXXI
Chapter 1: Introduction to LSL 35
   State Machines...35
   Handling Events..37
   Communicating 38
   Modifying Objects 40
   Understanding Dialogs..41
   Implementing Basic Security..43
   Summary 46
Chapter 2: String Handling 49
   Recipe 2.1: String Comparison 49
   Recipe 2.2: String Sets 56
   Recipe 2.3: String Parsing..61
   Summary 64
Chapter 3: Components for Buildings 67
   Recipe 3.1: Splashing Water 67
   Recipe 3.2: Open Door..70
   Recipe 3.3: Owner Locked Door 76
   Recipe 3.4: Multi-User Lockable Door 79
   Variables Needed for the Door..85
   Recipe 3.5: Teleport Pad 88
   Recipe 3.6: Elevator..90
   Summary 96
Chapter 4: Particle Effects..99
   Recipe 4.1: Basic Particle Emitter...99
   Recipe 4.2: Chimney..106
   Recipe 4.3: Leaf Generator 110
   Recipe 4.4: Jewelry 114
   Recipe 4.5: Explosion..118
   Summary 121
Chapter 5: Vehicles 123
   Recipe 5.1: Car..124
   Recipe 5.2: Boat..143

Recipe 5.3: Helicopter 157
Recipe 5.4: Super Car 167
Summary 174
Chapter 6: Scanners 177
Recipe 6.1: Avatar Radar 178
Recipe 6.2: Notecard Giver 182
Recipe 6.3: Automatic Door 184
Recipe 6.4: Traffic Scanner 187
Summary 193
Chapter 7: Miscellaneous Recipes 195
Recipe 7.1: Avatar Cannon 195
Recipe 7.2: Analog Clock 199
Recipe 7.3: Weather Station 202
Recipe 7.4: Slide Show 205
Recipe 7.5: Notecard Controlled Slide Show 207
Recipe 7.6: Announcer Script 211
Recipe 7.7: Online Indicator 214
Summary 221
Chapter 8: Commerce 223
Recipe 8.1: Camping Pad 223
Recipe 8.2: Simple Tip Jar 238
Recipe 8.3: Club Tip Jar 243
Recipe 8.4: Vendor Script 257
Summary 266
Chapter 9: Rental Property 269
Recipe 9.1: Rental Script 270
Other Rental Considerations 284
Summary 286
Chapter 10: Weapons 289
Recipe 10.1: Basic Gun 290
Recipe 10.2: Multi Bullet Gun 300
Bullets for the Multi Bullet Gun..306
Summary 314
Chapter 11: Wearable Objects 317
Recipe 11.1: Parachute 317
Recipe 11.2: HUD Parachute...328
Recipe 11.3: Jet Pack 334
Recipe 11.4: Anti-Push Bracelet 340

Summary 343
Appendix A: Downloading Examples 345
Appendix B: Built In Animations 347
Appendix C: Event Functions..351

Table of Figures

Figure 1.1: Second Life Dialogs..42
Figure 1.2: Setting the Group of an Object..45
Figure 3.1: Beach Front Land in Second Life...68
Figure 3.2: Swimming Pool...69
Figure 3.3: Door with Center..71
Figure 3.4: An Elevator...91
Figure 4.1: Basic Particle Emitter...100
Figure 4.2: Chimney..107
Figure 4.3: Fall Leafs..111
Figure 4.4: Jewelry...115
Figure 4.5: Explosion 118
Figure 5.1: Second Life Vehicles..124
Figure 5.2: A Car in Second Life...125
Figure 5.3: Setting the Material Type..126
Figure 5.4: A Car with Two Passengers..140
Figure 5.5: A Boat in Second Life...144
Figure 5.6: A Boat with Wake...156
Figure 5.7: A Helicopter..157
Figure 6.1: Avatar Radar...179
Figure 6.2: Notecard Giver..182
Figure 6.3: Automatic Door...185
Figure 6.4: Traffic Scanner...188
Figure 7.1: Avatar Cannon..196
Figure 7.2: Analog Clock...199
Figure 7.3: Weather Station..202
Figure 7.4: Slide Show..205
Figure 7.5: Online Indicator..214
Figure 8.1: Traffic...224
Figure 8.2: A Camping Pad...225
Figure 8.3: A Tip Jar...238
Figure 8.4: A Pay Dialog...244
Figure 8.5: A Second Life Store..257
Figure 8.6: Using a Vendor Script...258
Figure 9.1: An Apartment Building...269
Figure 9.2: The Primary Door..271
Figure 9.3: The Secondary Door...283

Figure 9.4: Setting a Landing Point 285

Figure 10.1: An Area that Allows Damage 290

Figure 10.2: Mouselook Mode 291

Figure 10.3: Holding a Gun 292

Figure 10.4: Basic Bullet 298

Figure 10.5: Load the Gun 301

Figure 10.6: An Avatar in a Cage 313

Figure 11.1: Wearing a Parachute 318

Figure 11.2: Parachuting in Second Life 319

Figure 11.3: Avatar on the Ground at Low Altitude...323

Figure 11.4: Avatar on the Ground at High Altitude 324

Figure 11.5: A HUD Display 329

Figure 11.6: A Jet Pack 334

Table of Listings

Listing 2.1: String Comparison (StringCompare.lsl)..49

Listing 2.2: String Set Comparison (StringSetCompare.lsl) 56

Listing 2.3: String Parsing (StringParse.lsl)..61

Listing 3.1: Splashing Water (Splash.lsl) 69

Listing 3.2: Open Door (OpenDoor.lsl) 71

Listing 3.3: Owner Locked Door (OwnerLockedDoor.lsl) 77

Listing 3.4: Multi-User Lockable Door (SmartDoor.lsl)................................80

Listing 3.5: Teleport Pad (Teleport.lsl)..88

Listing 3.6: Elevator Car (Elevator.lsl) 91

Listing 3.7: Call Elevator (Call.lsl) 96

Listing 4.1: Basic Particle Emitter (BasicParticle.lsl) 100

Listing 4.2: Chimney (Smoke.lsl) 107

Listing 4.3: Fall Leafs (Leafs.lsl) 111

Listing 4.4: Jewelry (Bling.lsl)...115

Listing 4.5: Explosion (Explode.lsl) 118

Listing 5.1: Main Car Script for the Root Prim (Car.lsl) 127

Listing 5.2: Car Passenger Seat (CarSeat.lsl) 140

Listing 5.3: Can't Sit Here (DontSitHere.lsl)...140

Listing 5.4: Car Wheel (WheelScript.lsl)..142

Listing 5.5: The Boat Script (Boat.lsl) 144

Listing 5.6: Boat Wake (BoatWake.lsl) 153

Listing 5.7: Helicopter Script (Helicopter.lsl)...158

Listing 5.8: Helicopter Rotors (Blade.lsl) 166

Listing 5.9: The Super Car (SuperCar.lsl) 167

Listing 6.1: Avatar Radar (Radar.lsl) 179

Listing 6.2: Notecard Giver (NotecardGiver.lsl)...182

Listing 6.3: Automatic Door (AutoDoor.lsl) 185

Listing 6.4: Traffic Scanner (TrafficScanner.lsl) 188

Listing 7.1: Avatar Cannon (Cannon.lsl)..196

Listing 7.2: Analog Clock (AnalogClock.lsl)...200

Listing 7.3: Weather Station (Weather.lsl)..203

Listing 7.4: Slide Show (SlideShow.lsl)...205

Listing 7.5: Slide Control Notecard (SlideControl.not) 208

Listing 7.6: A Notecard Controlled Slide Show (NotecardSlideShow.lsl) 208

Listing 7.7: An Announcer Script (NotecardReader.lsl) 211

Listing 7.8: Online Indicator (OnlineIndicator.lsl) 214

Listing 8.1: Camping Pad Configuration (CampConfig.not) 225

Listing 8.2: Camping Pad Dancing (CampDance.lsl) 226

Listing 8.3: Camping Pad Control (Camp.lsl) 229

Listing 8.4: Simple Tip Jar (TipJar.lsl) 239

Listing 8.5: Club Tip Jar (ClubTipJar.not) 243

Listing 8.6: Club Tip Jar (TipJarClub.lsl) 244

Listing 8.7: Vendor Notecard (Vendor.not) 258

Listing 8.8: Main Vendor Script (Vendor.not) 259

Listing 8.9: The Forward Button (VendorForward.lsl) 265

Listing 8.10: The Backward Button (VendorBack.lsl) 265

Listing 8.11: The Buy Button (VendorBuy.lsl) 265

Listing 10.1: Basic Gun (BasicGun.lsl) 292

Listing 10.2: Basic Bullet (BulletBasic.lsl) 298

Listing 10.3: Multi Bullet Gun (MultiGun.lsl) 301

Listing 10.4: Blank Bullet (BulletBlank.lsl) 306

Listing 10.5: 20% Bullet (Bullet20.lsl) 307

Listing 10.6: Kill Bullet (BulletKill.lsl) 308

Listing 10.7: Explosion Bullet (BulletExplode.lsl) 309

Listing 10.8: Push Bullet (BulletPush.lsl) 311

Listing 10.9: Cage Bullet (BulletCage.lsl) 313

Listing 11.1: Parachute (Parachute.lsl) 319

Listing 11.2: HUD Parachute (ParachuteHUD.lsl) 329

Listing 11.3: Close Parachute (ParaClose.lsl) 333

Listing 11.4: Open Parachute (ParaOpen.lsl) 333

Listing 11.5: Jet Pack (JetPack.lsl) 334

Listing 11.6: Anti Push Script (NoPush.lsl) 340

Table of Tables

Table 1.1: Communication Distances..40

Table 4.1: PSYS_PART_FLAGS Flags 103

Table 4.2: PSYS_SRC_PATTERN Values...104

Table 4.3: Remaining Particle Emitter Name-Value Pairs 105

Table 4.4: Parameters for fakeMakeExplosion 120

Table 5.1: Vehicle Types 135

Table 5.2: Floating Point Vehicle Parameters..136

Table 5.3: Vector Vehicle Parameters 137

Table 5.4: Rotation Point Vehicle Parameters 138

Table 5.4: Vector Vehicle Parameters 149

Table 6.1: Scan Types 177

Table 10.1: Bullet Types 300

INTRODUCTION

This book provides many reusable recipes for the Linden Scripting Language (LSL). These recipes can be used as fully functioning objects in Second Life, or they can be used as starting points for other projects. The recipes presented in the book span a wide range of scripts that are commonly programmed in Second Life.

Chapter 1 begins the book by introducing the Linden Scripting Language. This chapter is not intended to teach the Linden Scripting Language. Rather, this chapter will give a general overview of the Linden Scripting Language to someone who already has previous programming experience.

Chapter 2 introduces several useful functions. These useful functions can be reused in many different scripting projects. These functions will be used by many of the recipes later in this book. Functions are provided that process both numbers and strings.

Chapter 3 introduces scripts for buildings. Buildings are a major part of Second Life. Scripts can greatly enhance a buildings utility. Scripts often control doors, elevators and other aspects of a building. This chapter also shows how to create "fake" water above sea level. Additionally, a teleport pad is introduced that can quickly transport a user anywhere in the building.

Chapter 4 introduces particle effects. Particles allow explosions, smoke, glisten effects and many other visual effects. Scripts are provided that produces explosions, falling leaves. Particles can also be used to create flashy jewelry.

Chapter 5 introduces vehicles. This chapter shows how to create land, air and sea vehicles. A car is used to demonstrate land vehicles. A helicopter is used to demonstrate air vehicles. A boat is used to demonstrate water vehicles. Additionally, a super car is provided that shares characteristics of a car, boat and helicopter.

Chapter 6 introduces scanner scripts. Scanners allow the script to be aware of the world around it. Scanners usually scan for avatars around them. However, scanners can also scan for objects. This chapter shows how to create a notecard giver, a traffic monitor, and an automatic door. All of these make use of scanners.

Chapter 7 introduces several miscellaneous scripts that did not fall into other categories. Yet some of their techniques will be built upon in the remaining chapters of the book. This chapter shows how to create slideshows and a cannon to shoot an avatar from. An online status indicator is also presented that displays the availability of an avatar. An analog clock, with moving hands, is also demonstrated. This chapter also introduces how to use notecards as configuration files.

Chapter 8 introduces commerce scripts. Commerce occurs when any two Second Life users exchange money. This is a very important part of Second Life. This chapter shows how to create a vendor, for a store, as well as tip jars. Chapter 9 continues discussion of e-commerce by showing how to create an apartment rental script.

Chapter 10 introduces weapon scripts. Weapons inflict damage on avatars. An avatar has a health rating form 0 to 100%. If this value drops to zero, then the avatar dies. Death is no big deal in Second Life, an avatar simply teleports back to its home location when it dies. This chapter focuses on guns and bullets. The type of bullet fired is more important than the gun that fires it. This chapter provides bullets that damage avatars, as well as blanks that do no damage. Additionally, bullets are provided that trap and push avatars.

Chapter 11 introduces scripts that can be used with wearable objects. This chapter includes scripts for anti-push bracelets, jet packs and parachutes.

The examples are listed in this book. However, it is not necessary to type them out. All recipes can be obtained, from Second Life, in fully working form. To obtain any of the recipes, visit the Heaton Research HQ on Encogia Island. The Heaton Research HQ can be found at the following location.

`http://slurl.com/secondlife/Encogia/200/196/23`

CHAPTER 1: INTRODUCTION TO LSL

- Understanding State Machines
- Implementing Basic Security
- Changing the Appearance of an Object
- Communicating
- Using Dialogs

This book is designed for those who understand the basics of building and scripting in Second Life. For these people this book will provide many useful Linden Scripting Language (LSL) examples. These examples are very useful in their own right, but also serve as starting points for more complex Linden Scripting Language projects.

Chapter 1 begins with a quick review of the Linden Scripting Language. This chapter is not designed to teach the Linden Scripting Language to someone without programming experience. If you have already programmed a language, e.g.., C, C++, Java or C#, this chapter will provide sufficient introduction to the Linden Scripting Language to get you started.

If you have no programming experience, review one of the many tutorials for the Linden Scripting Language. A Google search on "LSL Tutorial" will reveal a few.

This chapter will now introduce the Linden Scripting Language, beginning with state machines.

State Machines

The concept of a state machine is not unique to Second Life. State machines are a common programming paradigm. However, no language makes the concept of a state machine as integral as the Linden Scripting Language. Many of the recipes in this book use state machines. As a result, it is very important to understand the concept of a state machine.

To see state machines in action, consider the default script, which is automatically generated by Second Life, when a new script is created. This script is shown here.

```
default
{
    state_entry()
    {
        llSay(0, "Hello, Avatar!");
    }
```

```
    touch_start(integer total_number)
    {
        llSay(0, "Touched.");
    }
}
```

This script starts with the word **default**. The word **default** specifies the name of the state that the enclosed code belongs to. For this script there is only one state. This state, which is named **default**, is the starting state for any script in Second Life.

Many scripts are constructed entirely within their **default** state. This is often bad design in Second Life. Consider the following script, which implements a simple switch that can be turned on or off.

```
integer value;

default
{
    state_entry()
    {
        value = TRUE;
    }

    touch_start(integer total_number)
    {
        if( value==TRUE )
        {
            llSay(0,"On");
            value = FALSE;
        }
        else
        {
            llSay(0,"Off");
            value = TRUE;
        }
    }
}
```

As can be seen, a global variable, named **value**, is set to either **TRUE** or **FALSE**. As the user touches the object, the object will say either "On" or "Off". As the object is touched these values alternate. Also, a note on global variables. Global variables are normally considered bad programming practice. However in Second Life, there is really little choice as to whether to use them or not. Because the Linden Scripting Language does not support user defined classes, global variables are the primary way for a script to hold values long-term.

This same functionality could be created using a state machine. The following lines of code do this.

```
default
{
    touch_start(integer total_number)
    {
        llSay(0,"On");
        state off;
    }
}

state off
{
    touch_start(integer total_number)
    {
        llSay(0,"Off");
        state default;
    }
}
```

The above code creates a second state, named **off**. This gives the above script two states: **default** and **off**. Both states contain their own **touch_start** event handler. Both states use the **state** command to switch to the opposite state when the object is touched.

The Linden Scripting Language is optimized for state engines. Because of this, state engines should be used when possible.

Handling Events

The last section showed how the **touch_start** function is called whenever an avatar touches an object. The **touch_start** function is an event handler. Second Life includes many different event handlers. The recipes in this book make use of many of these event handlers.

There are many different event handlers in the Linden Scripting Language. Appendix C, "Event Types" provides a listing of all of the event types in the Linden Scripting Language.

Another very common event type is the **timer** event. Many of the recipes in this book use **timer** events. The following script uses **timer** events.

```
default
{
    state_entry()
    {
        llSetTimerEvent(1);
    }
```

```
touch_start(integer total_number)
{
    llSetTimerEvent(0);
}

timer()
{
    llSay(0,"Timer");
}
}
```

The above script starts with a **state_entry** event handler. The **state_entry** event handler is called when the object enters the state associated with the event handler. In this case, the **state_entry** event handler is called when the **default** state is entered.

The provided **state_entry** event handler begins by calling the **llSetTimerEvent** function to establish a timer. The parameter passed to the **llSetTimerEvent** function call specifies the number of seconds between timer events. To disable the timer call the **llSetTimerEvent** function with a value of zero.

Every time a **timer** event occurs, the **timer** event handler is called. The above script says "Timer" each time that the timer event occurs.

Communicating

Objects in Second Life can communicate in many of the same ways that avatars communicate. Objects listen to conversations going on around them. Objects can also speak and participate in those conversations. Additionally, objects can send instant messages to avatars. However, instant messages between an avatar and an object are one-way. An avatar cannot send an instant message back to an object.

The following script demonstrates how an object can listen to conversations going on around it. The object will wait for someone to say either "hello" or "goodbye". Once the object detects either of these words, the object makes an appropriate greeting to the avatar that spoke to the object.

```
integer CHANNEL = 0;

default
{
    state_entry()
    {
        llListen(CHANNEL, "", NULL_KEY, "");
    }
```

```
listen(integer channel, string name, key id,
  string message)
{
    if( llToLower(message) == "hello" )
    {
        llSay(CHANNEL,"Hello " + name );
    }
    else if( llToLower(message) == "goodbye" )
    {
        llSay(CHANNEL,"Goodbye " + name );
    }
  }
}
```

For an object to begin listening, the object must call the **llListen** function. This function specifies the channel the object would like to listen on. The above script calls the **llListen** function in the **state_entry** event handler. The script specifies that it would like to listen to the channel specified by the **CHANNEL** variable. The Linden Scripting Language does not have user defined constants. As a result, the above declaration of **CHANNEL** is as close as we can come to a constant.

Channel zero is the normal conversation channel in Second Life. All communication between avatars is on channel zero. Therefore, by requesting to listen on channel zero, the object will be notified anytime something is said near the object.

The above script contains a **listen** event handler. This event handler is called each time something is said near the object. The object checks for either "hello" or "goodbye". Because the strings are converted to lower case, the user could also enter "Hello" or any mixture of upper and lower case characters. The script responds with a greeting directed to the avatar's name. The avatar's name was passed in as a parameter named **name**.

The **llSay** function is used when a script wants to say something. The above calls to **llSay** use channel zero. However, often objects want to communicate with each other, and not allow nearby avatars to listen. To do this, the script should specify a channel other than zero. Many recipes in this book communicate on channels other than zero.

In addition to **llSay**, there are three other functions allow a script to talk. The only difference between the four communication functions is the distance they cover. Table 1.1 summarizes the communication functions.

Table 1.1: Communication Distances

Communication Function	Distance
llWhisper	10m
llSay	20m
llShout	100m
llRegionSay	Entire region, cannot be used on channel 0.

There is a fifth communication function, with unlimited range. The **llInstantMessage** function allows an instant message to be sent to the specified avatar.

```
default
{
    touch_start(integer total_num)
    {
      // get the key of the objects owner.
      key owner=llGetOwner();
        llInstantMessage(owner,llKey2Name(owner)+", "
        + (string)total_num +" Avatar(s) touched me!");
    }
}
```

The above script sends a message to the object's owner every time the object is touched. It is also possible to send a message to the object's owner by using the **llOwnerSay** function. However, **llOwnerSay** does not have the unlimited distance of a **llInstantMessage** function call.

Modifying Objects

It is possible to modify objects using the Linden Scripting Language. Every aspect of an object can be modified using script. A large number of functions in the Linden Scripting Language allow the script to change the numerous properties available.

A number of these functions will be used by later recipes in this book. A script that changes the color of an object is shown here. This script will change the object to red, blue or green, depending on what the user says.

```
integer CHANNEL = 0;

default
{
    state_entry()
    {
        llListen(CHANNEL, "", NULL_KEY, "");
    }
```

```
listen(integer channel, string name, key id,
  string message)
{
    if( llToLower(message) == "red" )
    {
        llSetColor(<255,0,0>,ALL_SIDES);
    }
    else if( llToLower(message) == "green" )
    {
        llSetColor(<0,255,0>,ALL_SIDES);
    }
    else if( llToLower(message) == "blue" )
    {
        llSetColor(<0,0,255>,ALL_SIDES);
    }
  }
}
```

To change the color of an object, the above code uses the **llSetColor** function. This function must be passed two parameters. The first is a vector specifying the desired color. The second parameter specifies to which side this color should be applied. For this example, the **ALL_SIDES** constant is used, which specifies that all of the sides should be set to the specified color.

The color value is specified as a **vector**. For example, **<255,0,0>** specifies the color red. The first number is red, the second green, and the third blue. Using red, green and blue values of nearly any color can be specified. The valid range for each color component is between zero and 255.

Understanding Dialogs

The Linden Scripting Language allows much more direct interaction with avatars than simple touch events. It is also possible to create a dialog. A Second Life dialog can be seen in Figure 1.1.

Figure 1.1: Second Life Dialogs

The following script makes use if a dialog to allow the user to select a color.

```
integer CHANNEL = 10;

default
{
    state_entry()
    {
        llListen(CHANNEL, "", NULL_KEY, "");
    }

    touch_start(integer total_num)
    {
        list l = ["red","green","blue"];
        key who = llDetectedKey(0);
        llDialog(who, "Where to?", l, CHANNEL);
    }
```

```
listen(integer channel, string name, key id,
   string message)
{
    if( llToLower(message) == "red" )
    {
        llSetColor(<255,0,0>,ALL_SIDES);
    }
    else if( llToLower(message) == "green" )
    {
        llSetColor(<0,255,0>,ALL_SIDES);
    }
    else if( llToLower(message) == "blue" )
    {
        llSetColor(<0,0,255>,ALL_SIDES);
    }
}
}
```

This script is very similar to the script presented in the previous section. There are two main differences. First, this script makes use of channel 10, rather than channel zero. The second difference is that this script uses a dialog.

The dialog is used at the end of the **touch_start** event handler. Calling the **llDialog** function creates a dialog. The dialog displays buttons that correspond to the **list** that was passed into the **llDialog** function.

Once the user selects one of the options from the dialog, the name of that button is "said" over the specified channel. This causes the user's choice to be picked up by the **listen** event handler. In this way, implementing a dialog is very similar to implementing a script that listens to user conversation.

Implementing Basic Security

Some objects will only function when their owner is trying to use them. It is also possible to program an object to only function with group members. The following sections show how to implement basic security both for the owner and for groups.

Implementing Owner Security

Sometimes an object will only work with the owner of that object. This is particularly true of vehicles. The following script shows how to detect if someone, other than the owner, is trying to use the object.

```
default
{
    touch_start(integer total_number)
    {
```

```
integer i;
for(i=0;i<total_number;i++)
{
    if( llDetectedKey(i)!=llGetOwner() )
    {
        llSay(0, llDetectedName(i)
            + " you are not my owner.");
    }
    else
    {
        llSay(0, llDetectedName(i)
            + " you are my owner.");
    }
}
    }
}
```

When the above script is touched, the above script's **touch_start** event handler is called. The **touch_start** event handler is passed a value that indicates how many avatar's are touching it at once. It is very rare that more than one avatar will be touching the object at once. However, if the object is likely to have more than one avatar touching at once, the script should use the **total_number** parameter.

This script makes use of the **total_number** parameter. A loop counts through all the avatars that have touched the object. The **key** to each touching avatar is obtained with **llDetectedKey**. This **key** is compared against the owner of the object. If the owner and touching avatar are not the same, the avatar is informed that they are not welcome. This is a quick method to determine whether an avatar is the owner or not.

Implementing Group Security

Sometimes a object will only work with the group of that object. The following script shows how to detect if someone, other than the group, is trying to use the object.

The group that an object is in can be set from the object properties window. Figure 1.2 shows an object with a group set.

Figure 1.2: Setting the Group of an Object

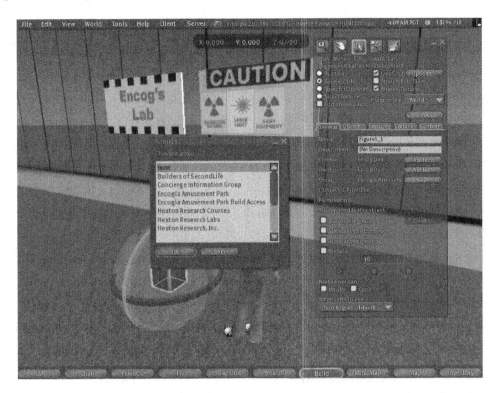

The following script checks to see if the user that touched the object is in the same group as the object being touched.

```
default
{
    touch_start(integer total_number)
    {
        integer i;
        for(i=0;i<total_number;i++)
        {
            if( llDetectedGroup(i)==FALSE )
            {
                llSay(0, llDetectedName(i)
+ " you must be in correct group.");
            }
            else
            {
                llSay(0, llDetectedName(i)
+ " you are in my group.");
            }
        }
    }
```

```
        }
}
```

To detect whether the touching avatar is in the same group as the object, the **llDetectGroup** function is called. If the avatar is in the same group, a value of **TRUE** is returned, otherwise **FALSE** is returned.

Summary

This chapter introduced some basic concepts that will be used by later chapters in this book. Very short scripts that introduced key concepts were presented. None of the scripts presented in this chapter would be very useful by themselves. However, they illustrate techniques that recipes in future chapters will use.

In this chapter object communication was demonstrated. Objects can both talk and listen to avatars. Additionally, an object can send an instant message. However, it is impossible for an object to receive an instant message. Objects can neither receive instant messages from other objects nor avatars. Dialogs can also be presented to communicate with avatars.

Objects can modify their appearance. There are many functions available to modify the appearance of an object. This chapter showed how to change the color of an object. Many of the recipes presented later in this book will change the appearance of an object in other ways.

Sometimes an object should only function with the owner of that object or the group to which an object belongs. It is possible to compare the avatar that is trying to use the object to the owner of the object. If the avatar using the object does not match the owner, then the object will not allow itself to be used. The same check can be performed on groups.

The Linden Scripting Language allows user functions to be created. The next chapter presents useful functions that may be useful in other scripts. Recipes presented later in this book will use some of these functions.

Chapter 2: String Handling

- Comparing Strings
- Determining String Set Membership
- Parsing Strings

The Linden Scripting Language contains many useful functions. However, it is also possible for a script programmer to add functions of their own. This chapter presents several useful functions that can be used in conjunction with larger scripts.

This chapter presents functions for string processing. These string functions deal with three areas. Firstly, string comparison functions will be demonstrated. These functions allow the script to compare strings in various ways. Secondly, string set functions will be demonstrated. These allow the script to determine whether a string is numeric, alphanumeric or any other combination of allowed characters. Finally, string parsing will be demonstrated.

Other recipes in this book make use of the recipes presented in this chapter.

Recipe 2.1: String Comparison

The Linden Scripting Language makes it very easy to compare two strings. To compare two strings, named **stra** and **strb**, use the following code:

```
if( stra == strb )
{
  llSay(0,"Equal.");
}
```

While this method of string comparison is good for determining whether two strings are exactly equal to each other, sometimes more advanced string comparison is called for. A script might need to determine whether two strings are equal, and ignore the case. Additionally, it might be necessary to determine which string would appear first in a dictionary.

Recipe 2.1 meets these needs. This recipe can be seen in Listing 2.1.

Listing 2.1: String Comparison (StringCompare.lsl)

```
string CHARS = "!\"#$%&'()*+,-./0123456789:;<=>?@ABCDEFGHIJKLM-
NOPQRSTUVWXYZ[\]^_`abcdefghijklmnopqrstuvwxyz{|}~";
```

```
integer compareLen(string a, string b,integer len)
{
    integer result = 0;
    if(a != b)
    {
        integer index = 0;
        do
        {
            string chara = llGetSubString(a,index,index);
            string charb = llGetSubString(b,index,index);

            integer posa = llSubStringIndex(CHARS ,chara);
            integer posb = llSubStringIndex(CHARS ,charb);

            if((posa >= 0) && (posb >= 0))
            {
                result = posa - posb;
            }
            else if(posa >= 0)
            {
                result = 1;
            }
            else if(posb >= 0)
            {
                result = -1;
            }

            if(result != 0) index = len;
            ++index;

        }
        while(index < len);
    }

    return result;
}

integer compareNoCaseLen(string a, string b,integer len)
{
    string stra = llToLower(a);
    string strb = llToLower(b);
    return compareLen(stra,strb,len);
}
```

```
integer compare(string a, string b)
{
    integer lena = llStringLength(a);
    integer lenb = llStringLength(b);
    integer result;
    if(lena < lenb)
        result =  compareLen(a,b,lena);
    else
        result =  compareLen(a,b,lenb);

    return result;
}


integer compareNoCase(string a, string b)
{
    integer la = llStringLength(a);
    integer lb = llStringLength(b);
    string stra = llToLower(a);
    string strb = llToLower(b);
    integer result;
    if(la < lb)
        result =  compareNoCaseLen(stra,strb,la);
    else
        result =  compareNoCaseLen(stra,strb,lb);

    return result;
}

// Some test uses
default
{
    state_entry()
    {
        llSay(0, "compareNoCase(hello,HELLO): "
            + (string)compareNoCase("jeff","Jeff") );
        llSay(0, "compare(hello,HELLO): "
            + (string)compare("jeff","Jeff") );
        llSay(0, "compare(aaa,bbb): "
            + (string)compare("aaa","bbb") );
        llSay(0, "compare(aaa,bbb): "
            + (string)compare("bbb","aaa") );
    }
}
```

This recipe begins by defining a variable, **CHARS**, which holds all of the characters that can be compared. This variable also defines the order in which characters will be sorted. This variable is declared as follows:

```
string CHARS = "!\"#$%&'()*+,-./0123456789:;<=>?@ABCDEFGHIJKLM-
NOPQRSTUVWXYZ[\]^_`abcdefghijklmnopqrstuvwxyz{|}~";
```

For example, if the character "!" were to be compared to "#", the string comparison function would report that "!" occurs first, and "#" second. This is because of the order of these two characters in the above list.

Using the compareLen Function

To compare two strings, the **compareLen** function is provided.

```
integer compareLen(string a, string b,integer len)
{
```

The **compareLen** function accepts three parameters. The first two are the strings to compare. The third parameter is the length of characters to compare. For example, if five were specified as the **len** variable, then characters zero through four would be compared.

The **compareLen** function returns one of these three values.

- Less than zero, string **a** is less than string **b**
- Zero, string **a** and string **b** are equal
- Greater than zero, string **a** is greater than string **b**

A variable, named **result** is created to hold the result of the comparison. If the two strings are not equal, the program begins the process of determining which string occurs first alphabetically.

```
    integer result = 0;
    if(a != b)
    {
        integer index = 0;
        do
        {
```

To determine which string occurs first alphabetically, a **do/loop** is used to loop across all of the characters in the string.

```
            string chara = llGetSubString(a,index,index);
            string charb = llGetSubString(b,index,index);
```

The individual characters for each position are extracted from the strings.

```
            integer posa = llSubStringIndex(CHARS ,chara);
            integer posb = llSubStringIndex(CHARS ,charb);
```

The position of each character is calculated. This numeric value allows the program to determine the alphabetical order of the two characters.

If both **posa** and **posb** are greater than zero, both characters were found in the **CHARS** variable. If this is the case, the **result** variable will be the difference between them. If they are equal, this will result in a value of zero. If they are not equal, the **result** variable will hold a value either greater or less than zero, depending on whether **posa** or **posb** was greater.

```
if((posa >= 0) && (posb >= 0))
{
    result = posa - posb;
}
```

If character **a** was found, but not character **b** then return a value of one, which indicates that string **a** is greater than string **b**.

```
else if(posa >= 0)
{
    result = 1;
}
```

If character **b** was found, but not character a then return a value of negative one, which indicates that string **b** is greater than string **a**.

```
else if(posb >= 0)
{
    result = -1;
}
```

If the two characters were equal, continue with the loop.

```
if(result != 0) index = len;
++index;
```

Continue looping until the end of the string is reached.

```
    }
    while(index < len);
}
return result;
}
```

Finally, return the **result** variable.

Understanding the compareNoCaseLen Function

Sometimes it is useful to compare two strings and ignore case. The **compareNoCaseLen** function does this. The **compareNoCaseLen** function accepts three parameters. The first two are the strings to compare. The third parameter is the length of characters to compare.

```
integer compareNoCaseLen(string a, string b,integer len)
{
```

First, the two strings are converted to lower case.

```
    string stra = llToLower(a);
    string strb = llToLower(b);
    return compareLen(stra,strb,len);
}
```

Finally, they are compared using the **compareLen** function discussed in the previous section.

Understanding the compare Function

The two string functions presented so far allow a length to be specified. This can be very useful if only the first part of the strings should be compared. However, usually the entire string should be compared. The **compare** function compares the entire string.

```
integer compare(string a, string b)
{
```

First, the length of each string is calculated.

```
    integer lena = llStringLength(a);
    integer lenb = llStringLength(b);
```

The **compareLen** method is called to perform the comparison. The length of the smallest string is used in the comparison.

```
    integer result;
    if(lena < lenb)
        result =  compareLen(a,b,lena);
    else
        result =  compareLen(a,b,lenb);

    return result;
}
```

Finally, the **result** variable is returned.

Understanding the compareNoCase Function

The **compareNoCase** function works just like **compareNoCaseLen**, except that no length is provided. The entire string will be compared.

```
integer compareNoCase(string a, string b)
{
```

First the length of each string is calculated.

```
    integer la = llStringLength(a);
    integer lb = llStringLength(b);
```

Next, the strings are converted into lowercase.

```
    string stra = llToLower(a);
    string strb = llToLower(b);
    integer result;
```

The **compareLen** method is called to perform the actual comparison. The length of the smallest string is used in the comparison.

```
    if(la < lb)
        result =  compareLen(stra,strb,la);
    else
        result =  compareLen(stra,strb,lb);

    return result;
}
```

Finally, the **result** is returned.

Comparing Strings

The script includes a simple **state_entry** function that tests the functions presented in this recipe.

```
default
{
    state_entry()
    {
        llSay(0, "compareNoCase(hello,HELLO): "
            + (string)compareNoCase("jeff","Jeff") );
        llSay(0, "compare(hello,HELLO): "
            + (string)compare("jeff","Jeff") );
        llSay(0, "compare(aaa,bbb): "
            + (string)compare("aaa","bbb") );
        llSay(0, "compare(aaa,bbb): "
            + (string)compare("bbb","aaa") );
    }
}
```

The output the above script is shown here.

```
[20:52]  Object: compareNoCase(hello,HELLO): 0
[20:52]  Object: compare(hello,HELLO): 31
[20:52]  Object: compare(aaa,bbb): -1
[20:52]  Object: compare(aaa,bbb): 1
```

The above output demonstrates how the functions can be used.

Recipe 2.2: String Sets

Often it is desirable to test whether a string is in a specific set of characters. Recipe 2.2 allows a string to be tested to see whether the string is a member of one of the following sets:

- Numeric
- Alphabetic
- Alphanumeric

Recipe 2.2 is shown in Listing 2.2.

Listing 2.2: String Set Comparison (StringSetCompare.lsl)

```
string CHARS = "!\"#$%&'()*+,-./0123456789:;<=>?@ABCDEFGHIJKLM
NOPQRSTUVWXYZ[\]^_`abcdefghijklmnopqrstuvwxyz{|}~";


integer compareLen(string a, string b,integer len)
{
    integer result = 0;
    if(a != b)
    {
        integer index = 0;
        do
        {
            string chara = llGetSubString(a,index,index);
            string charb = llGetSubString(b,index,index);

            integer posa = llSubStringIndex(CHARS ,chara);
            integer posb = llSubStringIndex(CHARS ,charb);

            if((posa >= 0) && (posb >= 0))
            {
                result = posa - posb;
            }
            else if(posa >= 0)
            {
                result = 1;
            }
            else if(posb >= 0)
```

```
        {
            result = -1;
        }

        if(result != 0) index = len;
        ++index;

    }
    while(index < len);
}

return result;
}

integer compareNoCaseLen(string a, string b,integer len)
{
    string stra = llToLower(a);
    string strb = llToLower(b);
    return compareLen(stra,strb,len);
}

integer compare(string a, string b)
{
    integer lena = llStringLength(a);
    integer lenb = llStringLength(b);
    integer result;
    if(lena < lenb)
        result =  compareLen(a,b,lena);
    else
        result =  compareLen(a,b,lenb);

    return result;
}


integer compareNoCase(string a, string b)
{
    integer la = llStringLength(a);
    integer lb = llStringLength(b);
    string stra = llToLower(a);
    string strb = llToLower(b);
    integer result;
    if(la < lb)
        result =  compareNoCaseLen(stra,strb,la);
    else
        result =  compareNoCaseLen(stra,strb,lb);
```

```
        return result;
}

// Some test uses
default
{
    state_entry()
    {
        llSay(0, "compareNoCase(hello,HELLO): "
            + (string)compareNoCase("jeff","Jeff") );
        llSay(0, "compare(hello,HELLO): "
            + (string)compare("jeff","Jeff") );
        llSay(0, "compare(aaa,bbb): "
            + (string)compare("aaa","bbb") );
        llSay(0, "compare(aaa,bbb): "
            + (string)compare("bbb","aaa") );
    }
}
```

This recipe begins by defining several different character sets. The variable named **CHARS** holds all of the characters that this recipe deals with. The variable **LETTERS** holds the upper and lower case letters. The variable **NUMBERS** holds the ten digits.

```
string CHARS = " !\"#$%&'()*+,-./0123456789:;<=>?@ABCDEFGHIJKLM
NOPQRSTUVWXYZ[\]^_`abcdefghijklmnopqrstuvwxyz{|}~";
string LETTERS= "ABCDEFGHIJKLMNOPQRSTUVWXYZabcdefghijklmnopqrstu
vwxyz";
string NUMBERS = "0123456789";
```

These character sets will be used by the functions in this recipe.

Understanding the onlyContains Function

The **onlyContains** function determines whether one string only contains characters from a second string. All of the other set functions are based upon the **onlyContains** function.

```
integer onlyContains(string a, string b)
{
```

The **onlyContains** function accepts two parameters. The first parameter, **a**, specifies the string that is to be examined. The second parameter, **b**, is the set of characters that a should contain. If the **a** string only contains the characters in **b**, then the value of **TRUE** is returned, otherwise **FALSE** is returned.

The function begins by obtaining the length of string **a**.

```
integer l = llStringLength(a);
integer result = FALSE;
if(l != 0)
{
```

If string **a** has a zero length value, return **FALSE**, because string **a** contains no characters, let alone those specified in string **b**.

```
result = TRUE;
integer index = 0;
do
{
```

The characters from string **a** are separated one by one and checked against string **b**.

```
string chara = llGetSubString(a,index,index);
integer posa = llSubStringIndex(b,chara);
```

If the character is not found in string **b**, return **FALSE**.

```
if(posa < 0)
{
    result = FALSE;
    index = l;
}
++index;
```

Continue looping until the end of string **a** is reached.

```
}
while(index < l);
}
return result;
}
```

Finally, return the **result**. Using the **containsOnly** function, a variety of useful set membership functions can be created. These will be discussed in the next sections.

Understanding the isNumeric Function

The **isNumeric** function uses the **onlyContains** function to determine whether the specified string only contains digits. To do this, the **NUMBERS** variable, which contains the digits, is used in conjunction with the **onlyContains** function.

```
integer isNumeric(string a)
{
    return onlyContains(a,NUMBERS);
}
```

This function allows a script to quickly determine whether a string is numeric.

Understanding the isAlpha Function

The **isAlpha** function determines whether the specified string is a set of only letters. Either capital or lowercase is acceptable. The **isAlpha** function works by ensuring that the string only contains characters from the **LETTERS** string.

```
integer isAlpha(string a)
{
    return onlyContains(a,LETTERS);
}
```

This function allows a script to quickly determine whether a string only contains letters.

Understanding the isAlphanumeric Function

The **isAlphanumeric** function determines whether the specified string is a set of only letters and digits. Either capital or lowercase is acceptable. The **isAlphanumeric** function works by ensuring that the string only contains characters from the **LETTERS** or **NUMBERS** strings.

```
integer isAlphanumeric(string a)
{
    return onlyContains(a,LETTERS + NUMBERS);
}
```

This function allows a script to quickly determine whether a string contains only digits and letters.

Testing String Sets

The script includes a simple **state_entry** function that tests the functions presented in this recipe. This shows how the functions in this recipe behave when passed various types of data.

```
default
{
    state_entry()
    {
        llSay(0,"isNumeric(abc): " + (string)isNumeric("abc") );
        llSay(0,"isNumeric(123): " + (string)isNumeric("123") );
        llSay(0,"isAlpha(abc): " + (string)isAlpha("abc") );
        llSay(0,"isAlpha(123): " + (string)isAlpha("123") );
        llSay(0,"isAlphanumeric(abc123): "
            + (string)isAlphanumeric("abc123") );
        llSay(0,"isAlphanumeric(123!!!!): "
            + (string)isAlphanumeric("123!!!!") );
    }
}
```

When run the above code will produce the following output.

```
[3:24]   Object: isNumeric(abc): 0
[3:24]   Object: isNumeric(123): 1
[3:24]   Object: isAlpha(abc): 1
[3:24]   Object: isAlpha(123): 0
[3:24]   Object: isAlphanumeric(abc123): 1
[3:24]   Object: isAlphanumeric(123!!!!): 0
```

It is also possible to parse strings. This will be discussed in the next section.

Recipe 2.3: String Parsing

String parsing is the process whereby a string is divided into substrings so that the computer can understand the string. To see why string parsing is needed, consider a future example in this book. Later in this book recipes that allow a locking door to be installed will be demonstrated. This locking door allows the owner of the door to add other users to a list of allowed users.

To add users to this door the owner must say their names. For example, to add the user "Encog Dod" the owner must say the following to the door.

```
door add Encog Dod
```

To process this command properly, the door must divide the string into the words that make it up. This allows the door to make sure that the command starts with the word "door". String parsing also allows the door to evaluate the command that was given to it.

Listing 2.3 shows a simple script that parses strings.

Listing 2.3: String Parsing (StringParse.lsl)

```
string text;

string pop()
{
    string result;
    integer i = llSubStringIndex(text, " ");

    if( i!=-1 )
    {
        i -=1;
        result = llGetSubString(text,0,i);
        text = llGetSubString(text,i+2,-1);
        return result;
    }
    else
    {
```

```
            result = text;
            text = "";
        }

    text = llStringTrim(text, STRING_TRIM);
    result = llStringTrim(result, STRING_TRIM);

    return result;
}



default
{
    state_entry()
    {
        text = "Now is the time for all good men to come to the
aid of their country.";
        string str;

        while( (str=pop())!="" )
        {
            llSay(0,str);
        }
    }
}
```

This recipe takes a string, such as "Testing one two three", and then provides a method that breaks the string up by spaces. The previous string would become the following four strings: "Testing", "one", "two", and "three".

To do this, the global variable **text**, must be set to the string to be parsed. Then, each time one element from text is needed, the **pop** function should be called. The **pop** function returns the first space delimited substring from the **text** variable and also removes what was returned from the **text** variable.

Implementing the pop Function

The **pop** function accepts no parameters and returns a string. The returned string will be the next string parsed from the **text** variable.

```
string pop()
{
```

This function begins by searching for the first occurrence of the space character.

```
    string result;
    integer i = llSubStringIndex(text, " ");
```

If a space is found, extract the data from the **text** variable up to where the space was found. Also remove this string from the **text** variable.

```
if( i!=-1 )
{
    i -=1;
    result = llGetSubString(text,0,i);
    text = llGetSubString(text,i+2,-1);
    return result;
}
```

If no spaces are found, return the remaining characters in the **text** variable. The **text** variable is also set to an empty string, since there are no additional characters to parse.

```
else
{
    result = text;
    text = "";
}
```

Trim extra spaces from both the remaining text and the string just extracted.

```
text = llStringTrim(text, STRING_TRIM);
result = llStringTrim(result, STRING_TRIM);

return result;
}
```

Finally, the **result** variable is returned.

Testing String Parsing

The script includes a simple **state_entry** function that tests the functions presented in this recipe. This demonstrates how the **pop** function behaves when passed a sentence.

```
default
{
    state_entry()
    {
        text = "Now is the time for all good men to come to the
aid of their country.";
        string str;

        while( (str=pop())!="" )
        {
            llSay(0,str);
        }
    }
}
```

}

The results from parsing the above sentence are:

```
[3:22]   Object: Now
[3:22]   Object: is
[3:22]   Object: the
[3:22]   Object: time
[3:22]   Object: for
[3:22]   Object: all
[3:22]   Object: good
[3:22]   Object: men
[3:22]   Object: to
[3:22]   Object: come
[3:22]   Object: to
[3:22]   Object: the
[3:22]   Object: aid
[3:22]   Object: of
[3:22]   Object: their
[3:22]   Object: country.
```

This recipe shows how to break up a string by spaces. It could also be easily modified to parse a string in other ways. This is very similar to the built in function **llParseString2List**, except that the **pop** function does not require that every string be delimited by the space. At any point, the remaining text can be accessed by using the **text** value. For example "door add Encog Dod", the parsing could stop after add and "Encog Dod" remains in the **text** string. If **llParseString2List** were used "Encog Dod" would have been split into two strings: "Encog" and "Dod". If this functionality is not required, the **llParseString2List** function should be used.

Summary

This chapter showed how to parse and compare strings. Second Life scripts often receive data directly from users as they type. The functions presented in this chapter help scripts to make sense of this data. The functions in this chapter are of little use alone. These functions will usually be incorporated into larger scripts.

Functions were provided that determined set membership of strings. The **isNumeric** function allows a script to determine whether a string only contains numeric values. The **isAlpha** function allows a script to determine whether a string only contains alphabetic characters. The **isAlphanumeric** function allows a script to determine whether a string is alphanumeric.

Chapters one and two presented scripts that speak to the user. The scripts presented so far do not directly interact with the Second Life world. Chapter three will introduce scripts that directly interact with the Second Life world. The recipes in Chapter 3 show how to create building components. This includes items such as doors and elevators.

CHAPTER 3: COMPONENTS FOR BUILDINGS

- Creating Splashing Water
- Creating an Open Door
- Creating an Owner-Locked Door
- Creating a Smart Door
- Creating a Teleport Pad
- Creating an Elevator

Buildings are very common in Second Life. As an avatar flies over the Second Life world, they encounter many different buildings. Scripts have their place in buildings. Scripts provide doors and other building elements. Lockable doors control access to buildings.

Multi-floor buildings need a way to quickly take the user from one floor to another. Elevators are a common solution. Elevators work similarly to real-world elevators. However, elevators and stairs take up valuable space inside a building. Many buildings in Second Life use teleport pads. A teleport pad transports the user to a specified location.

This chapter presents several Recipes for scripts that are common either in or around buildings. The first Recipe shows how to create water that splashes when an avatar enters it.

Recipe 3.1: Splashing Water

The Second Life world includes water. However, all water in Second Life is at exactly the same level. Water is usually at 20 meters on the z-coordinate. However, this is not always the case, as private islands can set the water height to any level desired. Second life water can be seen in Figure 3.1.

Figure 3.1: Beach Front Land in Second Life

Sometimes water is needed at a higher altitude than "sea level". A good example of this is a swimming pool. A swimming pool could be above sea level if it occurs inland. To give the swimming pool the effect of water, a phantom rectangle is created with a water texture. A small swimming pool can be seen in Figure 3.2.

Figure 3.2: Swimming Pool

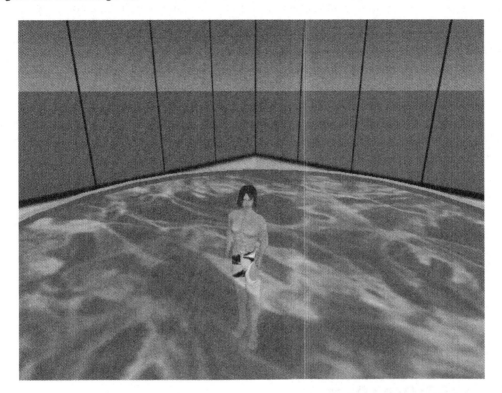

However, the water in the swimming pool is fairly boring without a script. A script allows the water to "flow" and also produce a "splash" sound when an avatar enters the water. Listing 3.1 shows the script used for water.

Listing 3.1: Splashing Water (Splash.lsl)

```
default
{
    state_entry()
    {
        llSetTextureAnim(ANIM_ON | ROTATE | LOOP
            | SMOOTH, ALL_SIDES, 0, 0, 0, 100, .05);
        llVolumeDetect(TRUE);
    }

    collision_start( integer num_detected )
    {
        llTriggerSound("splash", 1);
    }

}
```

The **state_entry** function sets up both the flow of the water and the splash sound effect. First, a texture animation is created. Texture animations are created once by calling **llSetTextureAnim**. Once the texture animation is started, it continues with no further interaction required from the script. The texture animation for the water is started with the following command:

```
llSetTextureAnim(ANIM_ON | ROTATE | LOOP
        | SMOOTH, ALL_SIDES, 0, 0, 0, 100, .05);
```

The above function call rotates the texture every 0.05 frames. This causes the water to slowly rotate. Next, a call to **llVolumeDetect** instructs Second Life to call the collision event handlers whenever an avatar comes into contact with the object. The following function call does this.

```
llVolumeDetect(TRUE);
```

Whenever the **collision_start** event handler is called, the "splash" sound should be played. The following lines do this.

```
collision_start( integer num_detected )
{
    llTriggerSound("splash", 1);
}
```

The **llTriggerSound** plays the sound "splash" at the maximum volume of one. The sound must be stored in the object's inventory.

Recipe 3.2: Open Door

Doors are very common in the Second Life world. Most doors open as soon as an avatar touches them. Some doors only open for specific users. Many doors open for any avatar.

A door in Second Life usually opens by rotating the door's object by 90 degrees. This means a simple flat cube is insufficient for a door. This is because objects in Second Life are always rotated about their center. Think about a door in real life. Does the door rotate about its center when opened? No. A door rotates about its hinges when it opens. The hinges are on the side. Because of this, a door in Second Life is normally a cube with a cut path to remove one side of the rectangle. This causes the center of the door to appear to be on its side.

To create such a door, create a rectangular cube and set a cut path begin of 0.375 and a cut path end of 0.875. Additionally, set the texture's repeats per face horizontal to 2, and the horizontal texture offset to 0.5. All other values can remain at their default state. If the sample objects are obtained from this book, a perfectly setup door object can be seen. Refer to Appendix A on how to obtain sample objects and code for this book. Figure 3.3 shows a door and the center point.

Figure 3.3: Door with Center

This Recipe shows how to create an open door that will open for any avatar. The script for such a door is shown in Listing 3.2.

Listing 3.2: Open Door (OpenDoor.lsl)

```
float          TIMER_CLOSE = 5.0;
integer        DIRECTION   = -1;
// direction door opens in. Either 1 (outwards) or -1 (inwards);

integer        DOOR_OPEN   = 1;
integer        DOOR_CLOSE  = 2;

vector         originalPos;

door(integer what)
{
    rotation       rot;
    rotation       delta;
    vector eul;

    llSetTimerEvent(0);
```

```
      if ( what == DOOR_OPEN )
      {
          llTriggerSound("doorOpen", 1);
          eul = <0, 0, 90*DIRECTION>;
//90 degrees around the z-axis, in Euler form

      } else if ( what == DOOR_CLOSE)
      {
          llTriggerSound("doorClose", 1);
          eul = <0, 0, 90*-DIRECTION>;
//90 degrees around the z-axis, in Euler form
      }

      eul *= DEG_TO_RAD; //convert to radians rotation
      rot = llGetRot();
      delta = llEuler2Rot(eul);
      rot = delta * rot;
      llSetRot(rot);
}


default
{
    on_rez(integer start_param)
    {
        llResetScript();
    }

    state_entry()
    {
        originalPos = llGetPos();
    }

    touch_start(integer total_number)
    {
        door(DOOR_OPEN);
        state open_state;

    }

    moving_end()
    {
        originalPos = llGetPos();
    }
}
```

```
state open_state
{
    state_entry()
    {
        llSetTimerEvent(TIMER_CLOSE);
    }

    touch_start(integer num)
    {
        door(DOOR_CLOSE);
        llSetPos(originalPos);
        state default;
    }

    timer()
    {
        door(DOOR_CLOSE);
        llSetPos(originalPos);
        state default;
    }

    moving_start()
    {
        door(DOOR_CLOSE);
        state default;
    }
}
```

The door script begins by defining a number of variables. The **TIMER_CLOSE** variable defines how long until the door swings closed. The **DIRECTION** variable specifies the direction the door opens, either 1 (outwards) or -1 (inwards). The **DOOR_OPEN** and **DOOR_CLOSE** variables are used as constants to tell the **door** function what state the door should move to. The **originalPos** variable holds the original position of the door. This is useful because sometimes the door will slightly change positions when opening or closing. Doors are particularly prone to changing positions when they hit something in the process of opening or closing. These variables can be seen here.

```
float        TIMER_CLOSE = 5.0;
integer      DIRECTION   = -1;
integer      DOOR_OPEN   = 1;
integer      DOOR_CLOSE  = 2;
vector       originalPos;
```

The door script defines one global function, named **door**. This function should be passed either **DOOR_OPEN** or **DOOR_CLOSE** for its single parameter. The **door** function begins by creating a few variables that will be needed as the door is rotated.

```
door(integer what)
{
    rotation    rot;
    rotation    delta;
    vector eul;

    llSetTimerEvent(0);
```

Next, the **open** state is handled. The door is rotated by 90 degrees. To do this, a **vector** is created that specifies a rotation of zero in both the x and y coordinate system, but a value of -90 or +90 in the z-coordinate. Additionally, the door open sound is played.

```
    if ( what == DOOR_OPEN )
    {
        llTriggerSound("doorOpen", 1);
        eul = <0, 0, 90*DIRECTION>;
```

Next, the **close** state is handled. The door is rotated by 90 degrees. To do this, a **vector** is created that specifies a rotation of zero in both the x and y coordinate system, but a value of -90 or +90 in the z-coordinate. The opposite direction of the **open** state is specified. Additionally, the door open sound is played.

```
    } else if ( what == DOOR_CLOSE)
    {
        llTriggerSound("doorClose", 1);
        eul = <0, 0, 90*-DIRECTION>;
    }
```

Second Life expresses rotations not in degrees or radians but in a form called a quaternion. This is a four component rotation that has x, y, z and s components. Most scripts do not deal with quaternions directly, but rather convert radians into quaternions using the **llEuler2Rot** function.

This can seen before the **eul** variable is converted into radians. Next, the current rotation is obtained by calling **llGetRot**. The change in rotation, called delta, is obtained by converting the radians into a quaternion rotation. This is done by calling the **llEuler2Rot** function.

```
    eul *= DEG_TO_RAD; //convert to radians rotation
    rot = llGetRot();
    delta = llEuler2Rot(eul);
    rot = delta * rot;
    llSetRot(rot);
}
```

The above code is very common in Second Life scripts that need to deal with angles.

Next, the two states for the door must be handled. The **default** state is when the door is closed. The **open_state** state, as its name implies, handles the state where the door is opened. The door begins in the **default** closed state. The door includes an **on_rez** event that resets the script. This ensures that the script is properly setup if it is sold or transferred. For the simple open door this is not really necessary, since the open door does not care about its owner. However, for objects that operate differently for their owner, a call to **llResetScript** should always be set in the **on_rez** event handler.

```
default
{
    on_rez(integer start_param)
    {
        llResetScript();
    }

    state_entry()
    {
        originalPos = llGetPos();
    }
```

When the door is touched, and it is in the **closed** state, open the door and switch to the **open_state**.

```
    touch_start(integer total_number)
    {
        door(DOOR_OPEN);
        state open_state;
    }
```

If the user moves the door, grab a new copy of **originalPos**.

```
    moving_end()
    {
        originalPos = llGetPos();
    }
}
```

The open state begins by setting a timer. This door will close automatically after the time specified by **TIMER_CLOSE** elapses. If the user touches the closed door before the timer is up, immediately close and return to the **default** state.

```
state open_state
{
    state_entry()
    {
        llSetTimerEvent(TIMER_CLOSE);
    }
```

```
touch_start(integer num)
{
    door(DOOR_CLOSE);
    llSetPos(originalPos);
    state default;
}
```

Once the **timer** event occurs, return the door to a closed state and set the position back to the original position. Return to the **default** state.

```
timer()
{
    door(DOOR_CLOSE);
    llSetPos(originalPos);
    state default;
}
```

If the user begins to move the door, close the door and return to the **default** state.

```
moving_start()
{
    door(DOOR_CLOSE);
    state default;
}
}
```

This script implements a basic unlocked door. The next two Recipes demonstrate two different types of locking doors.

Recipe 3.3: Owner Locked Door

It is easy enough to create a simple locking door. The door presented in this Recipe will only open for its owner. Of course, in Second Life, locked doors are not totally secure. There are ways to get around them, due to limitations in the Second Life client program.

The easiest way to step around a locked door is to position the avatar right against it. Then press the cursor left or cursor right and rotate the avatar. When the correct angle reveals the inside of the building, find something to sit on and select it. The avatar will now be inside of the building!

Despite these limitations, locked doors are still popular in Second Life. They keep casual or inexperienced users out. However, if a user is really determined to enter, they will be able to. The only way to keep a user out is to use the land tools and setup access controls. To do this, right click on the land and choose about. Then, under the access tab specify who may access this land.

The owner locked door is presented in Listing 3.3.

Listing 3.3: Owner Locked Door (OwnerLockedDoor.lsl)

```
float        TIMER_CLOSE = 5.0;
integer      DIRECTION    = -1;
// direction door opens in. Either 1 (outwards) or -1 (inwards);

integer      DOOR_OPEN   = 1;
integer      DOOR_CLOSE  = 2;

vector       originalPos;

door(integer what)
{
    rotation    rot;
    rotation    delta;
    vector eul;

    llSetTimerEvent(0);

    if ( what == DOOR_OPEN )
    {
        llTriggerSound("doorOpen", 1);
        eul = <0, 0, 90*DIRECTION>;
//90 degrees around the z-axis, in Euler form

    } else if ( what == DOOR_CLOSE)
    {
        llTriggerSound("doorClose", 1);
        eul = <0, 0, 90*-DIRECTION>;
//90 degrees around the z-axis, in Euler form
    }

    eul *= DEG_TO_RAD; //convert to radians rotation
    rot = llGetRot();
    delta = llEuler2Rot(eul);
    rot = delta * rot;
    llSetRot(rot);
}


default
{
    on_rez(integer start_param)
    {
        llResetScript();
    }
```

```
    state_entry()
    {
        originalPos = llGetPos();
    }

    touch_start(integer total_number)
    {
        key who = llDetectedKey(0);
        if( who==llGetOwner() )
        {
            llSay(0,"Hello " + llDetectedName(0) );
            door(DOOR_OPEN);
            state open_state;
        }
        else
        {
            llSay(0,llDetectedName(0) + " is at the door." );
            llTriggerSound("doorbell", 0.8);
        }
    }

    moving_end()
    {
        originalPos = llGetPos();
    }
}

state open_state
{
    state_entry()
    {
        llSetTimerEvent(TIMER_CLOSE);
    }

    touch_start(integer num)
    {
        door(DOOR_CLOSE);
        llSetPos(originalPos);
        state default;
    }

    timer()
    {
        door(DOOR_CLOSE);
        llSetPos(originalPos);
        state default;
    }
```

```
moving_start()
{
    door(DOOR_CLOSE);
    state default;
}
}
```

A good part of this Recipe is the same as Recipe 3.2. Because of this, only the new code will be explained. This Recipe only explains the security aspects of the door. For a discussion on how the door opens, refer to Recipe 3.2.

All security for the owner-locked door is implemented inside the **touch_start** event handler. The first thing that the **touch_start** event handler does is to obtain the **key** to the avatar that touched the door. This **key** must match the owner of the door. The owner is obtained by calling **llGetOwner** and the touching user is obtained by calling **llDetectedKey**. If the owner is the one who touched the door, begin the opening procedure.

```
touch_start(integer total_number)
{
    key who = llDetectedKey(0);
    if( who==llGetOwner() )
    {
        llSay(0,"Hello " + llDetectedName(0) );
        door(DOOR_OPEN);
        state open_state;
    }
```

If the owner is not the one opening the door, play a doorbell sound and say who is at the door.

```
    else
    {
        llSay(0,llDetectedName(0) + " is at the door." );
        llTriggerSound("doorbell", 0.8);
    }
}
```

This door can only be opened by one person. To create a door that opens with a larger number of people, refer to the next Recipe.

Recipe 3.4: Multi-User Lockable Door

In the real world, a door rarely has only one key. Rather, a key will be given to each person trusted to open the door. This Recipe implements a door that can be opened by multiple users. The door starts being able only to be opened by the owner. However, the owner can grant access to additional users.

To add users to the door, say "door" followed by one of the commands. The door understands the following commands:

- door
- door add [user name]
- door list
- door clear

The "door" command displays the name of the door. The "door add" command adds the specified user to the access list. The "door list" shows all those who can access the door. The "door clear" command clears the list so that only the owner can open the door. The owner can always open the door, and is not on the list.

The following is a sample illustration of a conversation with the door.

```
[15:16]   You: door
[15:16]   Smart Door: I am the smart door!
[15:16]   You: door add Mandy Nakamura
[15:16]   Smart Door: Adding MANDY NAKAMURA
[15:16]   You: door add Aught Oh
[15:16]   Smart Door: Adding AUGHT OH
[15:16]   You: door list
[15:16]   Smart Door: The following people have access to open me:
[15:16]   Smart Door: MANDY NAKAMURA
[15:16]   Smart Door: AUGHT OH
```

This "smart door" is shown in Listing 3.4.

Listing 3.4: Multi-User Lockable Door (SmartDoor.lsl)

```
float       TIMER_CLOSE = 5.0;
integer     DIRECTION   = -1;
// direction door opens in. Either 1 (outwards) or -1 (inwards);

integer     DOOR_OPEN   = 1;
integer     DOOR_CLOSE  = 2;

vector      originalPos;
string text;
list allow;

door(integer what)
{
    rotation    rot;
    rotation    delta;
    vector eul;

    llSetTimerEvent(0);
```

```
    if ( what == DOOR_OPEN )
    {
        llTriggerSound("doorOpen", 1);
        eul = <0, 0, 90*DIRECTION>;
//90 degrees around the z-axis, in Euler form

    } else if ( what == DOOR_CLOSE)
    {
        llTriggerSound("doorClose", 1);
        eul = <0, 0, 90*-DIRECTION>;
//90 degrees around the z-axis, in Euler form
    }

    eul *= DEG_TO_RAD;
//convert to radians rotation
    rot = llGetRot();
    delta = llEuler2Rot(eul);
    rot = delta * rot;
    llSetRot(rot);
}

string pop()
{
    string result;
    integer i = llSubStringIndex(text, " ");

    if( i!=-1 )
    {
        i -=1;
        result = llGetSubString(text,0,i);
        text = llGetSubString(text,i+2,-1);
        return result;
    }
    else
    {
        result = text;
        text = "";
    }

    text = llStringTrim(text, STRING_TRIM);
    result = llStringTrim(result, STRING_TRIM);

    return result;
}
```

```
default
{
    on_rez(integer start_param)
    {
        llResetScript();
    }

    state_entry()
    {
        originalPos = llGetPos();
        llListen(0, "", NULL_KEY, "");
    }

    touch_start(integer total_number)
    {
        key who = llDetectedKey(0);
        integer shouldOpen = 0;

        if( who==llGetOwner() )
            shouldOpen = 1;

        string name = llToUpper(llDetectedName(0));
        if( llListFindList(allow,[name]) != -1 )
            shouldOpen = 1;

        if( shouldOpen == 1 )
        {
            llSay(0,"Hello " + llDetectedName(0) );
            door(DOOR_OPEN);
            state open_state;
        }
        else
        {
            llSay(0,llDetectedName(0) + " is at the door." );
            llTriggerSound("doorbell", 0.8);
        }
    }

    moving_end()
    {
        originalPos = llGetPos();
    }

    listen(integer channel, string name, key id, string message)
    {
        if( id==llGetOwner() )
```

```
        {
            text = message;
            string prefix = llToLower(pop());

            if( prefix=="door" )
            {
                string command = pop();
                if( command=="" )
                {
                    llSay(0,"I am the smart door!");
                }
                else if( command=="clear" )
                {
                    llSay(0,"Clearing access list.");
                    allow = [];
                }
                else if( command=="add" )
                {
                    if( llStringLength(text)> 0 )
                    {
                        text = llToUpper(text);
                        allow+=[text];
                        llSay(0,"Adding " + text );
                    }
                    else
                    {
                        llSay(0,
"You must also specify an avatar when using add.");
                    }
                }
                else if( command=="list" )
                {
                    integer length = llGetListLength(allow);
                    if( length==0 )
                    {
                        llSay(0,
"No one, other than my owner, may open me.");
                    }
                    else
                    {
                        integer i;
                        llSay(0,
"The following people have access to open me:");
```

```
                        for (i = 0; i < length; ++i)
                        {
                            llSay(0,llList2String(allow, i));
                        }
                    }
                }
                else
                {
                    llSay(0,"I did not understand that command,
say \"door\" for a list of commands.");
                }
            }
        }


    }
}

state open_state
{
    state_entry()
    {
        llSetTimerEvent(TIMER_CLOSE);
    }

    touch_start(integer num)
    {
        door(DOOR_CLOSE);
        llSetPos(originalPos);
        state default;
    }

    timer()
    {
        door(DOOR_CLOSE);
        llSetPos(originalPos);
        state default;
    }

    moving_start()
    {
        door(DOOR_CLOSE);
        state default;
    }
}
```

The next few sections explain how the smart door was implemented, starting with the variables needed for the door.

Variables Needed for the Door

Several variables are defined for the smart door. Some of the variables are the same as were used for the open door shown in Recipe 3.2. The new variable is shown here.

```
list allow;
```

The **allow** variable keeps a list of who is allowed to open the door. This Recipe only describes what was added to Recipe 3.2 to create the smart door. This includes the security features, but not the mechanics of how to open the door. For more information on the mechanics of opening the door, refer to Recipe 3.2.

The functionality for this Recipe is split among two event handlers. The **touch_start** event handler allows the door to be opened by touching it. The **listen** event handler allows the owner of the door to add users to the list of people who are allowed to open the door.

Controlling Access to the Door

All of the door security is handled by the **touch_start** event handler. First, the **start_touch** event handler checks to see who touched the door. If the owner of the door touched the door, the door should always be opened.

```
touch_start(integer total_number)
{
    key who = llDetectedKey(0);
    integer shouldOpen = 0;

    if( who==llGetOwner() )
        shouldOpen = 1;
```

Next, the name of the touching user is converted to be entirely upper case. The list of allowed users is checked. If the user is found, the door will be opened. A Linden Scripting Language **list** can easily be searched by calling **llListFindList**.

```
    string name = llToUpper(llDetectedName(0));
    if( llListFindList(allow, [name]) != -1 )
        shouldOpen = 1;
```

If it has been determined that the door should be opened, the door says hello to the touching user. The door then opens.

```
    if( shouldOpen == 1 )
    {
        llSay(0,"Hello " + llDetectedName(0) );
        door(DOOR_OPEN);
        state open_state;
    }
```

If the door should not be opened, play a doorbell sound and say who is at the door.

```
else
{
        llSay(0,llDetectedName(0) + " is at the door." );
        llTriggerSound("doorbell", 0.8);
}
}
```

To determine whether users should be allowed or not, the **touch_start** event handler requires that all authorized users be added to the list. Users are added to the list by talking to the door. This is covered in the next section.

Listening for Commands

The **listen** event handler uses the **pop** function that was introduced in Recipe 2.3. For more information about how the **pop** function works, refer to Recipe 2.3. The **pop** function is used to break open the commands to the door.

The **listen** event handler begins by making sure that the one talking to it is the owner of the object. If the one talking is not the owner, the conversation is ignored.

```
listen(integer channel, string name, key id, string message)
{
        if( id==llGetOwner() )
        {
                text = message;
                string prefix = llToLower(pop());
```

The first space delimited word is extracted from what was said to the door. This string is converted into lower case. The script checks to see whether this word was door. Since all the commands to the door start with the word "door", if the prefix is not door, the door will do nothing further.

```
                if( prefix=="door" )
                {
```

Once it has been established that what the owner said is prefixed by door, the next space delimited word is the command. The command is obtained. If there is no command, the door simply identifies itself.

```
                        string command = pop();
                        if( command=="" )
                        {
                                llSay(0,"I am the smart door!");
                        }
```

If the command is clear, the list is set to an empty array, which clears it.

```
                        else if( command=="clear" )
```

```
        {
            llSay(0,"Clearing access list.");
            allow = [];
        }
```

If the command is add, the door obtains the rest of the text and adds that user. It is important to not use **pop** at this point. User names in Second Life are a first name, a space and the last name. If pop is used, only the first name would be obtained.

```
        else if( command=="add" )
        {
            if( llStringLength(text)> 0 )
            {
                text = llToUpper(text);
                allow+=[text];
                llSay(0,"Adding " + text );
            }
```

If no user is specified, display an error.

```
            else
            {
llSay(0,"You must also specify an avatar when using add.");
            }
        }
```

If the command list is given, the length of the list is obtained. If the list has a length equal to zero, the door reports that it can only opened by its owner.

```
        else if( command=="list" )
        {
            integer length = llGetListLength(allow);
            if( length==0 )
            {
llSay(0,"No one, other than my owner, may open me.");
            }
```

Otherwise, a **for** loop is used to display the entire list of allowed users.

```
            else
            {
                integer i;
llSay(0,"The following people have access to open me:");
                for (i = 0; i < length; ++i)
                {
                 llSay(0,llList2String(allow, i));
                }
            }
        }
```

If the command does not match any of the previous values, the door states that it did not understand the command.

```
                else
              {
llSay(0,"I did not understand that command.");
              }
           }
        }
}
```

The rest of the door recipe is the same as Recipe 3.2. To see the mechanics of opening and closing the door, Refer to Recipe 3.2.

Recipe 3.5: Teleport Pad

Buildings in Second Life often have more than one level. There are three common methods for allowing users to move from one level to another, they are:

- Stairs or Ramps
- Elevators
- Teleport Pads

Stairs and ramps do not require any scripting. The user walks up them. Elevators and teleport pads require scripting. This chapter provides a recipe for each.

This recipe provides a simple teleport pad. A teleport pad is more flexible than an elevator. The teleport pad can send the user to a specific point, within 300 meters, in the same region. The teleport pad recipe is shown in Listing 3.5.

Listing 3.5: Teleport Pad (Teleport.lsl)

```
vector target=<190, 197, 64>;

vector offset;

default
{
    moving_end()
    {
        offset = (target- llGetPos()) * (ZERO_ROTATION /
            llGetRot());
        llSitTarget(offset, ZERO_ROTATION);
    }

    state_entry()
    {
        llSetText("Teleport pad",<0,0,0>,1.0);
```

```
        offset = (target- llGetPos()) *
            (ZERO_ROTATION / llGetRot());
        llSetSitText("Teleport");
        llSitTarget(offset, ZERO_ROTATION);
    }

    changed(integer change)
    {
        if (change & CHANGED_LINK)
        {
            llSleep(0.5);
            if (llAvatarOnSitTarget() != NULL_KEY)
            {
                llUnSit(llAvatarOnSitTarget());
            }
        }
    }

    touch_start(integer i)
    {
        llSay(0, "Please right-click and select Teleport");
    }
}
```

The teleport script uses two global variables. They are.

```
vector target=<190, 197, 64>;
vector offset;
```

The **target** is the coordinate that the teleport script should send the user to. The **offset** is calculated based on the target and the current position of the teleporter. The **offset** is the distance that must be traveled to reach the target, starting from the teleporter.

Whenever the teleport pad is moved, the **offset** must be recalculated. The sit target is then updated.

```
moving_end()
{
        offset = (target- llGetPos()) *
            (ZERO_ROTATION / llGetRot());
        llSitTarget(offset, ZERO_ROTATION);
}
```

Likewise, when the teleport pad is first created, the offset must be recalculated. Additionally, the sit text is specified. Rotation is also taken into account and neutralized.

```
state_entry()
{
    llSetText("Teleport pad",<0,0,0>,1.0);
    offset = (target- llGetPos()) *
        (ZERO_ROTATION / llGetRot());
    llSetSitText("Teleport");
    llSitTarget(offset, ZERO_ROTATION);
}
```

When a user sits on the teleport pad, their avatar sits at the target location. The avatar is then stood up.

```
changed(integer change)
{
    if (change & CHANGED_LINK)
    {
        llSleep(0.5);
        if (llAvatarOnSitTarget() != NULL_KEY)
        {
            llUnSit(llAvatarOnSitTarget());
        }
    }
}
```

The teleport pad is a form of Linden Scripting Language trick. By specifying a distant co-ordinate for the sit target, the avatar is moved to that distant location and then stood up. This instantaneously moves the avatar to the new location. The avatar is able to move through walls and anything else that is in the way.

Recipe 3.6: Elevator

Elevators are a common mode of transportation in the Second Life world. The Heaton Research office building, where many of the examples from this book can be found, includes an elevator. It is the same elevator that will be covered in this recipe. The elevator in the Heaton Research Tower can be found at:

http://slurl.com/secondlife/Encogia/197/197/23

The above SLURL leads to the lobby of the Heaton Research tower. The elevator is located there. If the elevator is not present, click the green cone to call the elevator. Figure 3.4.

Figure 3.4: An Elevator

The elevator consists of two objects:

- The Elevator Car
- Elevator Call Cone

Each of these objects contains its own script and serves its own function.

The Elevator Car

The elevator car is the heart of the elevator system. It is also has the most complex script of any of the elevator parts. The elevator car can be seen in Figure 3.4. The script for the elevator car is shown in Listing 3.6.

Listing 3.6: Elevator Car (Elevator.lsl)

```
integer CHANNEL = 42; // dialog channel
list MENU_MAIN = ["Floor 1", "Floor 2", "Floor 3", "Floor 4",
"Floor 5", "Floor 6", "Floor 7", "Floor 8", "Floor 9", "Floor
10","Roof"]; // the main menu

float BOTTOM = 22.260;
float FLOOR_HEIGHT = 10;
```

```
float SPEED = 2;
float target;


default
{
    state_entry()
    {
        llListen(CHANNEL, "", NULL_KEY, ""); // listen for dialog
answers (from multiple users)
        llSitTarget(<0,-0.5,0.5>, llEuler2Rot(<0,0,-90>) );
        llSetText("Sit Here to Ride Elevator",<0,0,0>,1.0);
        target = BOTTOM;
    }

    listen(integer channel, string name, key id, string message)
    {
        integer idx = llListFindList(MENU_MAIN, [message]);
        if( idx!=-1 )
        {
            llSay(0,"Elevator heading to " + message + "." );
            target = BOTTOM + (idx*10);
            state moving;
        }
    }

    changed(integer Change)
    {
        llDialog(llAvatarOnSitTarget(), "Where to?", MENU_MAIN,
CHANNEL);
    }

}

state moving
{


    state_entry()
    {
        llSetTimerEvent(0.1);
    }

    timer()
    {
        vector pos = llGetPos();
```

```
if( pos.z!=target )
{
    if( pos.z>target )
    {
        pos.z = pos.z - SPEED;
    }
    else
    {
        pos.z = pos.z + SPEED;
    }
}

if(  llFabs(pos.z - target) < SPEED )
{
    pos.z = target;
    llSetTimerEvent(0);
    llSetPos(pos);
    llSay(0,"Elevator has reached its target." );
    state default;
}

llSetPos(pos);

    }
}
```

The elevator car begins by defining several global variables. These are.

```
integer CHANNEL = 42; // dialog channel
list MENU_MAIN = ["Floor 1", "Floor 2", "Floor 3", "Floor 4",
"Floor 5", "Floor 6", "Floor 7", "Floor 8", "Floor 9", "Floor
10","Roof"]; // the main menu
float BOTTOM = 22.260;
float FLOOR_HEIGHT = 10;
float SPEED = 2;
float target;
```

The first is the **CHANNEL.** The elevator needs its target floor communicated to it. This will be communicated using either a menu or one of the elevator call cones. The **MAIN_MENU** defines the labels for each of the floors. The **BOTTOM** variable defines the height of the ground floor. The **FLOOR_HEIGHT** variable defines the height of each of the floors in meters. The **SPEED** defines how fast the elevator travels, lower is slower. The target variable holds the target z-coordinate, in meters, when the elevator is in motion.

The **default** state of the elevator is to be still. After the **default** state is entered, the elevator sets up. It defines the sit target, as well as the sit text. The elevator also begins listening for commands.

```
default
{
    state_entry()
    {
        llListen(CHANNEL, "", NULL_KEY, "");
      // listen for dialog answers (from multiple users)
        llSitTarget(<0,-0.5,0.5>, llEuler2Rot(<0,0,-90>) );
        llSetText("Sit Here to Ride Elevator",<0,0,0>,1.0);
        target = BOTTOM;
    }
}
```

The **listen** event handler allows the elevator to receive commands from both the elevator's menu and the elevator call cones placed on each of the floors. The **listen** event handler begins by finding the index of the string sent to it. This tells the elevator which floor to visit. The elevator then announces which floor it is heading to and enters the moving state.

```
    listen(integer channel, string name, key id, string message)
    {
        integer idx = llListFindList(MENU_MAIN, [message]);
        if( idx!=-1 )
        {
            llSay(0,"Elevator heading to " + message + "." );
            target = BOTTOM + (idx*10);
            state moving;
        }
    }
```

When an avatar sits on the elevator car, a dialog is displayed to prompt for which floor to visit. This will be a list of floors specified in the **MAIN_MENU** variable. When the user picks one of these options, the text of that option is sent to the elevator car's **listen** event handler.

```
    changed(integer Change)
    {
        llDialog(llAvatarOnSitTarget(), "Where to?",
            MENU_MAIN, CHANNEL);
    }
}
```

Once the elevator enters the moving state, a timer is created that will occur ten times a second.

```
state moving
{
```

```
state_entry()
{
    llSetTimerEvent(0.1);
}
```

Each time the **timer** event handler is called, the elevator moves closer to its target. The **timer** event handler begins by obtaining the current position of the elevator.

```
timer()
{
    vector pos = llGetPos();
```

If the elevator is not at its target, the current z-coordinate will be increased or decreased, depending on which is necessary to move the elevator closer to its target.

```
    if( pos.z!=target )
    {
        if( pos.z>target )
        {
            pos.z = pos.z - SPEED;
        }
        else
        {
            pos.z = pos.z + SPEED;
        }
    }
```

If the elevator is reasonably close to its target, move the elevator directly to its target. The timer is then stopped and the elevator returns to its default state.

```
    if(  llFabs(pos.z - target) < SPEED )
    {
        pos.z = target;
        llSetTimerEvent(0);
        llSetPos(pos);
        llSay(0,"Elevator has reached its target." );
        state default;
    }

    llSetPos(pos);

}
}
```

The elevator car is only part of the elevator system. An elevator call must be placed on each of the floors to call the elevator to that floor.

Calling the Elevator

One of the elevator call cones is present in Figure 3.4. It is the green cone. Once clicked, it will call the elevator to the specified floor. The call elevator script is very simple. Once clicked, it calls the elevator to the floor specified in its script. The call elevator script can be seen in Listing 3.7.

Listing 3.7: Call Elevator (Call.lsl)

```
integer CHANNEL = 42; // dialog channel

default
{
    state_entry()
    {
        llSetText("Touch to Call Elevator",<0,0,0>,1.0);
    }

    touch_start(integer total_number)
    {

        llRegionSay(42, "Floor 1");
    }
}
```

Once the call elevator cone is clicked, the **touch_start** event handler announces the target floor to the region on the same channel to which the elevator is listening.

```
llRegionSay(42, "Floor 7");
```

The **llRegionSay** has much more distance than **llShout**. Commands sent with **llRegionSay** can be heard anywhere in the region. However, **llRegion** may say not be used on the general chat channel (0). The shout command sends the command to the elevator car.

Summary

Buildings are very common structures in Second Life. The vast majority of a building is usually non-scripted objects. However, some aspects of buildings require scripts. This chapter introduced several recipes that provide commonly used scripts for buildings.

Sometimes water is needed in locations other than the ocean. Second Life provides ocean water for any area below a specific altitude. However, to get water at other altitudes, that water must be built. The first recipe in this chapter showed how to build water. The script showed how to make a splash sound when an avatar enters the water. The recipe also showed how to animate the texture and make it appear that the water was flowing.

Doors are a very common part of buildings in Second Life. This chapter presented three recipes for doors. The first door recipe was a simple door that can be opened by any avatar. The second door could only be opened by its owner. The third door could be opened by its owner or any avatar that the owner adds to its access list.

Many buildings in Second Life contain more than one floor. If the building contains more than one floor, a means is required to move between floors. Common scriptless solutions include stairs and ramps. Scripts can be used to implement elevators and teleport pads. This chapter provides recipes for both.

The next chapter will introduce the Second Life particle system. Particles are small objects that can be emitted from a scripted object. Common uses for particles include leaving trails from vehicles, smoke, and allowing jewelry to glisten.

CHAPTER 4: PARTICLE EFFECTS

- Understanding the Basic Particle Emitter
- Creating Chimney Smoke
- Creating Jewelry Bling
- Creating Explosions
- Creating Falling Leafs

Any prim in Second Life can emit particles. Particles are 2D sprites emitted from their prim in definable ways. Particles are not objects in the sense that they can be touched or count against the land's maximum object count. Particles are generated completely on the client side, so they do not contribute to in-game lag.

Particle emitters are used for a wide range of purposes in Second Life. Some of their uses include:

- Creating insects and leaves in landscaped areas
- Creating flashy laser type effects in clubs
- Leaving smoke and wave trails behind vehicles
- Causing jewelry to sparkle
- Smoke from chimneys
- Creating explosions

This chapter provides several recipes for particle emitters. The first recipe shows a basic particle emitter script.

Recipe 4.1: Basic Particle Emitter

The basic particle emitter script shown in this recipe emits red particles that float upward. The basic particle emitter is designed to be a starting point from which other particle emitters can be created. Most of the particle emitters in this chapter used the basic particle emitter as a starting point. The basic particle emitter can be seen in action in Figure 4.1.

Figure 4.1: Basic Particle Emitter

The script for the basic particle emitter can be seen in Listing 4.1.

Listing 4.1: Basic Particle Emitter (BasicParticle.lsl)

```
generalParticleEmitterOn()
{
    llParticleSystem([
        PSYS_PART_FLAGS , 0
    //| PSYS_PART_BOUNCE_MASK
//Bounce on object's z-axis
    | PSYS_PART_WIND_MASK
//Particles are moved by wind
    | PSYS_PART_INTERP_COLOR_MASK
//Colors fade from start to end
    | PSYS_PART_INTERP_SCALE_MASK
//Scale fades from beginning to end
    | PSYS_PART_FOLLOW_SRC_MASK
//Particles follow the emitter
    | PSYS_PART_FOLLOW_VELOCITY_MASK
//Particles are created at the velocity of the emitter
    //| PSYS_PART_TARGET_POS_MASK   //Particles follow the target
```

```
    | PSYS_PART_EMISSIVE_MASK
//Particles are self-lit (glow)
    //| PSYS_PART_TARGET_LINEAR_MASK
//Undocumented--Sends particles in straight line?

    ,

    //PSYS_SRC_TARGET_KEY , NULL_KEY,
//The particles will head towards the specified key
    //Select one of the following for a pattern:
    //PSYS_SRC_PATTERN_DROP              Particles start at
emitter with no velocity
    //PSYS_SRC_PATTERN_EXPLODE           Particles explode from
the emitter
    //PSYS_SRC_PATTERN_ANGLE             Particles are emitted
in a 2-D angle
    //PSYS_SRC_PATTERN_ANGLE_CONE        Particles are emitted
in a 3-D cone
    //PSYS_SRC_PATTERN_ANGLE_CONE_EMPTY  Particles are emitted
everywhere except for a 3-D cone

    PSYS_SRC_PATTERN,               PSYS_SRC_PATTERN_ANGLE_CONE

    ,PSYS_SRC_TEXTURE,              ""
//UUID of the desired particle texture, or inventory name
    ,PSYS_SRC_MAX_AGE,              0.0
//Time, in seconds, for particles to be emitted. 0 = forever
    ,PSYS_PART_MAX_AGE,             4.0
//Lifetime, in seconds, that a particle lasts
    ,PSYS_SRC_BURST_RATE,           0.5
//How long, in seconds, between each emission
    ,PSYS_SRC_BURST_PART_COUNT,     6
//Number of particles per emission
    ,PSYS_SRC_BURST_RADIUS,         10.0
//Radius of emission
    ,PSYS_SRC_BURST_SPEED_MIN,      .4
//Minimum speed of an emitted particle
    ,PSYS_SRC_BURST_SPEED_MAX,      .5
//Maximum speed of an emitted particle
    ,PSYS_SRC_ACCEL,                <0,0,1>
//Acceleration of particles each second
    ,PSYS_PART_START_COLOR,         <1,0,0>
//Starting RGB color
    ,PSYS_PART_END_COLOR,           <1,0,0>
//Ending RGB color, if INTERP_COLOR_MASK is on
    ,PSYS_PART_START_ALPHA,         1.0
//Starting transparency, 1 is opaque, 0 is transparent.
```

```
        ,PSYS_PART_END_ALPHA,           1.0
//Ending transparency
        ,PSYS_PART_START_SCALE,         <.25,.25,.25>
//Starting particle size
        ,PSYS_PART_END_SCALE,           <1.5,1.5,1.5>
//Ending particle size, if INTERP_SCALE_MASK is on
        ,PSYS_SRC_ANGLE_BEGIN,          300 * DEG_TO_RAD
//Inner angle for ANGLE patterns
        ,PSYS_SRC_ANGLE_END,            60 * DEG_TO_RAD
//Outer angle for ANGLE patterns
        ,PSYS_SRC_OMEGA,                <0.0,0.0,0.0>
//Rotation of ANGLE patterns, similar to llTargetOmega()
            ]);
}

generalParticleEmitterOff()
{
    llParticleSystem([]);
}

default
{
    state_entry()
    {
        generalParticleEmitterOn();
    }

    touch_start( integer num )
    {
        // uncomment the following line to allow this
        // effect to be turned off state off;
    }
}

state off
{
    state_entry()
    {
        generalParticleEmitterOff();
    }

    touch_start( integer num )
    {
        state default;
    }
}
```

Nearly all of the work of the basic particle emitter is performed by the call to **llParticleSystem** inside of the **generalParticleEmitterOn** function.

Creating a Particle Emitter

A particle emitter is created by passing a list to the **llParticleSystem** function. This list is a series of name-value pairs. The majority of the code presented in Listing 4.1 creates this list.

The first name-value pair in the list is **PSYS_PART_FLAGS**. This defines a number of flags that define how the particles behave. These flags can be combined using the bit-wise or operator (|). These flags are summarized in Table 4.1.

Table 4.1: PSYS_PART_FLAGS Flags

Flag	Purpose
PSYS_PART_BOUNCE_MASK	Bounce on object's z-axis.
PSYS_PART_WIND_MASK	Particles are moved by wind.
PSYS_PART_INTERP_COLOR_MASK	Colors fade from start to end.
PSYS_PART_INTERP_SCALE_MASK	Scale fades from beginning to end.
PSYS_PART_FOLLOW_SRC_MASK	Particles follow the emitter.
PSYS_PART_FOLLOW_VELOCITY_MASK	Particles are created at the velocity of the emitter.
PSYS_PART_TARGET_POS_MASK	Particles follow the target.
PSYS_PART_EMISSIVE_MASK	Particles are self-lit (glow).
PSYS_PART_TARGET_LINEAR_MASK	Undocumented flag.

A particle system should specify a pattern using the **PSYS_SRC_PATTERN** name-value pair. Table 4.2 lists the possible patterns that can be specified.

Table 4.2: PSYS_SRC_PATTERN Values

Pattern	Purpose
PSYS_SRC_PATTERN_DROP	Particles start at emitter with no velocity.
PSYS_SRC_PATTERN_EXPLODE	Particles explode from the emitter.
PSYS_SRC_PATTERN_ANGLE	Particles are emitted in a 2-D angle.
PSYS_SRC_PATTERN_ANGLE_CONE	Particles are emitted in a 3-D cone.
PSYS_SRC_PATTERN_ANGLE_CONE_EMPTY	Particles are emitted everywhere except for a 3-D cone.

The remaining name-value pairs are simply a name and a simple value such as a number, texture key, or vector. These name-value pairs are summarized in Table 4.3.

Table 4.3: Remaining Particle Emitter Name-Value Pairs

Name-Value Pair	Purpose
PSYS_SRC_TARGET_KEY	Specifies the key of an object or avatar that the particles will move towards. The PSYS_PART_TARGET_POS_MASK flag must be specified for the PSYS_SRC_TARGET_KEY name-value pair to have any effect.
PSYS_SRC_TEXTURE	Specifies the UUID or inventory name of the desired particle texture.
PSYS_SRC_MAX_AGE	Specifies the maximum amount of time, in seconds, that the particle emitter should emit particles. Specify 0.0 for forever.
PSYS_PART_MAX_AGE	Specifies the amount of time, in seconds, that each particle should remain for.
PSYS_SRC_BURST_RATE	Specifies the amount of time, in seconds, between each emission of particles.
PSYS_SRC_BURST_PART_COUNT	Specifies the number of particles to be produced during each emission.
PSYS_SRC_BURST_RADIUS	Specifies the radius, in meters, of each particle emission.
PSYS_SRC_BURST_SPEED_MIN	Specifies the minimum burst speed of the particles.
PSYS_SRC_BURST_SPEED_MAX	Specifies the maximum burst speed of the particles.
PSYS_SRC_ACCEL	Specifies the acceleration vector for the particles.
PSYS_PART_START_COLOR	Specifies a starting RGB color for the particles. Only works if the INTERP_COLOR_MASK flag is on.
PSYS_PART_END_COLOR,	Specifies an ending RGB color for the particles. Only works if the INTERP_COLOR_MASK flag is on.
PSYS_PART_START_ALPHA	Specifies the starting transparency for particles. Specify a value of 1.0 for opaque and 0.0 for transparent.
PSYS_PART_END_ALPHA	Specifies the ending transparency for particles. Specify a value of 1.0 for opaque and 0.0 for transparent.

PSYS_PART_START_SCALE	Specifies the starting particle size, as a vector. Only works if the INTERP_SCALE_MASK flag was set.
PSYS_PART_END_SCALE	Specifies the ending particle size, as a vector. Only works if the INTERP_SCALE_MASK flag was set.
PSYS_SRC_ANGLE_BEGIN	Specifies the inner angle, in radians, for angle patterns.
PSYS_SRC_ANGLE_END	Specifies the outer angle, in radians, for angle patterns.
PSYS_SRC_OMEGA	Specifies the angle of rotation patterns.

By modifying these values, any sort of particle emitter script can be created. The basic particle emitter script presented in this recipe creates red particles. The script specifies a vector of `<1,0,0>` for the **PSYS_PART_START_COLOR** and **PSYS_PART_END_COLOR**. The value `<1,0,0>` is RGB for red. The particles start with a size of `<.25,.25,.25>` and end with a size of `<1.5,1.5,1.5>`. No texture is specified so the particles will be glowing spheres. To cause the particles to go up a **PSYS_SRC_ACCEL** of `<0,0,1>` is specified.

Many of the remaining recipes in this chapter will simply modify the values of the basic particle script to create other effects. Once a particle system has been specified for a prim, that prim will continue to emit particles until the amount of time specified by **PSYS_SRC_MAX_AGE** elapses. If a value of zero was specified, the prim will continue to create particles indefinably. To stop the prim from producing particles, the **llParticleSystem** function call should be called with an empty set, as seen here:

```
llParticleSystem([]);
```

Once an empty set has been specified to the particle system, no more particles will be produced.

Recipe 4.2: Chimney

Chimneys are a popular addition to many buildings in Second Life. By using a particle emitter script, a chimney can be made to produce smoke as well. This produces a very realistic looking chimney. The example chimney script, provided at the Heaton Research Tower is shown in Figure 4.2.

Figure 4.2: Chimney

The chimney script begins with the basic emitter script. The completed chimney script can be seen in Listing 4.2.

Listing 4.2: Chimney (Smoke.lsl)

```
generalParticleEmitterOn()
{
    llParticleSystem([
        PSYS_PART_FLAGS , 0
    //| PSYS_PART_BOUNCE_MASK
//Bounce on object's z-axis
    | PSYS_PART_WIND_MASK
//Particles are moved by wind
    | PSYS_PART_INTERP_COLOR_MASK
//Colors fade from start to end
    | PSYS_PART_INTERP_SCALE_MASK
//Scale fades from beginning to end
    | PSYS_PART_FOLLOW_SRC_MASK
//Particles follow the emitter
    | PSYS_PART_FOLLOW_VELOCITY_MASK
//Particles are created at the velocity of the emitter
```

```
    //| PSYS_PART_TARGET_POS_MASK
//Particles follow the target
    | PSYS_PART_EMISSIVE_MASK
//Particles are self-lit (glow)
    //| PSYS_PART_TARGET_LINEAR_MASK
//Undocumented--Sends particles in straight line?
    ,


    //PSYS_SRC_TARGET_KEY , NULL_KEY,
//The particles will head towards the specified key
    //Select one of the following for a pattern:
    //PSYS_SRC_PATTERN_DROP              Particles start at
emitter with no velocity
    //PSYS_SRC_PATTERN_EXPLODE          Particles explode from
the emitter
    //PSYS_SRC_PATTERN_ANGLE            Particles are emitted
in a 2-D angle
    //PSYS_SRC_PATTERN_ANGLE_CONE       Particles are emitted
in a 3-D cone
    //PSYS_SRC_PATTERN_ANGLE_CONE_EMPTY    Particles are emitted
everywhere except for a 3-D cone

    PSYS_SRC_PATTERN,               PSYS_SRC_PATTERN_ANGLE_CONE

    ,PSYS_SRC_TEXTURE,              "smoke"
//UUID of the desired particle texture, or inventory name
    ,PSYS_SRC_MAX_AGE,              0.0
//Time, in seconds, for particles to be emitted. 0 = forever
    ,PSYS_PART_MAX_AGE,             3.0
//Lifetime, in seconds, that a particle lasts
    ,PSYS_SRC_BURST_RATE,           0.5
//How long, in seconds, between each emission
    ,PSYS_SRC_BURST_PART_COUNT,     3
//Number of particles per emission
    ,PSYS_SRC_BURST_RADIUS,         10.0
//Radius of emission
    ,PSYS_SRC_BURST_SPEED_MIN,      .4
//Minimum speed of an emitted particle
    ,PSYS_SRC_BURST_SPEED_MAX,      .5
//Maximum speed of an emitted particle
    ,PSYS_SRC_ACCEL,                <0.0,0,.05>
//Acceleration of particles each second
    ,PSYS_PART_START_COLOR,         <1.0,1.0,1.0>
//Starting RGB color
    ,PSYS_PART_END_COLOR,           <1.0,1.0,1.0>
//Ending RGB color, if INTERP_COLOR_MASK is on
```

```
        ,PSYS_PART_START_ALPHA,         0.9
//Starting transparency, 1 is opaque, 0 is transparent.
        ,PSYS_PART_END_ALPHA,          0.0
//Ending transparency
        ,PSYS_PART_START_SCALE,        <.25,.25,.25>
//Starting particle size
        ,PSYS_PART_END_SCALE,          <.75,.75,.75>
//Ending particle size, if INTERP_SCALE_MASK is on
        ,PSYS_SRC_ANGLE_BEGIN,         0 * DEG_TO_RAD
//Inner angle for ANGLE patterns
        ,PSYS_SRC_ANGLE_END,           45 * DEG_TO_RAD
//Outer angle for ANGLE patterns
        ,PSYS_SRC_OMEGA,               <0.0,0.0,0.0>
//Rotation of ANGLE patterns, similar to llTargetOmega()
            ]);
}

generalParticleEmitterOff()
{
    llParticleSystem([]);
}


default
{
    state_entry()
    {
        generalParticleEmitterOn();
    }

    touch_start( integer num )
    {
    }
}

state off
{
    state_entry()
    {
        generalParticleEmitterOff();
    }

    touch_start( integer num )
    {
        state default;
    }
}
```

The most basic difference between the chimney script and the basic particle emitter script is that the chimney script uses textures. Located inside of the object inventory of the chimney object is a texture named "smoke". This texture is a puff of smoke, which will be used as the particle texture.

To produce the smoke, a **PSYS_PART_MAX_AGE** of three seconds is specified. The smoke will disappear relatively quickly as it rises from the chimney. The **PSYS_SRC_BURST_RATE** and **PSYS_SRC_BURST_PART_COUNT** specify the creation of three new puffs of smoke every half a second.

The **PSYS_SRC_BURST_SPEED_MIN** and **PSYS_SRC_BURST_SPEED_MAX** of .4 and .5 cause the smoke to rise relatively slowly. The values for **PSYS_PART_START_COLOR** and **PSYS_PART_END_COLOR** specify that the smoke both starts and stops as white. The **PSYS_SRC_ANGLE_BEGIN** and **PSYS_SRC_ANGLE_END** specify that the smoke will be emitted between zero and 45 degrees.

Recipe 4.3: Leaf Generator

Trees are a very common sight in Second Life. Some trees drop a stream of leaves to give a fall effect. This recipe will show how to create a leaf generator. The leaf generator can be seen in Figure 4.3.

Figure 4.3: Fall Leafs

The leaf generator was based on the basic particle script seen in Recipe 4.1. To learn more about the values that can be specified for a particle emitter, refer to Recipe 4.1. The script for the leaf particle emitter can be seen in Listing 4.3.

Listing 4.3: Fall Leafs (Leafs.lsl)

```
generalParticleEmitterOn()
{
    llParticleSystem([
        PSYS_PART_FLAGS , 0
    //| PSYS_PART_BOUNCE_MASK
//Bounce on object's z-axis
    | PSYS_PART_WIND_MASK
//Particles are moved by wind
    | PSYS_PART_INTERP_COLOR_MASK
//Colors fade from start to end
    | PSYS_PART_INTERP_SCALE_MASK
//Scale fades from beginning to end
    | PSYS_PART_FOLLOW_SRC_MASK
//Particles follow the emitter
    | PSYS_PART_FOLLOW_VELOCITY_MASK
```

```
//Particles are created at the velocity of the emitter
    //| PSYS_PART_TARGET_POS_MASK
//Particles follow the target
    | PSYS_PART_EMISSIVE_MASK
//Particles are self-lit (glow)
    //| PSYS_PART_TARGET_LINEAR_MASK
//Undocumented--Sends particles in straight line?
    ,

    //PSYS_SRC_TARGET_KEY , NULL_KEY,
//The particles will head towards the specified key
    //Select one of the following for a pattern:
    //PSYS_SRC_PATTERN_DROP                Particles start at
emitter with no velocity
    //PSYS_SRC_PATTERN_EXPLODE             Particles explode from
the emitter
    //PSYS_SRC_PATTERN_ANGLE               Particles are emitted
in a 2-D angle
    //PSYS_SRC_PATTERN_ANGLE_CONE          Particles are emitted
in a 3-D cone
    //PSYS_SRC_PATTERN_ANGLE_CONE_EMPTY    Particles are emitted
everywhere except for a 3-D cone

    PSYS_SRC_PATTERN,              PSYS_SRC_PATTERN_ANGLE_CONE

    ,PSYS_SRC_TEXTURE,             "leaf"
//UUID of the desired particle texture, or inventory name
    ,PSYS_SRC_MAX_AGE,             0.0
//Time, in seconds, for particles to be emitted. 0 = forever
    ,PSYS_PART_MAX_AGE,            10.0
//Lifetime, in seconds, that a particle lasts
    ,PSYS_SRC_BURST_RATE,          0.5
//How long, in seconds, between each emission
    ,PSYS_SRC_BURST_PART_COUNT,    6
//Number of particles per emission
    ,PSYS_SRC_BURST_RADIUS,        10.0
//Radius of emission
    ,PSYS_SRC_BURST_SPEED_MIN,     0.1
//Minimum speed of an emitted particle
    ,PSYS_SRC_BURST_SPEED_MAX,     0.5
//Maximum speed of an emitted particle
    ,PSYS_SRC_ACCEL,               <0,0,0>
//Acceleration of particles each second
    ,PSYS_PART_START_COLOR,        <1,1,1>
//Starting RGB color
    ,PSYS_PART_END_COLOR,          <0,0,0>
```

```
//Ending RGB color, if INTERP_COLOR_MASK is on
     ,PSYS_PART_START_ALPHA,        1.0
//Starting transparency, 1 is opaque, 0 is transparent.
     ,PSYS_PART_END_ALPHA,          1.0
//Ending transparency
     ,PSYS_PART_START_SCALE,        <.25,.25,.25>
//Starting particle size
     ,PSYS_PART_END_SCALE,          <.25,.25,.25>
//Ending particle size, if INTERP_SCALE_MASK is on
     ,PSYS_SRC_ANGLE_BEGIN,         90 * DEG_TO_RAD
//Inner angle for ANGLE patterns
     ,PSYS_SRC_ANGLE_END,           90 * DEG_TO_RAD
//Outer angle for ANGLE patterns
     ,PSYS_SRC_OMEGA,               <0.0,0.0,0.0>
//Rotation of ANGLE patterns, similar to llTargetOmega()
             ]);
}

generalParticleEmitterOff()
{
    llParticleSystem([]);
}

default
{
    state_entry()
    {
        generalParticleEmitterOn();
    }

    touch_start( integer num )
    {
    }
}

state off
{
    state_entry()
    {
        generalParticleEmitterOff();
    }

    touch_start( integer num )
    {
        state default;
    }
```

```
}
```

Unlike the basic particle script, the leaf emitter script uses a texture. This texture, named "leaf" is an image of a fall leaf. It is located in the object inventory of the leaf emitter. This allows the particles to appear as leaves.

To produce the leaves a **PSYS_PART_MAX_AGE** of 10 seconds is specified. The leaves disappear relatively slowly as they travel. The **PSYS_SRC_BURST_RATE** and **PSYS_SRC_BURST_PART_COUNT** specify the creation of six new leafs every half a second.

The **PSYS_SRC_BURST_SPEED_MIN** and **PSYS_SRC_BURST_SPEED_MAX** of .1 and .5 cause the leaves to travel relatively slowly. The **PSYS_SRC_ANGLE_BEGIN** and **PSYS_SRC_ANGLE_END** specify that the leaves will be emitted at 90 degrees.

Recipe 4.4: Jewelry

Jewelry is a popular accessory in Second Life. There are many types of jewelry in Second Life, such as necklaces, rings, ear-rings, bracelets and other forms. Some jewelry in Second Life appears to glitter. This glitter effect is done with a particle emitter. This recipe will show how to create a bracelet that uses a particle emitter to glitter. This glitter effect is sometimes called bling. This bracelet is shown in Figure 4.4.

Figure 4.4: Jewelry

The jewelry script was based on the basic particle script seen in Recipe 4.1. To learn more about the values that can be specified for a particle emitter, refer to Recipe 4.1. The script for the jewelry particle emitter can be seen in Listing 4.4.

Listing 4.4: Jewelry (Bling.lsl)

```
generalParticleEmitterOn()
{
    llParticleSystem([
        PSYS_PART_FLAGS , 0
    //| PSYS_PART_BOUNCE_MASK
//Bounce on object's z-axis
    //| PSYS_PART_WIND_MASK
//Particles are moved by wind
    | PSYS_PART_INTERP_COLOR_MASK
//Colors fade from start to end
    | PSYS_PART_INTERP_SCALE_MASK
//Scale fades from beginning to end
    | PSYS_PART_FOLLOW_SRC_MASK
//Particles follow the emitter
    | PSYS_PART_FOLLOW_VELOCITY_MASK
```

```
//Particles are created at the velocity of the emitter
    //| PSYS_PART_TARGET_POS_MASK
//Particles follow the target
    | PSYS_PART_EMISSIVE_MASK
//Particles will glow
    //| PSYS_PART_TARGET_LINEAR_MASK
//Undocumented--Sends particles in straight line?
    ,

    //PSYS_SRC_TARGET_KEY , NULL_KEY,
//The particles will head towards the specified key
    //Select one of the following for a pattern:
    //PSYS_SRC_PATTERN_DROP                Particles start at
emitter with no velocity
    //PSYS_SRC_PATTERN_EXPLODE            Particles explode from
the emitter
    //PSYS_SRC_PATTERN_ANGLE              Particles are emitted
in a 2-D angle
    //PSYS_SRC_PATTERN_ANGLE_CONE         Particles are emitted
in a 3-D cone
    //PSYS_SRC_PATTERN_ANGLE_CONE_EMPTY   Particles are emitted
everywhere except for a 3-D cone

    PSYS_SRC_PATTERN,               PSYS_SRC_PATTERN_EXPLODE

    ,PSYS_SRC_TEXTURE,              ""
//UUID of the desired particle texture, or inventory name
    ,PSYS_SRC_MAX_AGE,             0.0
//Time, in seconds, for particles to be emitted. 0 = forever
    ,PSYS_PART_MAX_AGE,            0.2
//Lifetime, in seconds, that a particle lasts
    ,PSYS_SRC_BURST_RATE,          0.5
//How long, in seconds, between each emission
    ,PSYS_SRC_BURST_PART_COUNT,    6
//Number of particles per emission
    ,PSYS_SRC_BURST_RADIUS,        10.0
//Radius of emission
    ,PSYS_SRC_BURST_SPEED_MIN,     .1
//Minimum speed of an emitted particle
    ,PSYS_SRC_BURST_SPEED_MAX,     .1
//Maximum speed of an emitted particle
    ,PSYS_SRC_ACCEL,               <0,0,0>
//Acceleration of particles each second
    ,PSYS_PART_START_COLOR,        <1,1,1>
//Starting RGB color
    ,PSYS_PART_END_COLOR,          <1,1,1>
```

```
//Ending RGB color, if INTERP_COLOR_MASK is on
     ,PSYS_PART_START_ALPHA,        1.0
//Starting transparency, 1 is opaque, 0 is transparent.
     ,PSYS_PART_END_ALPHA,          1.0
//Ending transparency
     ,PSYS_PART_START_SCALE,        <.04,.25,.01>
//Starting particle size
     ,PSYS_PART_END_SCALE,          <.03,.25,.01>
//Ending particle size, if INTERP_SCALE_MASK is on
     ,PSYS_SRC_ANGLE_BEGIN,         1.54
//Inner angle for ANGLE patterns
     ,PSYS_SRC_ANGLE_END,           1.55
//Outer angle for ANGLE patterns
     ,PSYS_SRC_OMEGA,               <0.0,0.0,0.0>
//Rotation of ANGLE patterns, similar to llTargetOmega()
             ]);
}

generalParticleEmitterOff()
{
    llParticleSystem([]);
}

default
{
    state_entry()
    {
        generalParticleEmitterOn();
    }
}
```

The jewelry script does not use any textures to produce the effect. A **PSYS_PART_MAX_AGE** of just 0.2 seconds is specified. This will make the jewelry glitter appear very briefly. The **PSYS_SRC_BURST_RATE** and **PSYS_SRC_BURST_PART_COUNT** specify the creation of six new flashes every half of a second.

The **PSYS_SRC_BURST_SPEED_MIN** and **PSYS_SRC_BURST_SPEED_MAX** of .1 and .1 cause the flash to barely move. The values for **PSYS_PART_START_COLOR** and **PSYS_PART_END_COLOR** specify that the flash starts and stops as white. The **PSYS_SRC_ANGLE_BEGIN** and **PSYS_SRC_ANGLE_END** specify a narrow emitter angle.

Recipe 4.5: Explosion

Explosions can be a useful effect in Second Life. This recipe implements an explosion that includes fire, smoke and a bang sound effect. To see the explosion in action, touch the black sphere that contains it. The object will explode, as seen in Figure 4.5.

Figure 4.5: Explosion

The explosion script is not based on the basic particle script, as were previous recipes. The script for the explosion script can be seen in Listing 4.5.

Listing 4.5: Explosion (Explode.lsl)

```
fakeMakeExplosion(integer particle_count, float particle_scale,
float particle_speed,
                float particle_lifetime, float source_cone,
string source_texture_id,
                vector local_offset)
{
    //local_offset is ignored
    llParticleSystem([
        PSYS_PART_FLAGS,                PSYS_PART_INTERP_COLOR_
```

```
MASK|PSYS_PART_INTERP_SCALE_MASK|PSYS_PART_EMISSIVE_MASK|
       PSYS_PART_WIND_MASK,
           PSYS_SRC_PATTERN,              PSYS_SRC_PATTERN_ANGLE_CONE,
           PSYS_PART_START_COLOR,         <1.0, 1.0, 1.0>,
           PSYS_PART_END_COLOR,           <1.0, 1.0, 1.0>,
           PSYS_PART_START_ALPHA,         0.50,
           PSYS_PART_END_ALPHA,           0.25,
           PSYS_PART_START_SCALE,         <particle_scale,
               particle_scale, 0.0>,
           PSYS_PART_END_SCALE,           <particle_scale * 2
               + particle_lifetime, particle_scale * 2
               + particle_lifetime, 0.0>,
           PSYS_PART_MAX_AGE,             particle_lifetime,
           PSYS_SRC_ACCEL,                <0.0, 0.0, 0.0>,
           PSYS_SRC_TEXTURE,              source_texture_id,
           PSYS_SRC_BURST_RATE,           1.0,
           PSYS_SRC_ANGLE_BEGIN,          0.0,
           PSYS_SRC_ANGLE_END,            source_cone * PI,
           PSYS_SRC_BURST_PART_COUNT,     particle_count / 2,
           PSYS_SRC_BURST_RADIUS,         0.0,
           PSYS_SRC_BURST_SPEED_MIN,      particle_speed / 3,
           PSYS_SRC_BURST_SPEED_MAX,      particle_speed * 2/3,
           PSYS_SRC_MAX_AGE,              particle_lifetime / 2,
           PSYS_SRC_OMEGA,                <0.0, 0.0, 0.0>
           ]);
}


default
{
    state_entry()
    {
        llPreloadSound("explosion");
        llSetText("Touch to Explode", <0.0, 1.0, 0.0>, 1.0);
    }



    touch_start(integer total_number)
    {
        fakeMakeExplosion(80, 1.0, 13.0, 2.2, 1.0, "fire",
            <0.0, 0.0, 0.0>);
        llTriggerSound("explosion", 10.0);
        llSleep(.5);
        fakeMakeExplosion(80, 1.0, 13.0, 2.2, 1.0, "smoke",
            <0.0, 0.0, 0.0>);
        llSleep(1);
```

```
            llParticleSystem([]);
    }
}
```

The explosion script uses a function named **fakeMakeExplosion**. The **fakeMakeExplosion** is a function that was posted to the Linden Scripting Language Wiki (**http://wiki.secondlife.com/wiki/**) and which emulates the behavior of the older function **llMakeExplosion**. The **llMakeExplosion** function has been deprecated and should no longer be used. However, the **fakeMakeExplosion** closely emulates the behavior of the original **llMakeExplosion**.

The **fakeMakeExplosion** function accepts the seven parameters. These parameters are specified in Table 4.4.

Table 4.4: Parameters for fakeMakeExplosion

Parameter	Purpose
particles	How many particles should be used for the explosion.
scale	How big should the particles be.
vel	What is the velocity for the explosion particles.
lifetime	How long, in seconds, should the explosion particles last.
arc	The explosion should occur between 0 and the angle specified.
texture	What texture should be used for the explosion particles.
offset	How far from the object should the explosion occur.

The following code is used in the explosion recipe to create an explosion effect. First **fakeMakeExplosion** is called to produce an initial blast of fire.

```
fakeMakeExplosion(80, 1.0, 13.0, 2.2, 1.0, "fire",
<0.0, 0.0, 0.0>);
```

Next the explosion sound is played.

```
llTriggerSound("explosion", 10.0);
```

The explosion lasts for about a half second before the smoke begins.

```
llSleep(.5);
```

Now a similar blast of smoke is produced.

```
fakeMakeExplosion(80, 1.0, 13.0, 2.2, 1.0, "smoke",
<0.0, 0.0, 0.0>);
```

The smoke is allowed to continue for a second.

```
llSleep(1);
```

The particle system is shut down.

```
llParticleSystem([]);
```

This produces a brief explosion that lasts for two seconds.

Summary

This chapter provided several recipes for the Linden Scripting Language particle emitter system. The particle emitter allows a prim to emit 2D particles. These particles can be used to create many different effects. This chapter provided recipes that demonstrate some of the most common uses for particle scripts.

A basic particle emitter script was presented that establishes all of the parameters necessary to begin emitting particles. Unmodified, the basic particle emitter script emits red particles upwards. However, the basic particle emitter script is meant to be a starting point for other particle emitter scripts. Many of the recipes in this chapter started with the basic particle emitter script.

Particle emitter scripts can be very useful for creating smoke. A recipe to create a chimney was presented in this chapter. The chimney script extended the basic particle script to produce puffs of smoke. When combined with a brick textured object, a chimney is produced.

Trees are very common in Second Life. An interesting fall effect can be created by causing leaves to fall from trees. A recipe is provided that creates a particle emitter that emits leafs. The leaves float gently in the wind.

Jewelry is another common user of particle scripts in Second Life. By using a particle script, Jewelry can be made to glitter. This effect is often called bling. Such "bling enabled" jewelry has become very popular in Second Life.

Particle emitter scripts can also be useful for causing vehicles to produce trails. The next chapter introduces Second Life vehicles. One of the vehicles will use a particle emitter script to leave waves behind a boat as it travels in the water.

CHAPTER 5: VEHICLES

- Create a Car
- Create a Boat
- Create a Helicopter
- Create a Super Car that is all Three
- Linear and Angular Motors

In a virtual world, such as Second Life, where people can fly and teleport, why would someone need a vehicle? Despite this, vehicles are very popular in Second Life where there are many different types of vehicles. In this chapter recipes will be presented for three different vehicle types. A fourth vehicle will combine all of the previous four and produce a "Super Car".

The recipes in this chapter cover three categories of vehicles. A car was selected to represent land vehicles. A boat was selected to represent water vehicles. A helicopter was selected to represent air vehicles. Finally, a super car was created that shares attributes with all of the previous vehicles. The super car is comfortable on land, sea or air. The vehicles covered by this chapter are presented in Figure 5.1.

Figure 5.1: Second Life Vehicles

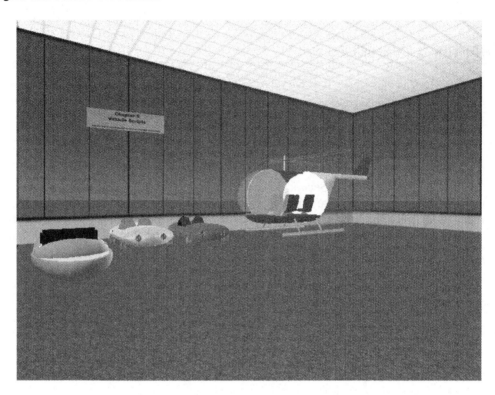

The first vehicle to be covered will be the car. Many of the vehicles share characteristics with the car. Implementation of these common characteristics will not be repeated in the later recipes. Therefore, it is important to review the car recipe, no matter what type of vehicle you are interested in creating.

Recipe 5.1: Car

The example car for this recipe is a bright-red two seater convertible. The car is not a true convertible, in that it does not convert. It is always in top-down mode. Because it never rains in Second Life, this is not a problem! The little red sports car is shown in Figure 5.2.

Figure 5.2: A Car in Second Life

The next few sections will explain different aspects of the car, and how it was constructed and scripted.

Vehicle Materials

All prims in Second Life have a material. The following materials are supported in Second Life: stone, metal, glass, wood, flesh, plastic and rubber. Materials affect the mass and friction of the vehicle. The majority of prims in Second Life are made of wood. This is because wood is the default material. Material type is specified in the object window. Figure 5.3 shows the material type being set.

Figure 5.3: Setting the Material Type

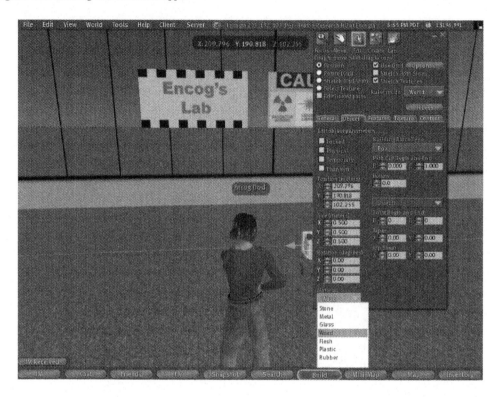

Material types are very important for vehicles in Second Life. The material type for the tires of the car is of particular importance. Which of the above material types should be chosen for the tires? It may seem that rubber is the logical choice. Rubber would create too much friction. Remember, that in the simplistic physics of Second Life, the tires do not really turn. They appear to turn, due to a trick used later in this recipe. But they are not really turning. Imagine a parked car being pushed along the ground. If the parking brake is on, that car will not move as well. The rubber would burn and the car would merely bump along. This is what happens when the tires are made of rubber in Second Life. The car barely moves.

The material of choice is surprising. It is the material with the least friction - glass. Any part of the vehicle that comes into contact with the ground should be made of glass. Durability is not an issue with a prim! Glass wheels are the norm in Second Life. Don't think of the materials as the actual materials. Rather, think of the material types as specifying the amount of friction the prim will cause.

The Root Prim

The car, like any other object in Second Life, consists of several primitives. However, not all primitives are equal. The most important primitive, or prim, is the root prim. When an object is selected, the root prim is shown outlined in yellow. The root prim is a very important concept for vehicles.

The root prim is the last prim selected when the vehicle was linked together. Therefore, it is very easy to accidentally change the root prim when new prims are being added to the object. For example, consider adding a bumper sticker to the car. Consider if the car was selected, the bumper sticker shift-selected and a link created. The bumper sticker would now be a part of the car object. However, the bumper sticker would now be the root prim! The bumper sticker was the last prim selected, so it is now the root prim. This would prevent the car from functioning properly. This is because the car is designed for the driver's seat to be the root prim.

The correct way to add the bumper sticker to the car would be to do the procedure described above in reverse. First, select the bumper sticker. Then shift-select the car and create the link. Now the car is the last object selected and the root prim will not change.

The root primitive is critical to a vehicle because the root prim is where the main vehicle script resides. Think of the root prim as the motor for the vehicle. It is the root prim that is moving, everything else is only attached to the root prim. It is also convenient if the driver sits on the root prim. This is why most vehicles in Second Life always make the root prim the driver's seat.

It also makes vehicle creation considerably easier if the root prim is at zero rotation in all three directions. At the very least, the root prim should only be rotated in 90-degree intervals in the three dimensions.

The root prim must be made a physical object for the vehicle to operate. Normally, this is done in code using a call to **llSetStatus**. However, being physical imposes an important limitation on vehicles. Physical objects in Second Life can contain no more than 31 prims. Because of this, no vehicle can contain more than 31 prims. If prim number 32 is added, the vehicle will stop.

The root prim is where the main car script resides. The car script can be seen in Listing 5.1.

Listing 5.1: Main Car Script for the Root Prim (Car.lsl)

```
float forward_power = 15; //Power used to go forward (1 to 30)
float reverse_power = -15; //Power used to go reverse (-1 to -30)
float turning_ratio = 2.0; //How sharply the vehicle turns. Less
is more sharply. (.1 to 10)
string sit_message = "Ride"; //Sit message
```

```
string not_owner_message = "You are not the owner of this vehicle
..."; //Not owner message

default
{
    state_entry()
    {
        llSetSitText(sit_message);
        // forward-back,left-right,updown
        llSitTarget(<0.2,0,0.45>, ZERO_ROTATION );

        llSetCameraEyeOffset(<-8, 0.0, 5.0>);
        llSetCameraAtOffset(<1.0, 0.0, 2.0>);

        llPreloadSound("car_start");
        llPreloadSound("car_run");

        //car
        llSetVehicleType(VEHICLE_TYPE_CAR);
        llSetVehicleFloatParam(
VEHICLE_ANGULAR_DEFLECTION_EFFICIENCY, 0.2);
        llSetVehicleFloatParam(
VEHICLE_LINEAR_DEFLECTION_EFFICIENCY, 0.80);
        llSetVehicleFloatParam(
VEHICLE_ANGULAR_DEFLECTION_TIMESCALE, 0.10);
        llSetVehicleFloatParam(
VEHICLE_LINEAR_DEFLECTION_TIMESCALE, 0.10);
        llSetVehicleFloatParam(
VEHICLE_LINEAR_MOTOR_TIMESCALE, 1.0);
        llSetVehicleFloatParam(
VEHICLE_LINEAR_MOTOR_DECAY_TIMESCALE, 0.2);
        llSetVehicleFloatParam(
VEHICLE_ANGULAR_MOTOR_TIMESCALE, 0.1);
        llSetVehicleFloatParam(
VEHICLE_ANGULAR_MOTOR_DECAY_TIMESCALE, 0.5);
        llSetVehicleVectorParam(
VEHICLE_LINEAR_FRICTION_TIMESCALE, <1000.0, 2.0, 1000.0>);
        llSetVehicleVectorParam(
VEHICLE_ANGULAR_FRICTION_TIMESCALE, <10.0, 10.0, 1000.0>);
        llSetVehicleFloatParam(
VEHICLE_VERTICAL_ATTRACTION_EFFICIENCY, 0.50);
        llSetVehicleFloatParam(
VEHICLE_VERTICAL_ATTRACTION_TIMESCALE, 0.50);
    }

    changed(integer change)
    {
```

```
    if (change & CHANGED_LINK)
    {

        key agent = llAvatarOnSitTarget();
        if (agent)
        {
            if (agent != llGetOwner())
            {
                llSay(0, not_owner_message);
                llUnSit(agent);
                llPushObject(agent, <0,0,50>,
ZERO_VECTOR, FALSE);
            }
            else
            {
                llTriggerSound("car_start",1);


                llMessageLinked(LINK_ALL_CHILDREN , 0,
"WHEEL_DRIVING", NULL_KEY);
                llSleep(.4);
                llSetStatus(STATUS_PHYSICS, TRUE);
                llSleep(.1);
                llRequestPermissions(agent,
PERMISSION_TRIGGER_ANIMATION | PERMISSION_TAKE_CONTROLS);

                llLoopSound("car_run",1);
            }
        }
        else
        {
            llStopSound();

            llSetStatus(STATUS_PHYSICS, FALSE);
            llSleep(.4);
            llReleaseControls();
            llTargetOmega(<0,0,0>,PI,0);

            llResetScript();
        }
    }

}
```

```
run_time_permissions(integer perm)
{
    if (perm)
    {
        llTakeControls(CONTROL_FWD | CONTROL_BACK |
CONTROL_DOWN | CONTROL_UP | CONTROL_RIGHT |
                          CONTROL_LEFT | CONTROL_ROT_RIGHT |
CONTROL_ROT_LEFT, TRUE, FALSE);
    }
}

control(key id, integer level, integer edge)
{
    integer reverse=1;
    vector angular_motor;

    //get current speed
    vector vel = llGetVel();
    float speed = llVecMag(vel);

    //car controls
    if(level & CONTROL_FWD)
    {
        llSetVehicleVectorParam(
VEHICLE_LINEAR_MOTOR_DIRECTION, <forward_power,0,0>);
        reverse=1;
    }
    if(level & CONTROL_BACK)
    {
        llSetVehicleVectorParam(
VEHICLE_LINEAR_MOTOR_DIRECTION, <reverse_power,0,0>);
        reverse = -1;
    }

    if(level & (CONTROL_RIGHT|CONTROL_ROT_RIGHT))
    {
        angular_motor.z -= speed / turning_ratio * reverse;
    }

    if(level & (CONTROL_LEFT|CONTROL_ROT_LEFT))
    {
        angular_motor.z += speed / turning_ratio * reverse;
    }

    llSetVehicleVectorParam(VEHICLE_ANGULAR_MOTOR_DIRECTION,
        angular_motor);
```

```
    } //end control


} //end default
```

The following sections explain the various parts of the car script.

Obtaining Permission

The car will be driven in a similar way to how an avatar walks. Cursor keys will turn and move it forward and backward. However, for a script to do this, it must get permission from the avatar. This is done with the **run_time_permissions** event handler. This event handler is shown here.

```
run_time_permissions(integer perm)
{
    if (perm)
    {
        llTakeControls(CONTROL_FWD | CONTROL_BACK |
        CONTROL_DOWN | CONTROL_UP | CONTROL_RIGHT |
    CONTROL_LEFT | CONTROL_ROT_RIGHT |
        CONTROL_ROT_LEFT, TRUE, FALSE);
    }
}
```

The same event handler is used for all of the vehicles in this chapter.

Sitting Down as the Driver

When an avatar sits down to drive the car, the car must perform a setup before the avatar can begin driving the car. The **changed** event handler is called when an avatar sits on an object. First, the **changed** event handler checks to see whether it was called because an object was linked to it. In this case, it was the avatar that was linked to the car object.

```
changed(integer change)
{
    if (change & CHANGED_LINK)
    {
```

Next, the script checks to see what avatar sat on it. If it was an avatar that sat on the car, the car checks to see whether the avatar is the car's owner.

```
        key agent = llAvatarOnSitTarget();
        if (agent)
        {
            if (agent != llGetOwner())
            {
```

If it is not the car's owner, the car informs the avatar that they are not allowed to drive the car. The avatar is pushed away.

```
llSay(0, not_owner_message);
llUnSit(agent);
llPushObject(agent, <0,0,50>,
        ZERO_VECTOR, FALSE);
}
```

If it is the car's owner, it is time to set up the car so that it can be driven. First, the **car_start** sound is played. The car is then enabled as a physical object. A physical object can be pushed by external or internal forces. Permission to take the controls is then requested. Finally, the **car_run** sound is looped.

```
else
{
        llTriggerSound("car_start",1);

        llSleep(.4);
    llSetStatus(STATUS_PHYSICS, TRUE);
    llSleep(.1);
    llRequestPermissions(agent,
PERMISSION_TRIGGER_ANIMATION | PERMISSION_TAKE_CONTROLS);

        llLoopSound("car_run",1);
    }
}
```

If the avatar is getting up, stop the sound and turn off physics. Controls are released. If physics are left on, any avatar who bumped into the parked car would move it.

```
else
{
        llStopSound();

        llSetStatus(STATUS_PHYSICS, FALSE);
        llSleep(.1);
        llSleep(.4);
        llReleaseControls();
        llTargetOmega(<0,0,0>,PI,0);
        llResetScript();
    }
    }
}
```

The call to **llTargetOmega** is very important. Without this call, the parked car will sometimes begin to rotate. This is a very strange, undesirable effect.

This script is very similar to the changed script used for all other vehicles in this chapter. The only changes will be in the sounds played and in the case of the helicopter starting, the blades rotating. The boat will also start a "wave trail" behind it. These differences will be covered in the other recipes in this chapter.

Controlling the Car

The **control** event handler is called when the user interacts with the control keys. The control keys are the cursor keys and page up/down, as well as other control keys. The car will only use the cursor keys.

Vehicles in Second Life are moved by two motors; the linear motor and the angular motor. The linear motor can move the vehicle in any direction in the x, y and z coordinate planes. The angular motor can rotate the object in any of the x, y and z coordinate planes. The car uses both motors. The linear motor moves the car forwards and backwards. The angular motor turns the car.

The **control** event handler begins by setting up some variables that will be needed by the handler. Because cars turn differently when in reverse, a flag is required to indicate if we are in reverse. Also, a variable is created to hold the direction of the angular motor.

```
control(key id, integer level, integer edge)
{
        integer reverse=1;
        vector angular_motor;
```

The current speed is obtained. This will be used with turning. Cars need to be in motion to turn.

```
        //get current speed
        vector vel = llGetVel();
        float speed = llVecMag(vel);
```

Next, each of the relevant controls will be checked. The first control to be checked is the forward control. When the user presses forward, the linear motor is used to apply the force to move the car forward. Note also that the car is moving forward by setting the reverse variable to one.

```
        //car controls
        if(level & CONTROL_FWD)
        {
                llSetVehicleVectorParam(
        VEHICLE_LINEAR_MOTOR_DIRECTION, <forward_power,0,0>);
                reverse=1;
        }
```

If the user presses back, apply power in the opposite direction. Note also that the car has been put in reverse by setting the reverse variable to -1.

```
if(level & CONTROL_BACK)
{
        llSetVehicleVectorParam(
VEHICLE_LINEAR_MOTOR_DIRECTION, <reverse_power,0,0>);
        reverse = -1;
}
```

For a right turn, rotate the car in the z-coordinate. Rotate by the specified angle and take into account whether the car is going in reverse.

```
if(level & (CONTROL_RIGHT|CONTROL_ROT_RIGHT))
{
        angular_motor.z -= speed /
                turning_ratio * reverse;
}
```

For a left turn, rotate the car in the z-coordinate. Rotate by the specified angle and take into account whether the car is going in reverse.

```
if(level & (CONTROL_LEFT|CONTROL_ROT_LEFT))
{
        angular_motor.z += speed /
                turning_ratio * reverse;
}
```

Now the angular motor can be set.

```
llSetVehicleVectorParam(
        VEHICLE_ANGULAR_MOTOR_DIRECTION, angular_motor);
```

```
}
```

The **control** event handler in the script is different for each vehicle type. This is because each vehicle handles differently. However, each vehicle shares some similarity in the **control** event handler.

Initializing the Car

The **state_entry** event handler initializes the car. Initialization is very different for each vehicle type. The car begins by setting the sit text and sit target.

```
state_entry()
{
    llSetSitText(sit_message);
    // forward-back,left-right,updown
    llSitTarget(<0.2,0,0.45>, ZERO_ROTATION );
```

Next, the camera is placed. The camera is offset behind and above the car. Now the camera looks into the car.

```
llSetCameraEyeOffset(<-8, 0.0, 5.0>);
llSetCameraAtOffset(<1.0, 0.0, 2.0>);
```

The two sounds that are used are preloaded. This prevents any pause when the sounds are played for the first time.

```
llPreloadSound("car_start");
llPreloadSound("car_run");
```

Next the vehicle parameters are set. The first is the vehicle type, which is set by calling **llSetVehicleType**. Valid values for **llSetVehicleType** are listed in Table 5.1.

Table 5.1: Vehicle Types

Vehicle Type	Purpose
VEHICLE_TYPE_NONE	Not a vehicle.
VEHICLE_TYPE_SLED	Simple vehicle that bumps along the ground, has a tendency to move along its local x-axis.
VEHICLE_TYPE_CAR	Vehicle that bounces along the ground but requires motors to be driven from external controls or other source.
VEHICLE_TYPE_BOAT	Hovers over water with a great deal of friction and some angular deflection.
VEHICLE_TYPE_AIRPLANE	Uses linear deflection for lift, no hover, and must bank to turn.
VEHICLE_TYPE_BALLOON	Hover, and friction, and no deflection.

Additionally vehicle parameters are set using the **llSetVehicleFloatParam**, **llSetVehicleVectorParam** and **llSetVehicleRotationParam** function calls. Table 5.2 summarizes the values that can be set with the **llSetVehicleFloatParam**.

Table 5.2: Floating Point Vehicle Parameters

Parameter	Purpose
VEHICLE_ANGULAR_DEFLECTION_EFFICIENCY	Value between 0 (no deflection) and 1 (maximum strength).
VEHICLE_ANGULAR_DEFLECTION_TIMESCALE	Exponential timescale for the vehicle to achieve full angular deflection.
VEHICLE_ANGULAR_MOTOR_DECAY_TIMESCALE	Exponential timescale for the angular motor's effectiveness to decay toward zero.
VEHICLE_ANGULAR_MOTOR_TIMESCALE	Exponential timescale for the vehicle to achieve its full angular motor velocity.
VEHICLE_BANKING_EFFICIENCY	Value between -1 (leans out of turns), 0 (no banking), and +1 (leans into turns).
VEHICLE_BANKING_MIX	Value between 0 (static banking) and 1 (dynamic banking).
VEHICLE_BANKING_TIMESCALE	Exponential timescale for the banking behavior to take full effect.
VEHICLE_BUOYANCY	Value between -1 (double-gravity) and 1 (full anti-gravity).
VEHICLE_HOVER_HEIGHT	Height at which the vehicle will try to hover.
VEHICLE_HOVER_EFFICIENCY	Value between 0 (bouncy) and 1 (critically damped) hover behavior.
VEHICLE_HOVER_TIMESCALE	The period of time for the vehicle to achieve its hover height.
VEHICLE_LINEAR_DEFLECTION_EFFICIENCY	Value between 0 (no deflection) and 1 (maximum strength).

VEHICLE_LINEAR_DEFLECTION_TIMESCALE	An exponential timescale for the vehicle to redirect its velocity along its x-axis.
VEHICLE_LINEAR_MOTOR_DECAY_TIMESCALE	An exponential timescale for the linear motor's effectiveness to decay toward zero.
VEHICLE_LINEAR_MOTOR_TIMESCALE	An exponential timescale for the vehicle to achieve its full linear motor velocity.
VEHICLE_VERTICAL_ATTRACTION_EFFICIENCY	Value between 0 (bouncy) and 1 (critically damped) attraction of vehicle z-axis to world z-axis (vertical).
VEHICLE_VERTICAL_ATTRACTION_TIMESCALE	An exponential timescale for the vehicle to align its z-axis to the world z-axis (vertical).

Table 5.3 summarizes the values that can be set with the **llSetVehicleVectorParam**.

Table 5.3: Vector Vehicle Parameters

Parameter	Purpose
VEHICLE_ANGULAR_FRICTION_TIMESCALE	The vector of timescales for exponential decay of angular velocity about the three vehicle axes.
VEHICLE_ANGULAR_MOTOR_DIRECTION	The angular velocity that the vehicle will try to achieve.
VEHICLE_LINEAR_FRICTION_TIMESCALE	The vector of timescales for exponential decay of linear velocity along the three vehicle axes.
VEHICLE_LINEAR_MOTOR_DIRECTION	The linear velocity that the vehicle will try to achieve.
VEHICLE_LINEAR_MOTOR_OFFSET	The offset from the center of mass of the vehicle where the linear motor is applied.

Table 5.4 summarizes the values that can be set with the **llSetVehicleRotationParam**.

Table 5.4: Rotation Point Vehicle Parameters

Parameter	Purpose
VEHICLE_REFERENCE_FRAME	The rotation of vehicle axes relative to local frame. Useful for when the root prim must be rotated.

The settings for the vehicle parameters of the car will now be reviewed. First, the vehicle type is set to car. Angular deflection is the tendency of a vehicle to move in certain directions. For example, a car will not tend to move in the z-coordinate (up and down). The angular deflection efficiency determines how effective angular deflection is. A value of 0.2 specifies angular deflection at 20%. This allows the car to turn fairly easily.

```
llSetVehicleType(VEHICLE_TYPE_CAR);
llSetVehicleFloatParam(
VEHICLE_ANGULAR_DEFLECTION_EFFICIENCY, 0.2);
```

A value of 0.8 specifies that linear deflection has 80% power. This means it takes more effort for the car to change its linear velocity.

```
llSetVehicleFloatParam(
VEHICLE_LINEAR_DEFLECTION_EFFICIENCY, 0.80);
```

It takes the car one tenth of a second for both linear and angular deflection to commence.

```
llSetVehicleFloatParam(
VEHICLE_ANGULAR_DEFLECTION_TIMESCALE, 0.10);
llSetVehicleFloatParam(
VEHICLE_LINEAR_DEFLECTION_TIMESCALE, 0.10);
```

It takes one second for the linear motor to reach full power.

```
llSetVehicleFloatParam(
VEHICLE_LINEAR_MOTOR_TIMESCALE, 1.0);
```

The linear motor will drop off in one fifth of a second. The car will not coast well.

```
llSetVehicleFloatParam(
VEHICLE_LINEAR_MOTOR_DECAY_TIMESCALE, 0.2);
```

The angular motor will reach full power in one tenth of a second.

```
llSetVehicleFloatParam(
VEHICLE_ANGULAR_MOTOR_TIMESCALE, 0.1);
```

The angular motor will drop off in 0.5 seconds. The car will stop turning fairly quickly when the user lets up on the control.

```
llSetVehicleFloatParam(
```

```
VEHICLE_ANGULAR_MOTOR_DECAY_TIMESCALE, 0.5);
```

Friction affects the car only in the y-coordinate, which is how the car moves forwards and backwards. The car can quickly fall or turn.

```
llSetVehicleVectorParam(
VEHICLE_LINEAR_FRICTION_TIMESCALE, <1000.0, 2.0, 1000.0>);
```

The car rotates fairly easily in the z-coordinate, but x and y are more difficult to rotate in.

```
llSetVehicleVectorParam(
VEHICLE_ANGULAR_FRICTION_TIMESCALE, <10.0, 10.0, 1000.0>);
```

A car should always stay right-side-up. The vertical attraction feature allows this.

```
llSetVehicleFloatParam(
VEHICLE_VERTICAL_ATTRACTION_EFFICIENCY, 0.50);
llSetVehicleFloatParam(
VEHICLE_VERTICAL_ATTRACTION_TIMESCALE, 0.50);
```

These values work well for a car. However, they will be considerably different for a boat or helicopter.

Who Sits Where

The car allows for one passenger, in addition to the driver. Additional passengers will be ejected. Figure 5.4 shows the car with a driver and one passenger.

Figure 5.4: A Car with Two Passengers

Extra seats must be provided to allow additional people, other than the driver to ride in a vehicle. The passenger seat has a simple **llSitTarget** function call in its **state_entry** event handler. The passenger seat can be seen here.

Listing 5.2: Car Passenger Seat (CarSeat.lsl)

```
default
{
    state_entry()
    {
        llSitTarget(<0.2,0,0.45>, ZERO_ROTATION );
    }
}
```

The driver's seat should be the root prim, which is the last prim selected. The passenger's seat should be the second to the last prim selected. A third script is also required, to disallow further seating. The third to the last prim selected should contain a script that prevents the user from sitting down. Such a script can be seen in Listing 5.3.

Listing 5.3: Can't Sit Here (DontSitHere.lsl)

```
default
```

```
{
    state_entry()
    {
        llSitTarget(<0.2,0,0.45>, ZERO_ROTATION );
    }

    changed(integer change)
    {

        if (change & CHANGED_LINK)
        {
            key agent = llAvatarOnSitTarget();
            if (agent)
            {
                llUnSit(agent);
                llSay(0,"Sorry, this vehicle is full.");
            }
        }
    }
}
```

The "don't sit here" script is needed because an avatar will try to choose a seat in the following order.

- If the exact prim selected can be sat on, choose it
- Next, try to sit on the root prim
- Next, try to sit on the prim selected just before the root prim
- Next, try to sit on the prim selected two before the root prim and so on

Because of this, the "chain" of sit targets must be broken just beyond the last passenger seat. The do not sit here script specifies a sit target in the **state_entry**, as for the passenger seat:

```
default
{
    state_entry()
    {
        llSitTarget(<0.2,0,0.45>, ZERO_ROTATION );
    }
```

Whenever the changed event handler is called, the avatar should be ejected with the **llUnSit** function call.

```
    changed(integer change)
    {
        if (change & CHANGED_LINK)
        {
            key agent = llAvatarOnSitTarget();
```

```
                    if (agent)
                    {
                        llUnSit(agent);
                        llSay(0,"Sorry, this vehicle is full.");
                    }
                }
            }
        }
    }
```

This prevents avatars from sitting on unintended parts of the vehicle.

Turning the Wheels

To appear more realistic, the car turns its wheels when in motion. There are several ways that this is commonly done in Second Life vehicles. The method used for this car is shown in Listing 5.4.

Listing 5.4: Car Wheel (WheelScript.lsl)

```
default
{
    state_entry()
    {
        llSetTimerEvent(0.20);
    }
    timer()
    {
        vector vel = llGetVel();
        float speed = llVecMag(vel);
        if(speed > 0)
        {
            llSetTextureAnim(ANIM_ON | SMOOTH | LOOP, 0, 0, 0,
                0, 1, speed*0.5);
        }
        else
        {
            llSetTextureAnim(ANIM_ON | SMOOTH | LOOP | REVERSE,
                           0, 0, 0, 0, 1, speed*0.5);
        }
    }
}
```

The above script is contained in all four wheels of the car. The script works by rotating the texture of the wheel in one direction when the car is moving forward, and in another direction when moving backwards. The speed of the car can be obtained by calling **llGetVel**, as seen here.

```
vector vel = llGetVel();
float speed = llVecMag(vel);
if(speed > 0)
{
      llSetTextureAnim(ANIM_ON | SMOOTH | LOOP, 0, 0, 0, 0, 1,
            speed*0.5);
}
else
{
      llSetTextureAnim(ANIM_ON | SMOOTH | LOOP | REVERSE,
            0, 0, 0, 0, 1, speed*0.5);
}
```

The hubcaps must be rotated too. The same script is used.

There quite a few parts to the car. Unlike previous recipes, one script can not handle the entire object. Individual scripts are needed in several of the prims that make up the car. Some parts of the scripts will be reused in other vehicles. However, the other vehicles in this chapter are either air or sea based. This introduces some differences from the land based car.

Recipe 5.2: Boat

Boats are also very popular in Second Life. The boat is designed to work with sea water. That is, the built-in water that is at a specific height, usually 20 meters. Sea areas can usually be found by examining the map. Or look for a "water sandbox" on the search. Sandboxes are public areas that allow anyone to build there. The boat shares some characteristics with the car. However, there are some important differences.

- The boat should roll slightly when it turns.
- The boat has buoyancy, and floats on the water.
- The boat leaves waves in its wake.
- The boat uses different sounds.
- The boat has no wheels to turn.

Most boats in Second Life will not work with artificial water. This is because the vehicle engine does not recognize artificial water as water. Artificial water is a prim that is textured to look like water. Recipe 3.1 shows how to create artificial water. To create a "boat" that traveled on artificial water, an "air vehicle" would need to be created to hover just above it.

All of the scripts necessary for the boat will be shown. However, only the aspects of the boat that are different from the car will be explained. If you have not reviewed the car, Recipe 5.1, should be reviewed prior to learning how to create a boat. The boat can be seen in Figure 5.5.

Figure 5.5: A Boat in Second Life

Most of the script necessary to handle the boat is contained in the root prim. The root prim is the driver's seat of the boat. This script is shown in Listing 5.5.

Listing 5.5: The Boat Script (Boat.lsl)

```
float forward_power = 25; //Power used to go forward (1 to 30)
float reverse_power = -15; //Power used to go reverse (-1 to -30)
float turning_ratio = 5.0; //How sharply the vehicle turns. Less
is more sharply. (.1 to 10)
string sit_message = "Ride"; //Sit message
string not_owner_message = "You are not the owner of this vehicle
..."; //Not owner message

default
{
    state_entry()
    {
        llSetSitText(sit_message);
        // forward-back,left-right,updown
        llSitTarget(<0.2,0,0.45>, ZERO_ROTATION );
```

```
llSetCameraEyeOffset(<-12, 0.0, 5.0>);
llSetCameraAtOffset(<1.0, 0.0, 2.0>);

llPreloadSound("boat_start");
llPreloadSound("boat_run");
    llSetVehicleFlags(0);
llSetVehicleType(VEHICLE_TYPE_BOAT);
llSetVehicleFlags(VEHICLE_FLAG_HOVER_UP_ONLY |
    VEHICLE_FLAG_HOVER_WATER_ONLY);
llSetVehicleVectorParam(
    VEHICLE_LINEAR_FRICTION_TIMESCALE, <1, 1, 1> );
llSetVehicleFloatParam(
    VEHICLE_ANGULAR_FRICTION_TIMESCALE, 2 );


    llSetVehicleVectorParam(
        VEHICLE_LINEAR_MOTOR_DIRECTION, <0, 0, 0>);
llSetVehicleFloatParam(VEHICLE_LINEAR_MOTOR_TIMESCALE, 1);
llSetVehicleFloatParam(
    VEHICLE_LINEAR_MOTOR_DECAY_TIMESCALE, 0.05);

llSetVehicleFloatParam( VEHICLE_ANGULAR_MOTOR_TIMESCALE,
        1 );
llSetVehicleFloatParam(
    VEHICLE_ANGULAR_MOTOR_DECAY_TIMESCALE, 5 );
llSetVehicleFloatParam( VEHICLE_HOVER_HEIGHT, 0.15);
llSetVehicleFloatParam( VEHICLE_HOVER_EFFICIENCY,.5 );
llSetVehicleFloatParam( VEHICLE_HOVER_TIMESCALE, 2.0 );
llSetVehicleFloatParam( VEHICLE_BUOYANCY, 1 );
llSetVehicleFloatParam(
    VEHICLE_LINEAR_DEFLECTION_EFFICIENCY, 0.5 );
llSetVehicleFloatParam(
    VEHICLE_LINEAR_DEFLECTION_TIMESCALE, 3 );
llSetVehicleFloatParam(
    VEHICLE_ANGULAR_DEFLECTION_EFFICIENCY, 0.5 );
llSetVehicleFloatParam(
    VEHICLE_ANGULAR_DEFLECTION_TIMESCALE, 10 );
llSetVehicleFloatParam(
    VEHICLE_VERTICAL_ATTRACTION_EFFICIENCY, 0.5 );
llSetVehicleFloatParam(
    VEHICLE_VERTICAL_ATTRACTION_TIMESCALE, 2 );
llSetVehicleFloatParam( VEHICLE_BANKING_EFFICIENCY, 1 );
llSetVehicleFloatParam( VEHICLE_BANKING_MIX, 0.1 );
llSetVehicleFloatParam( VEHICLE_BANKING_TIMESCALE, .5 );
llSetVehicleRotationParam( VEHICLE_REFERENCE_FRAME,
```

```
                ZERO_ROTATION );
        }

    changed(integer change)
    {

        if (change & CHANGED_LINK)
        {
            key agent = llAvatarOnSitTarget();
            if (agent)
            {
                if (agent != llGetOwner())
                {
                    llSay(0, not_owner_message);
                    llUnSit(agent);
                    llPushObject(agent, <0,0,50>,
                        ZERO_VECTOR, FALSE);
                }
                else
                {
                    llTriggerSound("boat_start",1);


                    llMessageLinked(LINK_ALL_CHILDREN , 0,
                        "start", NULL_KEY);
                    llSleep(.4);
                    llSetStatus(STATUS_PHYSICS, TRUE);
                    llSleep(.1);
                    llRequestPermissions(agent,
                        PERMISSION_TRIGGER_ANIMATION |
                        PERMISSION_TAKE_CONTROLS);

                    llLoopSound("boat_run",1);
                }
            }
            else
            {
                llStopSound();

                llSetStatus(STATUS_PHYSICS, FALSE);
                llSleep(.1);
                llMessageLinked(LINK_ALL_CHILDREN , 0,
                        "stop", NULL_KEY);
                llSleep(.4);
```

```
            llReleaseControls();
            llTargetOmega(<0,0,0>,PI,0);

            llResetScript();
        }
    }

}

run_time_permissions(integer perm)
{
    if (perm)
    {
        llTakeControls(CONTROL_FWD | CONTROL_BACK |
            CONTROL_DOWN | CONTROL_UP | CONTROL_RIGHT |
            CONTROL_LEFT | CONTROL_ROT_RIGHT |
            CONTROL_ROT_LEFT, TRUE, FALSE);
    }
}

control(key id, integer level, integer edge)
{
    integer reverse=1;
    vector angular_motor;

    //get current speed
    vector vel = llGetVel();
    float speed = llVecMag(vel);

    //car controls
    if(level & CONTROL_FWD)
    {
        llSetVehicleVectorParam(
        VEHICLE_LINEAR_MOTOR_DIRECTION, <forward_power,0,0>);
        reverse=1;
    }
    if(level & CONTROL_BACK)
    {
        llSetVehicleVectorParam(
        VEHICLE_LINEAR_MOTOR_DIRECTION, <reverse_power,0,0>);
        reverse = -1;
    }

    if(level & (CONTROL_RIGHT|CONTROL_ROT_RIGHT))
    {
        angular_motor.z -= speed / turning_ratio * reverse;
```

```
            angular_motor.x += 15;
        }

        if(level & (CONTROL_LEFT|CONTROL_ROT_LEFT))
        {
            angular_motor.z += speed / turning_ratio * reverse;
            angular_motor.x -= 15;
        }


        llSetVehicleVectorParam(VEHICLE_ANGULAR_MOTOR_DIRECTION,
angular_motor);

    } //end control


} //end default
```

The next few sections explain how the boat functions.

Initialization of the Boat

The car was initialized by setting its vehicle parameters to values that work well for a car. The boat works similarly. The boat is setup in the **state_entry** event handler. First, the boat sets the sit target and sit text.

```
state_entry()
{
    llSetSitText(sit_message);
    // forward-back,left-right,updown
    llSitTarget(<0.2,0,0.45>, ZERO_ROTATION );
```

Next, the camera is moved to a good distance behind the boat and above it. The camera looks into the boat. The camera for the boat is placed further back than the car because the boat is longer than the car.

```
        llSetCameraEyeOffset(<-12, 0.0, 5.0>);
        llSetCameraAtOffset(<1.0, 0.0, 2.0>);
```

The boat's two sounds are preloaded.

```
        llPreloadSound("boat_start");
        llPreloadSound("boat_run");
```

Next, the vehicle parameters are set. For more information on vehicle parameters refer to Tables 5.1, 5.2 and 5.3.

```
llSetVehicleType(VEHICLE_TYPE_BOAT);
llSetVehicleFlags(VEHICLE_FLAG_HOVER_UP_ONLY | VEHICLE_FLAG_HOVER_
WATER_ONLY);
llRemoveVehicleFlags( VEHICLE_FLAG_HOVER_TERRAIN_ONLY
```

```
| VEHICLE_FLAG_LIMIT_ROLL_ONLY
| VEHICLE_FLAG_HOVER_GLOBAL_HEIGHT);
```

The boat sets two of the vehicle flags using the **llSetVehicleFlags** function. These flags are summarized in Table 5.4.

Table 5.4: Vector Vehicle Parameters

Flag	Purpose
VEHICLE_FLAG_NO_DEFLECTION_UP	Prevents ground vehicles from deflecting up. Also prevents ground vehicles from "climbing" low prims in their path.
VEHICLE_FLAG_LIMIT_ROLL_ONLY	Allows the vehicle to climb and dive. Useful for airplanes.
VEHICLE_FLAG_HOVER_WATER_ONLY	Ignore terrain height when hovering.
VEHICLE_FLAG_HOVER_TERRAIN_ONLY	Ignore water height when hovering.
VEHICLE_FLAG_HOVER_GLOBAL_HEIGHT	Hover at global height instead of height above ground or water.
VEHICLE_FLAG_HOVER_UP_ONLY	Always stay at hover height, but go up. Useful for hover vehicles that need to jump.
VEHICLE_FLAG_LIMIT_MOTOR_UP	Keep ground vehicles on the ground.
VEHICLE_FLAG_MOUSELOOK_STEER	Use mouselook to steer the vehicle.
VEHICLE_FLAG_MOUSELOOK_BANK	Use mouselook to bank the vehicle.
VEHICLE_FLAG_CAMERA_DECOUPLED	The camera moves independently of the vehicle.

Friction affects the boat equally in all three coordinate planes.

```
llSetVehicleVectorParam(
VEHICLE_LINEAR_FRICTION_TIMESCALE, <1, 1, 1> );
```

It will take two seconds for angular friction to have its full effect on the boat.

```
llSetVehicleFloatParam(
VEHICLE_ANGULAR_FRICTION_TIMESCALE, 2 );
```

The linear motor will operate with no rotation.

```
llSetVehicleVectorParam(
VEHICLE_LINEAR_MOTOR_DIRECTION, <0, 0, 0>);
llSetVehicleFloatParam(
VEHICLE_LINEAR_MOTOR_TIMESCALE, 1);
```

The linear motor will decay very quickly.

```
llSetVehicleFloatParam(
VEHICLE_LINEAR_MOTOR_DECAY_TIMESCALE, 0.05);
```

The angular motor will take one second to reach full effect.

```
llSetVehicleFloatParam(
VEHICLE_ANGULAR_MOTOR_TIMESCALE, 1 );
```

The angular motor will decay in five seconds.

```
llSetVehicleFloatParam( VEHICLE_ANGULAR_MOTOR_DECAY_TIMESCALE,
5 );
```

The center of the boat will hover slightly above the water. This accounts for the underside of the boat, which should only be partially under water.

```
llSetVehicleFloatParam(
VEHICLE_HOVER_HEIGHT, 0.15);
```

The boat has 50% hover efficiency.

```
llSetVehicleFloatParam(
VEHICLE_HOVER_EFFICIENCY,.5 );
```

It will take two seconds for the hover to reach full effect.

```
llSetVehicleFloatParam(
VEHICLE_HOVER_TIMESCALE, 2.0 );
```

A boat has 100% buoyancy.

```
llSetVehicleFloatParam(
VEHICLE_BUOYANCY, 1 );
```

Linear deflection will be at 50% for the boat.

```
llSetVehicleFloatParam(
VEHICLE_LINEAR_DEFLECTION_EFFICIENCY, 0.5 );
```

It will take three seconds for linear deflection to have its full effect.

```
llSetVehicleFloatParam(
VEHICLE_LINEAR_DEFLECTION_TIMESCALE, 3 );
```

Angular deflection will be at 50% for the boat.

```
llSetVehicleFloatParam(
VEHICLE_ANGULAR_DEFLECTION_EFFICIENCY, 0.5 );
```

It will take ten seconds for angular deflection to reach full effect.

```
llSetVehicleFloatParam(
VEHICLE_ANGULAR_DEFLECTION_TIMESCALE, 10 );
```

A boat should always stay right-side-up. The vertical attraction feature allows this.

```
llSetVehicleFloatParam(
VEHICLE_VERTICAL_ATTRACTION_EFFICIENCY, 0.5 );
llSetVehicleFloatParam(
VEHICLE_VERTICAL_ATTRACTION_TIMESCALE, 2 );
```

The boat will have 100% banking effectiveness. A boat banks slightly when turning, this setting allows this.

```
llSetVehicleFloatParam(
VEHICLE_BANKING_EFFICIENCY, 1 );
```

The boat's banking will be only 10% dynamic. This allows a smooth controlled bank.

```
llSetVehicleFloatParam(
VEHICLE_BANKING_MIX, 0.1 );
```

It will take the boat only half a second to reach full banking. This allows the bank to be seen quickly when the boat begins to turn.

```
llSetVehicleFloatParam(
VEHICLE_BANKING_TIMESCALE, .5 );
```

There is no rotation on the root prim.

```
llSetVehicleRotationParam(
VEHICLE_REFERENCE_FRAME, ZERO_ROTATION );
```

There are some variables the boat has that the boat does not. These variables generally deal with banking, which is something the boat does not support. Additionally, the values were set to numbers that make sense for a boat.

Controlling the Boat

The controls for the boat are similar to the controls for the boat. However, there are some important differences for banking. Because of these differences, the entire control event handler will be reviewed.

The control event handler begins by setting up some variables that will be needed by the handler. Because boats, like cars, turn differently when in reverse, a flag must be kept to indicate if the boat is in reverse. A variable is also created to hold the direction of the angular motor.

```
control(key id, integer level, integer edge)
{
    integer reverse=1;
    vector angular_motor;
```

The current speed is obtained. This will be used with turning. Boats do not turn when they are not in motion.

```
//get current speed
vector vel = llGetVel();
float speed = llVecMag(vel);
```

Next, each of the relevant controls will be checked. The first control to be checked is the forward control. When the user presses forward, the linear motor is used to apply force to move the boat forward. Note also that the boat moves forward when reverse is set to one.

```
//boat controls
if(level & CONTROL_FWD)
{
    llSetVehicleVectorParam(
VEHICLE_LINEAR_MOTOR_DIRECTION, <forward_power,0,0>);
    reverse=1;
}
```

If the user presses back, apply power in the opposite direction. Note also that the boat moves in reverse when the reverse variable is set to -1.

```
if(level & CONTROL_BACK)
{
    llSetVehicleVectorParam(
VEHICLE_LINEAR_MOTOR_DIRECTION, <reverse_power,0,0>);
    reverse = -1;
}
```

For a right turn, rotate the boat in the z-coordinate. Rotate by the specified angle and take into account if the boat is going in reverse. Also roll the boat by 15 degrees on the x coordinate.

```
if(level & (CONTROL_RIGHT|CONTROL_ROT_RIGHT))
{
    angular_motor.z -= speed / turning_ratio * reverse;
    angular_motor.x += 15;
}
```

For a left turn, rotate the boat in the z-coordinate. Rotate by the specified angle and take into account if the boat is going in reverse. Also roll the boat by 15 degrees on the x coordinate.

```
if(level & (CONTROL_LEFT|CONTROL_ROT_LEFT))
{
    angular_motor.z += speed / turning_ratio * reverse;
    angular_motor.x -= 15;
}
```

Now the angular motor can be set.

```
llSetVehicleVectorParam(
    VEHICLE_ANGULAR_MOTOR_DIRECTION, angular_motor);
```

```
} //end control
```

The primary difference between the boat's control event handler and the car's is that the boat must take banking into account.

Waves in the Wake

The boat is designed to leave waves in its wake. This is done with a particle emitter script. The particle emitter script is based on the basic particle emitter script found in Recipe 4.1. The boat's wake script can be seen in Listing 5.6.

Listing 5.6: Boat Wake (BoatWake.lsl)

```
generalParticleEmitterOn()
{
    llParticleSystem([
        PSYS_PART_FLAGS , 0
    //| PSYS_PART_BOUNCE_MASK
//Bounce on object's z-axis
    //| PSYS_PART_WIND_MASK
//Particles are moved by wind
    | PSYS_PART_INTERP_COLOR_MASK
//Colors fade from start to end
    | PSYS_PART_INTERP_SCALE_MASK
//Scale fades from beginning to end
    | PSYS_PART_FOLLOW_SRC_MASK
//Particles follow the emitter
    | PSYS_PART_FOLLOW_VELOCITY_MASK
//Particles are created at the velocity of the emitter
    //| PSYS_PART_TARGET_POS_MASK
//Particles follow the target
    | PSYS_PART_EMISSIVE_MASK
//Particles are self-lit (glow)
    //| PSYS_PART_TARGET_LINEAR_MASK
//Undocumented--Sends particles in straight line?

    ,

    //PSYS_SRC_TARGET_KEY , NULL_KEY,
//The particles will head towards the specified key
    //Select one of the following for a pattern:
    //PSYS_SRC_PATTERN_DROP                Particles start at
emitter with no velocity
    //PSYS_SRC_PATTERN_EXPLODE            Particles explode from
the emitter
    //PSYS_SRC_PATTERN_ANGLE              Particles are emitted
in a 2-D angle
    //PSYS_SRC_PATTERN_ANGLE_CONE         Particles are emitted
```

```
in a 3-D cone
    //PSYS_SRC_PATTERN_ANGLE_CONE_EMPTY      Particles are emitted
everywhere except for a 3-D cone

    PSYS_SRC_PATTERN,               PSYS_SRC_PATTERN_ANGLE

    ,PSYS_SRC_TEXTURE,              "wake"
//UUID of the desired particle texture, or inventory name
    ,PSYS_SRC_MAX_AGE,              0.0
//Time, in seconds, for particles to be emitted. 0 = forever
    ,PSYS_PART_MAX_AGE,             4.0
//Lifetime, in seconds, that a particle lasts
    ,PSYS_SRC_BURST_RATE,           0.5
//How long, in seconds, between each emission
    ,PSYS_SRC_BURST_PART_COUNT,  6
//Number of particles per emission
    ,PSYS_SRC_BURST_RADIUS,         10.0
//Radius of emission
    ,PSYS_SRC_BURST_SPEED_MIN,   0.75
//Minimum speed of an emitted particle
    ,PSYS_SRC_BURST_SPEED_MAX,   1.5
//Maximum speed of an emitted particle
    ,PSYS_SRC_ACCEL,                <0,0,0>
//Acceleration of particles each second
    ,PSYS_PART_START_COLOR,         <0.85,0.85,1.0>
//Starting RGB color
    ,PSYS_PART_END_COLOR,           <1,1,1>
//Ending RGB color, if INTERP_COLOR_MASK is on
    ,PSYS_PART_START_ALPHA,       0.0
//Starting transparency, 1 is opaque, 0 is transparent.
    ,PSYS_PART_END_ALPHA,           1.0
//Ending transparency
    ,PSYS_PART_START_SCALE,         <2.5,1,0.0>
//Starting particle size
    ,PSYS_PART_END_SCALE,           <2.5,1,0.0>
//Ending particle size, if INTERP_SCALE_MASK is on
    ,PSYS_SRC_ANGLE_BEGIN,          0 * DEG_TO_RAD
//Inner angle for ANGLE patterns
    ,PSYS_SRC_ANGLE_END,            0 * DEG_TO_RAD
//Outer angle for ANGLE patterns
    ,PSYS_SRC_OMEGA,                <0.0,0.0,0.0>
//Rotation of ANGLE patterns, similar to llTargetOmega()
            ]);
}

generalParticleEmitterOff()
```

```
{
    llParticleSystem([]);
}

default
{
    state_entry()
    {
            generalParticleEmitterOff();
    }
    link_message(integer sender_num, integer num, string str,
            key id)
    {
        if(str=="stop")
        {
            generalParticleEmitterOff();
        }
        if(str=="start")
        {
            generalParticleEmitterOn();
        }
    }
}
```

The boat, with a wake behind it, can be seen in Figure 5.6.

Figure 5.6: A Boat with Wake

The wake script turns on and off as commanded by the main boat script in the root prim. To turn the wake on, the following command is issued by the main boat script.

```
llMessageLinked(LINK_ALL_CHILDREN , 0, "start", NULL_KEY);
```

To turn the wake script off, the following command is issued by the main boat script.

```
llMessageLinked(LINK_ALL_CHILDREN , 0, "stop", NULL_KEY);
```

Both commands are issued in the changed event handler. The wake trail will begin when the driver sits. The wake trail will end when the driver stands. This communication is done with a linked message. A linked message is sent to all linked prims. The wake script handles the linked message in the **link_message** event handler.

```
link_message(integer sender_num, integer num, string str, key id)
{
        if(str=="stop")
        {
                generalParticleEmitterOff();
        }
        if(str=="start")
        {
```

```
        generalParticleEmitterOn();
    }
}
```

If the message is to stop, the particle script is turned off. If the message is to start, the particle script is turned on. For more information on how the particle script is constructed, refer to Chapter 4.

Recipe 5.3: Helicopter

Helicopters and other flying vehicles are very popular in Second Life. This recipe shows how to create a helicopter. The helicopter is capable of carrying up to four avatars at once. The helicopter is flown very similarly to how an avatar is flown.

Figure 5.7: A Helicopter

The helicopter shares some characteristics with the car. However, there are some important differences.

- The helicopter should roll slightly when it turns.
- The helicopter hovers in the air.
- The helicopter spins its rotors whenever a driver is seated.

- The helicopter uses different sounds.
- The helicopter has no wheels to turn.
- The helicopter can leave the ground.

The main script for the helicopter is located in the root prim. This script is shown in Listing 5.7.

Listing 5.7: Helicopter Script (Helicopter.lsl)

```
float forward_power = 15; //Power used to go forward (1 to 30)
float reverse_power = -15; //Power used to go reverse (-1 to -30)
float turning_ratio = 2.0; //How sharply the vehicle turns. Less
is more sharply. (.1 to 10)
string sit_message = "Ride"; //Sit message
string not_owner_message =
"You are not the owner of this vehicle ..."; //Not owner message
float VERTICAL_THRUST = 7;
float ROTATION_RATE = 2.0;        //  Rate of turning

resetY()
{
    rotation rot = llGetRot();
    llSetRot(rot);
}

default
{
    state_entry()
    {
        llSetSitText(sit_message);
        // forward-back,left-right,updown
        llSitTarget(<0.2,0,0.45>, ZERO_ROTATION );

        llSetCameraEyeOffset(<-8, 0.0, 5.0>);
        llSetCameraAtOffset(<1.0, 0.0, 2.0>);

        llPreloadSound("helicopter_run");

        //helicopter
        llSetVehicleType(VEHICLE_TYPE_AIRPLANE);

        llSetVehicleFloatParam(
VEHICLE_ANGULAR_DEFLECTION_EFFICIENCY, 0.1);
        llSetVehicleFloatParam(
VEHICLE_LINEAR_DEFLECTION_EFFICIENCY, 0.1);
        llSetVehicleFloatParam(
VEHICLE_ANGULAR_DEFLECTION_TIMESCALE, 10);
        llSetVehicleFloatParam(
```

```
VEHICLE_LINEAR_DEFLECTION_TIMESCALE, 10);

        llSetVehicleFloatParam(
VEHICLE_LINEAR_MOTOR_TIMESCALE, 0.2);
        llSetVehicleFloatParam(
VEHICLE_LINEAR_MOTOR_DECAY_TIMESCALE, 10);
        llSetVehicleFloatParam(
VEHICLE_ANGULAR_MOTOR_TIMESCALE, 0.2);
        llSetVehicleFloatParam(
VEHICLE_ANGULAR_MOTOR_DECAY_TIMESCALE, 0.1);

        llSetVehicleVectorParam(
VEHICLE_LINEAR_FRICTION_TIMESCALE, <1,1,1>);
        llSetVehicleVectorParam(
VEHICLE_ANGULAR_FRICTION_TIMESCALE, <1,1000,1000>);

        llSetVehicleFloatParam(
VEHICLE_BUOYANCY, 0.9);

        llSetVehicleFloatParam(
VEHICLE_VERTICAL_ATTRACTION_EFFICIENCY, 1 );
        llSetVehicleFloatParam(
VEHICLE_VERTICAL_ATTRACTION_TIMESCALE, 2 );

        llSetVehicleFloatParam( VEHICLE_BANKING_EFFICIENCY, 1 );
        llSetVehicleFloatParam( VEHICLE_BANKING_MIX, 0.5 );
        llSetVehicleFloatParam( VEHICLE_BANKING_TIMESCALE, .5 );


    }

    changed(integer change)
    {


        if (change & CHANGED_LINK)
        {

            key agent = llAvatarOnSitTarget();
            if (agent)
            {
                if (agent != llGetOwner())
                {
                    llSay(0, not_owner_message);
                    llUnSit(agent);
                    llPushObject(agent, <0,0,50>,
```

```
                                ZERO_VECTOR, FALSE);
                }
                else
                {
                    llMessageLinked(LINK_ALL_CHILDREN , 0,
                        "start", NULL_KEY);

                    llSleep(.4);
                    llSetStatus(STATUS_PHYSICS, TRUE);
                    llSetStatus(STATUS_ROTATE_Y,TRUE);
                    llSleep(.1);
                    llRequestPermissions(agent,
PERMISSION_TRIGGER_ANIMATION | PERMISSION_TAKE_CONTROLS);

                    llLoopSound("helicopter_run",1);
                }
            }
            else
            {
                llStopSound();
                llMessageLinked(LINK_ALL_CHILDREN , 0, "stop",
                    NULL_KEY);

                llSetStatus(STATUS_PHYSICS, FALSE);
                llSleep(.4);
                llReleaseControls();
                llTargetOmega(<0,0,0>,PI,0);

                llResetScript();
            }
        }

    }

    run_time_permissions(integer perm)
    {
        if (perm) {
            llTakeControls(CONTROL_FWD | CONTROL_BACK |
            CONTROL_RIGHT | CONTROL_LEFT | CONTROL_ROT_RIGHT |
            CONTROL_ROT_LEFT | CONTROL_UP | CONTROL_DOWN,
            TRUE, FALSE);
        }
    }

    control(key id, integer level, integer edge)
    {
```

```
vector angular_motor;


// going forward, or stop going forward
if(level & CONTROL_FWD)
{
    llSetVehicleVectorParam(
        VEHICLE_LINEAR_MOTOR_DIRECTION,
        <forward_power,0,0>);
} else if(edge & CONTROL_FWD)
{
    llSetVehicleVectorParam(
        VEHICLE_LINEAR_MOTOR_DIRECTION, <0,0,0>);
}


// going back, or stop going back
if(level & CONTROL_BACK)
{
    llSetVehicleVectorParam(
        VEHICLE_LINEAR_MOTOR_DIRECTION,
        <reverse_power,0,0>);
}
else if(edge & CONTROL_BACK)
{
    llSetVehicleVectorParam(
        VEHICLE_LINEAR_MOTOR_DIRECTION, <0,0,0>);
}

// turning
if(level & (CONTROL_RIGHT|CONTROL_ROT_RIGHT))
{
    angular_motor.x += 25;
}

if(level & (CONTROL_LEFT|CONTROL_ROT_LEFT))
{
    angular_motor.x -= 25;
}


// going up or stop going up
if(level & CONTROL_UP) {
    llSetVehicleVectorParam(VEHICLE_LINEAR_MOTOR_DIREC-
TION, <0,0,VERTICAL_THRUST>);
} else if (edge & CONTROL_UP) {
```

```
            llSetVehicleVectorParam(
                 VEHICLE_LINEAR_MOTOR_DIRECTION, <0,0,0>);
        }

        // going down or stop going down

        if(level & CONTROL_DOWN) {
            llSetVehicleVectorParam(
                 VEHICLE_LINEAR_MOTOR_DIRECTION,
                 <0,0,-VERTICAL_THRUST>);
        } else if (edge & CONTROL_DOWN) {
            llSetVehicleVectorParam(
                 VEHICLE_LINEAR_MOTOR_DIRECTION, <0,0,0>);
        }

        angular_motor.y = 0;
        llSetVehicleVectorParam(
            VEHICLE_ANGULAR_MOTOR_DIRECTION, angular_motor);
    } //end control
} //end default
```

The next few sections will examine helicopter script in detail.

Initializing the Helicopter

The helicopter, like the car, is initialized in the **state_entry** event handler. First, the vehicle type is set to airplane. Airplane includes all air-based vehicles. For more information on airplane parameters refer to Tables 5.1, 5.2 and 5.3.

```
llSetVehicleType(VEHICLE_TYPE_AIRPLANE);
```

Angular deflection is the tendency of a vehicle to move in certain directions. The angular deflection efficiency determines how effective angular deflection is. A value of 0.1 specifies angular deflection at 10%. This allows the helicopter to turn fairly easily.

```
llSetVehicleFloatParam(
VEHICLE_ANGULAR_DEFLECTION_EFFICIENCY, 0.1);
```

A value of 0.1 specifies that linear deflection has 10% power. This means it takes little effort for the helicopter to change its linear velocity.

```
llSetVehicleFloatParam(
VEHICLE_LINEAR_DEFLECTION_EFFICIENCY, 0.1);
```

It will take ten seconds for angular deflection to reach full effect.

```
llSetVehicleFloatParam(
VEHICLE_ANGULAR_DEFLECTION_TIMESCALE, 10);
llSetVehicleFloatParam(
VEHICLE_LINEAR_DEFLECTION_TIMESCALE, 10);
```

It will take one fifth of a second for the linear motor to reach full power.

```
llSetVehicleFloatParam(
VEHICLE_LINEAR_MOTOR_TIMESCALE, 0.2);
```

It takes ten seconds for the linear motor to drop from full power. However, the controls for the helicopter will stop the linear motor if the direction of the helicopter is changed. This makes the helicopter easier to control. Because of this, the linear motor may not always have a full ten seconds to slow down.

```
llSetVehicleFloatParam(
VEHICLE_LINEAR_MOTOR_DECAY_TIMESCALE, 10);
```

It takes one fifth of a second for the angular motor to reach full power.

```
llSetVehicleFloatParam(
VEHICLE_ANGULAR_MOTOR_TIMESCALE, 0.2);
```

It takes one tenth of a second for the angular motor's power to drop off. This causes the helicopter to stop turning quickly.

```
llSetVehicleFloatParam(
VEHICLE_ANGULAR_MOTOR_DECAY_TIMESCALE, 0.1);
```

There is little friction in any of the three directions.

```
llSetVehicleVectorParam(
VEHICLE_LINEAR_FRICTION_TIMESCALE, <1,1,1>);
```

There is little angular friction in the x and z coordinate systems.

```
llSetVehicleVectorParam(
VEHICLE_ANGULAR_FRICTION_TIMESCALE, <1,1000,1000>);
```

The helicopter is slightly heavier than air. It will sink very slowly when hovering. It will also be able to sit on the ground without floating away.

```
llSetVehicleFloatParam(
VEHICLE_BUOYANCY, 0.9);
```

The helicopter should stay right-side up. The following vertical attraction values ensure this.

```
llSetVehicleFloatParam( VEHICLE_VERTICAL_ATTRACTION_EFFICIENCY,
1 );
llSetVehicleFloatParam( VEHICLE_VERTICAL_ATTRACTION_TIMESCALE,
2 );
```

The helicopter will turn quickly once banked.

```
llSetVehicleFloatParam(
VEHICLE_BANKING_EFFICIENCY, 1 );
```

The helicopter banking mix is 50% realistic. This means that the helicopter does not necessarily need to be in motion to turn.

```
llSetVehicleFloatParam(
VEHICLE_BANKING_MIX, 0.5 );
```

It takes half a second for the bank to translate into a turn.

```
llSetVehicleFloatParam(
VEHICLE_BANKING_TIMESCALE, .5 );
```

These values produce a helicopter that is steady and easy to control.

Controlling the Helicopter

The helicopter is controlled differently to the car. To begin with, the helicopter must bank to turn. The car simply turns. Also, the helicopter must detect when the up/down and forward/backward controls are released. Otherwise, the helicopter would continue in those directions and be difficult to control. Finally, the helicopter can go up and down, whereas the car stays on the ground.

The **control** event handler begins by checking to see whether the user is applying forward pressure to the helicopter controls. If this is the case, apply power to the linear motor to go forward.

```
// going forward, or stop going forward
if(level & CONTROL_FWD)
{
     llSetVehicleVectorParam(
     VEHICLE_LINEAR_MOTOR_DIRECTION, <forward_power,0,0>);
```

If the user recently ceased applying forward pressure to the helicopter controls, stop the linear motor.

```
} else if(edge & CONTROL_FWD)
{
     llSetVehicleVectorParam(
     VEHICLE_LINEAR_MOTOR_DIRECTION, <0,0,0>);
}
```

Next, the control event handler checks to see whether the user is applying backward pressure to the helicopter controls. If so, apply backward power to make the linear motor go backward.

```
// going back, or stop going back
if(level & CONTROL_BACK)
{
     llSetVehicleVectorParam(
     VEHICLE_LINEAR_MOTOR_DIRECTION, <reverse_power,0,0>);
}
```

If the user recently ceased applying backward pressure to the helicopter controls, stop the linear motor.

```
else if(edge & CONTROL_BACK)
{
     llSetVehicleVectorParam(
     VEHICLE_LINEAR_MOTOR_DIRECTION, <0,0,0>);
}
```

If the user is turning to the right, apply positive power to the angular motor in the x coordinate system. This rolls the helicopter to the right.

```
// turning
if(level & (CONTROL_RIGHT|CONTROL_ROT_RIGHT))
{
     angular_motor.x += 25;
}
```

If the user is turning to the left, apply negative power to the angular motor in the x coordinate system. This rolls the helicopter to the left.

```
if(level & (CONTROL_LEFT|CONTROL_ROT_LEFT))
{
     angular_motor.x -= 25;
}
```

Next, the control event handler checks to see whether the user is applying upward pressure to the helicopter controls. If so, apply upward power to the linear motor to make it go upwards.

```
// going up or stop going up
if(level & CONTROL_UP)
{
     llSetVehicleVectorParam(
VEHICLE_LINEAR_MOTOR_DIRECTION, <0,0,VERTICAL_THRUST>);
```

If the user recently ceased applying upward pressure to the helicopter controls, stop the linear motor.

```
} else if (edge & CONTROL_UP) {
     llSetVehicleVectorParam(
VEHICLE_LINEAR_MOTOR_DIRECTION, <0,0,0>);
}
```

Next the control event handler checks to see whether the user is applying downward pressure to the helicopter controls. If so, apply downward power to the linear motor to make it go downwards.

```
// going down or stop going down
```

```
if(level & CONTROL_DOWN)
{
     llSetVehicleVectorParam(
VEHICLE_LINEAR_MOTOR_DIRECTION, <0,0,-VERTICAL_THRUST>);
```

If the user has recently ceased applying upward pressure to the helicopter controls, stop the linear motor.

```
} else if (edge & CONTROL_DOWN) {
     llSetVehicleVectorParam(
VEHICLE_LINEAR_MOTOR_DIRECTION, <0,0,0>);
}
```

Finally, apply the correct power to the angular motor.

```
angular_motor.y = 0;
llSetVehicleVectorParam(
VEHICLE_ANGULAR_MOTOR_DIRECTION, angular_motor);
```

The control system for an air vehicle is different to a land or sea vehicle.

Spinning the Rotors

The helicopter has a spinning rotor, similar to a real helicopter. This blade is turned on and off by the main helicopter script's changed event handler. To start the rotor, use this command.

```
llMessageLinked(LINK_ALL_CHILDREN , 0, "start", NULL_KEY);
```

To stop the rotor, use this command.

```
llMessageLinked(LINK_ALL_CHILDREN , 0, "stop", NULL_KEY);
```

The script that drives the rotor is shown in Listing 5.8.

Listing 5.8: Helicopter Rotors (Blade.lsl)

```
float rad = 0.0;
float radinc = 0.05;
float time_inc = .2;
float rotspeed = 3.2;

default
{

    state_entry()
    {
        llSetTextureAnim(0, ALL_SIDES, 0, 0, 0, 0, 0);
    }

    link_message(integer sender_num, integer num, string str,
```

```
        key id)
{
    if(str=="stop")
    {
        llSetTextureAnim(0, ALL_SIDES, 0, 0, 0, 0, 0);
    }
    if(str=="start")
    {
        llSetTextureAnim(ANIM_ON | ROTATE | LOOP |
            SMOOTH, ALL_SIDES, 0, 0, 0, 100, 20);
    }
}

}
```

The rotor script does most of its work inside of the link_message event handler.

```
link_message(integer sender_num, integer num, string str, key id)
{
    if(str=="stop")
    {
        llSetTextureAnim(0, ALL_SIDES, 0, 0, 0, 0, 0);
    }
    if(str=="start")
    {
        llSetTextureAnim(ANIM_ON | ROTATE | LOOP
            |SMOOTH, ALL_SIDES, 0, 0, 0, 100, 20);
    }
}
```

When the event handler receives the message "stop", the rotor animation is stopped. When the event handler receives the message "start" the animation starts.

Recipe 5.4: Super Car

The last recipe in this chapter is a super car. The super car combines aspects from the previous three recipes. The super car can function as a car, a boat or a helicopter. By talking to the super car, the vehicle parameters can be switched out between any of the previous three vehicles. The super car looks very similar to the regular car, except that it is yellow.

The script for the root prim of the Super Car is shown in Listing 5.9.

Listing 5.9: The Super Car (SuperCar.lsl)

```
float forward_power = 15; //Power used to go forward (1 to 30)
float reverse_power = -15; //Power used to go reverse (-1 to -30)
float turning_ratio = 2.0; //How sharply the vehicle turns. Less
is more sharply. (.1 to 10)
```

```
string sit_message = "Ride"; //Sit message
string not_owner_message = "You are not the owner of this vehicle
..."; //Not owner message
float VERTICAL_THRUST = 7;

float ROTATION_RATE = 2.0;         //  Rate of turning

becomeBoat()
{
    llSetVehicleType(VEHICLE_TYPE_BOAT);
    llSetVehicleFlags(VEHICLE_FLAG_HOVER_UP_ONLY | VEHICLE_FLAG_
HOVER_WATER_ONLY);
    llRemoveVehicleFlags( VEHICLE_FLAG_HOVER_TERRAIN_ONLY
                              | VEHICLE_FLAG_LIMIT_ROLL_ONLY
                              | VEHICLE_FLAG_HOVER_GLOBAL_HEIGHT);
    llSetVehicleVectorParam( VEHICLE_LINEAR_FRICTION_TIMESCALE,
            <1, 1, 1> );
    llSetVehicleFloatParam( VEHICLE_ANGULAR_FRICTION_TIMESCALE,
            2 );

    llSetVehicleVectorParam(VEHICLE_LINEAR_MOTOR_DIRECTION,
            <0, 0, 0>);
    llSetVehicleFloatParam(VEHICLE_LINEAR_MOTOR_TIMESCALE, 1);
    llSetVehicleFloatParam(VEHICLE_LINEAR_MOTOR_DECAY_TIMESCALE,
            0.05);

    llSetVehicleFloatParam( VEHICLE_ANGULAR_MOTOR_TIMESCALE, 1 );
    llSetVehicleFloatParam( VEHICLE_ANGULAR_MOTOR_DECAY_TIMESCALE,
            5 );
    llSetVehicleFloatParam( VEHICLE_HOVER_HEIGHT, 0.15);
    llSetVehicleFloatParam( VEHICLE_HOVER_EFFICIENCY,.5 );
    llSetVehicleFloatParam( VEHICLE_HOVER_TIMESCALE, 2.0 );
    llSetVehicleFloatParam( VEHICLE_BUOYANCY, 1 );
    llSetVehicleFloatParam( VEHICLE_LINEAR_DEFLECTION_EFFICIENCY,
            0.5 );
    llSetVehicleFloatParam( VEHICLE_LINEAR_DEFLECTION_TIMESCALE,
            3 );
    llSetVehicleFloatParam( VEHICLE_ANGULAR_DEFLECTION_EFFICIENCY,
            0.5 );
    llSetVehicleFloatParam( VEHICLE_ANGULAR_DEFLECTION_TIMESCALE,
            10 );
    llSetVehicleFloatParam(
            VEHICLE_VERTICAL_ATTRACTION_EFFICIENCY, 0.5 );
    llSetVehicleFloatParam(
            VEHICLE_VERTICAL_ATTRACTION_TIMESCALE, 2 );
    llSetVehicleFloatParam( VEHICLE_BANKING_EFFICIENCY, 1 );
```

```
    llSetVehicleFloatParam( VEHICLE_BANKING_MIX, 0.1 );
    llSetVehicleFloatParam( VEHICLE_BANKING_TIMESCALE, .5 );
    llSetVehicleRotationParam( VEHICLE_REFERENCE_FRAME,
            ZERO_ROTATION );
}

becomeCar()
{
    //car
    llSetVehicleType(VEHICLE_TYPE_CAR);
    llSetVehicleFloatParam(VEHICLE_ANGULAR_DEFLECTION_EFFICIENCY,
            0.2);
    llSetVehicleFloatParam(VEHICLE_LINEAR_DEFLECTION_EFFICIENCY,
            0.80);
    llSetVehicleFloatParam(VEHICLE_ANGULAR_DEFLECTION_TIMESCALE,
            0.10);
    llSetVehicleFloatParam(VEHICLE_LINEAR_DEFLECTION_TIMESCALE,
            0.10);
    llSetVehicleFloatParam(VEHICLE_LINEAR_MOTOR_TIMESCALE, 1.0);
    llSetVehicleFloatParam(
            VEHICLE_LINEAR_MOTOR_DECAY_TIMESCALE, 0.2);
    llSetVehicleFloatParam(VEHICLE_ANGULAR_MOTOR_TIMESCALE, 0.1);
    llSetVehicleFloatParam(
            VEHICLE_ANGULAR_MOTOR_DECAY_TIMESCALE, 0.5);
    llSetVehicleVectorParam(
            VEHICLE_LINEAR_FRICTION_TIMESCALE,
            <1000.0, 2.0, 1000.0>);
    llSetVehicleVectorParam(VEHICLE_ANGULAR_FRICTION_TIMESCALE,
<10.0, 10.0, 1000.0>);
    llSetVehicleFloatParam(VEHICLE_VERTICAL_ATTRACTION_EFFICIENCY,
0.50);
    llSetVehicleFloatParam(VEHICLE_VERTICAL_ATTRACTION_TIMESCALE,
0.50);
}

becomePlane()
{
            llSetVehicleType(VEHICLE_TYPE_AIRPLANE);

        llSetVehicleFloatParam(
VEHICLE_ANGULAR_DEFLECTION_EFFICIENCY, 0.1);
        llSetVehicleFloatParam(
VEHICLE_LINEAR_DEFLECTION_EFFICIENCY, 0.1);
        llSetVehicleFloatParam(
VEHICLE_ANGULAR_DEFLECTION_TIMESCALE, 10);
        llSetVehicleFloatParam(
```

```
VEHICLE_LINEAR_DEFLECTION_TIMESCALE, 10);

        llSetVehicleFloatParam(VEHICLE_LINEAR_MOTOR_TIMESCALE,
    0.2);
        llSetVehicleFloatParam(
            VEHICLE_LINEAR_MOTOR_DECAY_TIMESCALE, 10);
        llSetVehicleFloatParam(VEHICLE_ANGULAR_MOTOR_TIMESCALE,
            0.2);
        llSetVehicleFloatParam(
            VEHICLE_ANGULAR_MOTOR_DECAY_TIMESCALE, 0.1);

        llSetVehicleVectorParam(VEHICLE_LINEAR_FRICTION_TIMESCALE,
            <5,5,5>);
        llSetVehicleVectorParam(VEHICLE_ANGULAR_FRICTION_TIMESCALE,
            <1,1,1>);

        llSetVehicleFloatParam(VEHICLE_BUOYANCY, 1.0);

        llSetVehicleFloatParam(
            VEHICLE_VERTICAL_ATTRACTION_EFFICIENCY, 0.2);
        llSetVehicleFloatParam(
            VEHICLE_VERTICAL_ATTRACTION_TIMESCALE, 3.0);

        llSetVehicleFloatParam( VEHICLE_BANKING_EFFICIENCY, 1 );
        llSetVehicleFloatParam( VEHICLE_BANKING_MIX, 0.1 );
        llSetVehicleFloatParam( VEHICLE_BANKING_TIMESCALE, .5 );
}

default
{
    state_entry()
    {
        llSetSitText(sit_message);
        // forward-back,left-right,updown
        llSitTarget(<0.2,0,0.45>, ZERO_ROTATION );

        llSetCameraEyeOffset(<-8, 0.0, 5.0>);
        llSetCameraAtOffset(<1.0, 0.0, 2.0>);

        llPreloadSound("car_start");
        llPreloadSound("car_run");

        llListen(0, "", NULL_KEY, "");

        becomeCar();
    }
```

```
listen(integer channel, string name, key id, string message)
{
    if( id==llGetOwner() )
    {
        if( message == "drive" )
            becomeCar();
        else if (message == "fly" )
            becomePlane();
        else if (message == "float" )
            becomeBoat();
    }
}


changed(integer change)
{


    if (change & CHANGED_LINK)
    {

        key agent = llAvatarOnSitTarget();
        if (agent)
        {
            if (agent != llGetOwner())
            {
                llSay(0, not_owner_message);
                llUnSit(agent);
                llPushObject(agent, <0,0,50>,
                    ZERO_VECTOR, FALSE);
            }
            else
            {
                llTriggerSound("car_start",1);

                llSay(0,"Welcome to the super car, say 'drive'
to make me a car, 'fly' to make me fly, or 'float' to make me a
boat.");
                llSleep(.4);
                llSetStatus(STATUS_PHYSICS, TRUE);
                llSleep(.1);
                llRequestPermissions(agent, PERMISSION_TRIG-
GER_ANIMATION | PERMISSION_TAKE_CONTROLS);

                llLoopSound("car_run",1);
```

```
                }
            }
            else
            {
                llStopSound();

                llSetStatus(STATUS_PHYSICS, FALSE);
                llSleep(.4);
                llReleaseControls();
                llTargetOmega(<0,0,0>,PI,0);

                llResetScript();
            }
        }
    }
}


run_time_permissions(integer perm)
{
    if (perm) {
        llTakeControls(CONTROL_FWD | CONTROL_BACK |
                CONTROL_RIGHT | CONTROL_LEFT |
                CONTROL_ROT_RIGHT | CONTROL_ROT_LEFT |
                CONTROL_UP | CONTROL_DOWN, TRUE, FALSE);
    }
}

control(key id, integer level, integer edge)
{
    integer reverse=1;
    vector angular_motor;

    //get current speed
    vector vel = llGetVel();
    float speed = llVecMag(vel);


    //car controls
    if(level & CONTROL_FWD)
    {
        llSetVehicleVectorParam(
            VEHICLE_LINEAR_MOTOR_DIRECTION,
            <forward_power,0,0>);
        reverse=1;
    }
    if(level & CONTROL_BACK)
```

```
    {
        llSetVehicleVectorParam(
            VEHICLE_LINEAR_MOTOR_DIRECTION,
            <reverse_power,0,0>);
        reverse = -1;
    }

    if(level & (CONTROL_RIGHT|CONTROL_ROT_RIGHT))
    {
        angular_motor.z -= turning_ratio;
    }

    if(level & (CONTROL_LEFT|CONTROL_ROT_LEFT))
    {
        angular_motor.z += turning_ratio;
    }

    if(level & CONTROL_UP) {
        llSetVehicleVectorParam(
            VEHICLE_LINEAR_MOTOR_DIRECTION,
            <0,0,VERTICAL_THRUST>);
    } else if (edge & CONTROL_UP) {
        llSetVehicleVectorParam(
            VEHICLE_LINEAR_MOTOR_DIRECTION, <0,0,0>);
    }
    if(level & CONTROL_DOWN) {
        llSetVehicleVectorParam(
            VEHICLE_LINEAR_MOTOR_DIRECTION,
            <0,0,-VERTICAL_THRUST>);
    } else if (edge & CONTROL_DOWN) {
        llSetVehicleVectorParam(
            VEHICLE_LINEAR_MOTOR_DIRECTION, <0,0,0>);
    }

    llSetVehicleVectorParam(VEHICLE_ANGULAR_MOTOR_DIRECTION,
        angular_motor);


    }
}
```

The super car has three functions used to set vehicle parameters. They are:

- Become Boat
- Become Car
- Become Plane

The driver can easily switch between the three by talking to the car. By saying "drive" the car becomes a car. By saying "float" the car becomes a boat. Finally, by saying "fly" the car becomes a flying machine. The car starts out in drive mode.

The switch is handled inside of the **listen** event handler.

Summary

Vehicles are a popular part of Second Life. This chapter provided recipes that demonstrate land, air and sea vehicles. By setting the vehicle parameter types, the vehicle type and handling characteristics can be specified. There are two very important event handlers in most vehicles.

The **changed** event handler is called when an avatar sits on a vehicle. The **changed** event handler must first determine whether the avatar is authorized to operate the vehicle. Normally, to operate the vehicle, the avatar must be the owner. Next, the event handler starts the vehicle.

The control event handler is called when the avatar applies pressure to the controls of the vehicle. Normally, a vehicle is moved in the same way as an avatar. The control event handler must process all of the movement requests and apply power to the linear and angular motors.

The next chapter will introduce recipes for scanners. Scanners can detect avatars around the scanning device. Other types of scanners also gather information about their environment.

CHAPTER 6: SCANNERS

- Create a Radar
- Automatically Giving Notecards
- Automatic Doors
- Monitoring Traffic

Scripts can be aware of their environment. Using a scanner, a script can detect avatars and other objects around it. To sense the presence of an avatar or other object, the **llSensor** or **llSensorRepeat** functions are used. The **llSensor** function scans just once, whereas the **llSensorRepeat** function scans at regular intervals.

The **llSensor** function is called with the following parameters.

```
llSensor(string name, key id, integer type, float range, float
arc)
```

The parameter **name** allows the sensor to look only for objects that match the specified name. If **name** is an empty string, all objects will be scanned. The **id** parameter allows the scanner to specify which objects will be scanned using a key. The value of **NULL_KEY** specifies all objects.

The parameter **type** specifies the type of scan. The valid types can be combined with the logical or (|) operator. These values are summarized in Table 6.1.

Table 6.1: Scan Types

Flag	Purpose
AGENT	Agents/avatars (users).
ACTIVE	Physical objects that are moving or objects containing an active script.
PASSIVE	Non-scripted or script is inactive and non-physical or, if physical, not moving.
SCRIPTED	Objects containing an active script.

The parameter **range** specifies how many meters out the scanner should scan. A value of zero will not scan. The parameter arc specifies the **arc**, in radians, the scanner should scan. Specify a value of **PI** radians to scan in all directions. For example, to scan for every agent, within 96 meters of the scanner, use the following command:

```
llSensor("", "",AGENT, 96, PI )
```

Usually an object will want to scan at regular intervals. The above command could be performed every second with the following command:

```
llSensorRepeat("", "",AGENT, 96, PI, 1)
```

Notice the additional parameter of one at the end of the command? This specifies a scan is required every second. If an avatar or object is detected by either scan, the **sensor** event handler will be called. This event handler is shown here.

```
sensor(integer num_detected)
```

If nothing was found, the **no_sensor** event handler is called.

```
no_sensor()
```

This chapter demonstrates four recipes that make use of sensors. The first recipe is a radar that detects avatars.

Recipe 6.1: Avatar Radar

Radars are a common gadget in Second Life. A nearby radar will report all avatars in the area. The radar presented in this recipe lists all nearby avatars, and their distances, just above the radar. The radar can be seen in Figure 6.1.

Figure 6.1: Avatar Radar

The script needed to produce this radar is shown in Listing 6.1.

Listing 6.1: Avatar Radar (Radar.lsl)

```
integer freq = 1;

default
{
    state_entry()
    {
        llSensorRepeat("", "",AGENT, 96, PI, freq);
    }

    sensor(integer num_detected)
    {
        integer i;
        string name;
        integer distance;
        string result = "";
        list data = [];
```

```
                    vector pos = llGetPos();


                    for(i=0;i<num_detected;i++)
                    {
                        name = llKey2Name(llDetectedKey(i));
                        vector detPos = llDetectedPos(i);
                        distance = (integer)llVecDist(pos, detPos);
                        data += distance;
                        data += name;
                    }

                    llListSort(data,2,FALSE);

                    integer listLength = llGetListLength(data);
                    for( i=0;i<listLength;i+=2)
                    {
                        distance = llList2Integer(data,i);
                        name = llList2String(data,i+1);

                        result = result + name + " [" +
                        (string)distance + "m]\n";
                    }

                    llSetText(result,<1,1,1>,1);
            }
    }
```

This script begins by defining a variable, named **freq**, to hold the scanning frequency. For the radar, the scanning frequency is one second.

```
integer freq = 1;
```

When the script starts, a repeating sensor is created to scan for Avatars up to 96 meters away.

```
state_entry()
{
        llSensorRepeat("", "",AGENT, 96, PI, freq);
}
```

Nearly all of the work performed by this script is performed inside of the **sensor** event handler. First, certain variables are defined that will be used by the event handler.

```
sensor(integer num_detected)
{
        integer i;
        string name;
        integer distance;
```

```
string result = "";
list data = [];
```

First, the current position of the radar is obtained. This is used to calculate the distance that each avatar is at.

```
vector pos = llGetPos();
```

All detected avatars are looped through.

```
for(i=0;i<num_detected;i++)
{
        name = llKey2Name(llDetectedKey(i));
        vector detPos = llDetectedPos(i);
        distance = (integer)llVecDist(pos, detPos);
```

The name and distance is obtained for each avatar. The name and distance are stored as pairs into the data list.

```
        data += distance;
        data += name;
}
```

Next the list is sorted. A span of two is specified because the list contains pairs. Each pair is made up of the name and distance.

```
llListSort(data,2,FALSE);
```

Now that the list has been sorted, it must be displayed. Loop through each pair in the list, and extract the **name** and **distance**. Add the results to the **result** string.

```
integer listLength = llGetListLength(data);
for( i=0;i<listLength;i+=2)
{
        distance = llList2Integer(data,i);
        name = llList2String(data,i+1);

        result = result + name + " ["
                + (string)distance + "m]\n";
}
```

Once the loop completes, display the completed list.

```
llSetText(result,<1,1,1>,1);
}
```

This radar will continue indefinitely scanning for nearby avatars. Radars can be useful for tracking which avatars are nearby. Specific actions can be performed when avatars approach. The next two recipes demonstrate this.

Recipe 6.2: Notecard Giver

Notecard givers are very common in Second Life. When an avatar appears at a new location, the avatar will often be given a notecard. This notecard explains the rules for the area, or other important information. Figure 6.2 shows an avatar being given a notecard.

Figure 6.2: Notecard Giver

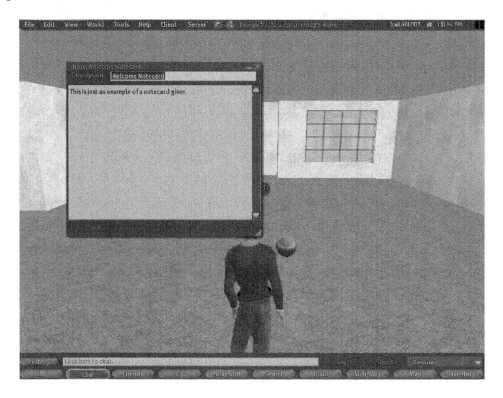

The script necessary to create the notecard giver is shown in Listing 6.2.

Listing 6.2: Notecard Giver (NotecardGiver.lsl)

```
string notecard = "Welcome Notecard";
integer freq = 1;
integer maxList = 100;
list given;


default
{
    state_entry()
    {
        llSensorRepeat("", "",AGENT, 20, PI, freq);
```

```
        llSetText("", <1.0, 1.0, 1.0>, 1.0);
    }

    sensor(integer num_detected)
    {
        integer i;
        key detected;

        for(i=0;i<num_detected;i++)
        {
            detected = llDetectedKey(i);

            if( llListFindList(given, [detected]) < 0 )
            {
                given += llDetectedKey(i);

                llGiveInventory(detected, notecard);
                if (llGetListLength(given) >= maxList)
                {
                    given = llDeleteSubList(given,0,10);
                }
            }
        }
    }
}
```

First, several variables are created that define how the notecard giver will operate. The name of the notecard must be defined. In this case, it is "Welcome Notecard". For the script to operate properly, a notecard, named "Welcome Notecard" is required in the object inventory of the notecard giver object. Additionally, a frequency of one second is specified. Every second, the notecard giver looks for new avatars.

It is important that the notecard giver does not keep giving the same avatars the same notecards. This quickly becomes annoying to the avatars. To achieve this, a list of the last 100 avatars is kept. This ensures that the same avatar does not immediately get the same notecard. Of course, if 100 other avatars visit after an avatar is given a notecard, that avatar will be given the notecard again, if he returns.

```
string notecard = "Welcome Notecard";
integer freq = 1;
integer maxList = 100;
list given;
```

When the script starts, a repeating sensor is created at the specified frequency.

```
state_entry()
{
    llSensorRepeat("", "",AGENT, 20, PI, freq);
```

```
}
```

The **sensor** event handler is called once a second, by default, and is responsible for distributing the notecards.

```
sensor(integer num_detected)
{
        integer i;
        key detected;
```

The event handler loops across all avatars that were detected.

```
        for(i=0;i<num_detected;i++)
        {
                detected = llDetectedKey(i);
```

The key for each detected avatar is obtained. This key is added to the given list, if the key is not already present in the list.

```
                if( llListFindList(given, [detected]) < 0 )
                {
                        given += llDetectedKey(i);

                        llGiveInventory(detected, notecard);
```

If the list has exceeded 100 avatars, shrink the list by 10. The function **llGiveInventory** allows inventory objects, in this case a notecard, to be given. Any item could be substituted here.

```
                if (llGetListLength(given) >= maxList)
                {
                        given = llDeleteSubList(given,0,10);
                }
```

This prevents the list from growing to an unmanageable length, and ensures that avatars are not given the same notecard too often.

Recipe 6.3: Automatic Door

Recipe 3.2 showed how to create a simple door. This door opens when an avatar touches it. This recipe builds on Recipe 3.2 by creating a door that automatically opens as the user approaches that door. Figure 6.3 shows the automatic door in action.

Figure 6.3: Automatic Door

The script necessary to produce the automatic door is shown in Listing 6.3.

Listing 6.3: Automatic Door (AutoDoor.lsl)

```
float        TIMER_CLOSE = 5.0;
integer      DIRECTION   = -1;
// direction door opens in. Either 1 (outwards) or -1 (inwards);

integer      DOOR_OPEN   = 1;
integer      DOOR_CLOSE  = 2;

vector       originalPos;

door(integer what)
{
    rotation    rot;
    rotation    delta;
    vector eul;

    llSetTimerEvent(0);
```

```
    if ( what == DOOR_OPEN )
    {
        llTriggerSound("doorOpen", 1);
        eul = <0, 0, 90*DIRECTION>; //90 degrees around the z-
axis, in Euler form

    } else if ( what == DOOR_CLOSE)
    {
        llTriggerSound("doorClose", 1);
        eul = <0, 0, 90*-DIRECTION>; //90 degrees around the z-
axis, in Euler form
    }

    eul *= DEG_TO_RAD; //convert to radians rotation
    rot = llGetRot();
    delta = llEuler2Rot(eul);
    rot = delta * rot;
    llSetRot(rot);
}


default
{
    on_rez(integer start_param)
    {
        llResetScript();
    }

    state_entry()
    {
        originalPos = llGetPos();
        llSensorRepeat("", "",AGENT, 5, PI, 1);
    }

    sensor(integer num_detected)
    {
        door(DOOR_OPEN);
        state open_state;
    }

    moving_end()
    {
        originalPos = llGetPos();
    }
}
```

```
state open_state
{
    state_entry()
    {
        llSensorRepeat("", "",AGENT, 5, PI, 1);
    }

    no_sensor()
    {
        door(DOOR_CLOSE);
        llSetPos(originalPos);
        state default;
    }

    sensor(integer num_detected)
    {
    }


    moving_start()
    {
        door(DOOR_CLOSE);
        state default;
    }
}
```

Few changes are required to Recipe 3.2 to create an automatic door. The mechanics of opening and closing the door are not explained in this recipe. For more information on that topic, refer to Recipe 3.2 in Chapter 3.

To automatically open the door, a simple sensor is used. This sensor moves the door to an opened state whenever it is called.

```
sensor(integer num_detected)
{
    door(DOOR_OPEN);
    state open_state;
}
```

This sensor will be called when any avatar approaches the door.

Recipe 6.4: Traffic Scanner

Traffic scanners are popular in Second Life. Traffic scanners perform a variety of tasks and provide a variety of statistics. The traffic scanner presented in this chapter counts the number of visitors per day. At the end of the day (midnight) the traffic scanner will Instant Message (IM) a visitor count to its owner.

Additionally, the traffic scanner reports a complete list of avatars that have visited for the day. To see this list of avatars, simply touch the traffic scanner. Figure 6.4 shows the traffic scanner reporting all unique visitors for a day.

Figure 6.4: Traffic Scanner

The script necessary to produce the traffic scanner is shown in Listing 6.4.

Listing 6.4: Traffic Scanner (TrafficScanner.lsl)

```
list known;
string parcelName;

integer DAYSEC = 86400;
integer visitorsYesterday;

setTimer()
{
    float now = llGetWallclock();
    integer secondsLeft = (DAYSEC - (integer)now);
    llSetTimerEvent(secondsLeft);
}
```

```
default
{
    on_rez(integer i)
    {
        llResetScript();
    }

    state_entry()
    {
        llSensorRepeat("", "", AGENT, 20.0, PI, 1.0);
        list lstParcelDetails = [PARCEL_DETAILS_NAME];

        list lstParcelName=llGetParcelDetails(llGetPos(),
            lstParcelDetails);

        parcelName =(string)lstParcelName;
        setTimer();
    }

    sensor(integer detected)
    {
        integer i;

        // Say the names of everyone the sensor detects
        for(i=0;i<detected;i++)
        {
            string name = llDetectedName(i);

            if( llListFindList(known,[name]) == -1 )
            {
                llSay(0,"Hello " + name + " welcome to " +
                  parcelName + "." );
                known += [name];
            }
        }
    }

    touch_start(integer total_number)
    {
        key owner = llGetOwner();
        key who = llDetectedKey(0);
        if( who==owner )
        {
            llSay(0, "Number of unique visitors today: " +
                (string)llGetListLength(known) );
```

```
            llSay(0, "Number of unique visitors yesterday: "
                 + (string)visitorsYesterday );
            string l = llList2CSV(known);
            llSay(0,"Visitors today:" + l );
        }
    }

    timer()
    {
        llSleep(60);
        visitorsYesterday = llGetListLength(known);
        setTimer();
        known = [];
        llInstantMessage(llGetOwner(),"You had "
            + (string)visitorsYesterday + " today at "
            + parcelName );
    }
}
```

The traffic scanner begins by defining variables that will be used by the script. The list named known keeps track of the avatars that have visited today. This prevents a returning avatar from being double counted. Next, the name of the land that the traffic counter is on is obtained. This is used when the traffic counter welcomes the avatar. The number of seconds in a day is defined so it is possible to know how long until midnight.

```
list known;
string parcelName;

integer DAYSEC = 86400;
integer visitorsYesterday;
```

These variables will be used by the entire script.

Setting Up the Traffic Scanner

The traffic scanner resets the script when it is rezzed. This makes sure the countdown to midnight is set correctly and no data is held from the last location of the scanner.

```
default
{
    on_rez(integer i)
    {
        llResetScript();
    }
```

A repeating sensor is created that scans for avatars. The name of the parcel is also obtained.

```
state_entry()
{
    llSensorRepeat("", "", AGENT, 20.0, PI, 1.0);
    list lstParcelDetails = [PARCEL_DETAILS_NAME];

    list lstParcelName=llGetParcelDetails(llGetPos(),
        lstParcelDetails);

    parcelName =(string)lstParcelName;
    setTimer();
}
```

Calling the **setTimer** function causes a timer to be set that will occur just after midnight. The **setTimer** function will be explained later in this recipe.

Detecting Avatars

All new avatars are detected inside of the sensor event handler.

```
sensor(integer detected)
{
    integer i;
```

The sensor event handler begins by looping across all detected avatars. If the avatar is not already in the list, that avatar is added. The traffic script also says "Hello" to each of the new avatars.

```
    // Say the names of everyone the sensor detects
    for(i=0;i<detected;i++)
    {
        string name = llDetectedName(i);

        if( llListFindList(known, [name]) == -1 )
        {
            llSay(0,"Hello " + name + " welcome to "
              + parcelName + "." );
            known += [name];
        }
    }
}
```

The list grows as new avatars visit during the day.

Displaying a List of Avatars

It is interesting to see the list of avatar names who have visited your area. Touching the traffic scanner displays this list. This is done by converting the visitor list to a string to display.

```
touch_start(integer total_number)
{
    key owner = llGetOwner();
    key who = llDetectedKey(0);
    if( who==owner )
    {
        llSay(0, "Number of unique visitors today: "
                + (string)llGetListLength(known) );
        llSay(0, "Number of unique visitors yesterday: "
                + (string)visitorsYesterday );
        string l = llList2CSV(known);
        llSay(0,"Visitors today:" + l );
    }
}
```

The owner of the traffic scanner is the only one allowed to display this list.

How Long Until Midnight

The list of known avatars is cleared out once a day. This occurs just after midnight. To do this, the script must calculate how many seconds until midnight, and then set a timer for that amount of time.

```
setTimer()
{
    float now = llGetWallclock();
    integer secondsLeft = (DAYSEC - (integer)now);
    llSetTimerEvent(secondsLeft);
}
```

To do this, the number of seconds since midnight is subtracted from the number of seconds in a day. A timer is set for that amount of time.

Resetting at Midnight

The traffic script should clear its list of known avatars just after midnight. This is done when the **timer** event handler is called. First, the event handler waits a minute to ensure that midnight has passed.

```
timer()
{
    llSleep(60);
    visitorsYesterday = llGetListLength(known);
    setTimer();
```

```
        known = [];
        llInstantMessage(llGetOwner(),"You had "
            + (string)visitorsYesterday + " today at "
            + parcelName );
    }
}
```

Next, the count of visitors for yesterday is updated. The timer is set for the next mid-night, which will be 24 hours ahead. Finally, a message is sent to the owner indicating how many people have visited.

Summary

This chapter showed how a script can be aware of its environment. This is done using scanners. Scanners allow a script to be notified whenever avatars or objects come into contact with it.

This chapter introduced four recipes that work with scanners. A radar shows the avatars that are nearby. A welcome card giver hands out welcome cards to avatars as they teleport in. An automatic door opens as soon as an avatar approaches. Finally, a traffic counter is provided to track who visits your land.

The next chapter introduces several miscellaneous scripting techniques that do not fit into the other chapters. Techniques for working with the weather are shown. Additionally analog clocks, cannons and other gadgets are explored.

CHAPTER 7: MISCELLANEOUS RECIPES

- Shooting an Avatar from a Cannon
- Creating an Analog Clock
- Reading the Weather
- Using Notecards for Configuration
- Tracking Avatar's On-Line Status
- Creating a Slideshow

The recipes presented in this chapter are not easily classified into one of the categories covered by the other chapters. This chapter covers a wide range of topics from shooting an avatar from a cannon to monitoring Second Life weather.

This chapter also introduces how to use notecards to store configuration information. Notecards were introduced in Chapter 6 and are very similar to text files. Using the notecard, the user can store configuration information about the script into the notecard. This allows the function of the script to change, without requiring the user to modify the actual script file.

Recipe 7.1: Avatar Cannon

The `llPushObject` function allows one object to apply force to another. This causes the second object to move in a specified direction. There are many uses for the `llPushObject` function. One simple demonstration of this is an avatar cannon. The avatar cannon allows an avatar to sit in its barrel and be blasted into the air.

Chapter 10 introduces a parachute recipe. The cannon recipe is useful for testing the parachute recipe. Strap on a parachute and blast your avatar into the air, with the cannon. Figure 7.1 shows an avatar waiting to be shot from the cannon.

Figure 7.1: Avatar Cannon

The script necessary to produce this cannon is shown in Listing 7.1.

Listing 7.1: Avatar Cannon (Cannon.lsl)

```
key target;
integer countdown;

default
{
    state_entry()
    {
        llSitTarget(<0,0,0.1>,ZERO_ROTATION);
        llSetText("Sit here to\nbe fired from the cannon!",
            <0.0, 1.0, 0.0>, 1.0);
    }

    timer()
    {
        llSay(0,"Cannon will fire in " + (string)countdown
            + " seconds.");
        countdown--;
```

```
        if( countdown<0 )
        {
            llSetTimerEvent(0);
            llPushObject(target, <0,0,2147483647>,
                ZERO_VECTOR, FALSE);
        }
    }

    changed(integer change)
    {

        if (change & CHANGED_LINK)
        {

            key agent = llAvatarOnSitTarget();

            if (agent)
            {
                countdown = 10;
                target = agent;
                llUnSit(target);
                llSetTimerEvent(1);
            }
        }
    }
}
}
```

The cannon recipe begins by declaring the following two variables:

```
key target;
integer countdown;
```

The **default** state of the cannon script begins by defining a sit target and instructional text to the avatar.

```
llSitTarget(<0,0,0.1>,ZERO_ROTATION);
llSetText("Sit here to\nbe fired from the cannon!",
<0.0, 1.0, 0.0>, 1.0);
```

Like previous chapters, the script is notified that an avatar has sat down through a call to the **changed** event handler.

```
changed(integer change)
{
```

The **changed** event handler begins by checking to see whether a new link has been added.

```
if (change & CHANGED_LINK)
{
```

Next, obtain the key of the avatar that sat in the cannon.

```
key agent = llAvatarOnSitTarget();
```

If the key was successfully obtained, then set up the cannon to blast the avatar from it. Begin by setting the countdown to 10. The cannon counts down from ten before shooting the avatar from its barrel. An avatar cannot be moved while sitting, so it is necessary to unseat the avatar by calling **llUnSit**. Finally, begin a **timer** event at one second intervals.

```
if (agent)
{
    countdown = 10;
    target = agent;
    llUnSit(target);
    llSetTimerEvent(1);
}
}
}
```

The timer will perform the countdown and ultimately shoot the avatar from its barrel.

```
timer()
{
    llSay(0,
"Cannon will fire in " + (string)countdown + " seconds.");
```

For each iteration of the timer, decrease the **countdown** by one.

```
countdown--;
```

When the **countdown** reaches zero, then prepare to fire the avatar. Set the timer interval to zero. This stops the timer. Next call **llPushObject** to push the avatar, whose key is stored in the target variable, to shoot the avatar straight up. The value 2,147,483,647 represents the maximum value that can be applied.

```
if( countdown<0 )
{
    llSetTimerEvent(0);
    llPushObject(target, <0,0,2147483647>,
        ZERO_VECTOR, FALSE);
}
}
```

This shoots the avatar high into the air.

Recipe 7.2: Analog Clock

An analog clock is a clock that has two hands that show the passage of minutes and hours. Digital clocks simply show times with numbers, such as 6:23. Digital clocks are not a complete replacement for analog clocks. Analog clocks are still considered desirable for decorative purposes. Additionally, analog clocks, with their moving hands, show the passage of time more clearly for some people.

This recipe will show how to create an analog clock in Second Life. The analog clock can be seen in Figure 7.2.

Figure 7.2: Analog Clock

An analog clock consists of three prims. Firstly the clock face and secondly, the hour and minute hands. The clock face contains the script that runs the clock. The textures of the hour and minute hands are rotated to give the appearance that they are rotating as time passes.

The script necessary to produce the analog clock is shown in Listing 7.2.

Listing 7.2: Analog Clock (AnalogClock.lsl)

```lsl
setClock()
{
    integer t = llRound(llGetWallclock());
    integer hours = t / 3600;
    integer minutes = (t % 3600) / 60;
     integer minutes_angle = minutes;
     integer hours_angle = hours;

    minutes_angle*=6;
    minutes_angle = 180-minutes_angle;

    hours_angle *= 30;
    hours_angle+= (minutes/12)*6;
    hours_angle =180 - hours_angle;


    llSetLinkPrimitiveParams(3,[PRIM_TEXTURE, 0, "hour", <1,1,1>,
<0,0,0>, hours_angle * DEG_TO_RAD ]);
    llSetLinkPrimitiveParams(2,[PRIM_TEXTURE, 0, "minute",
<1,1,1>, <0,0,0>, minutes_angle * DEG_TO_RAD]);
}

default
{
    state_entry()
    {

        llSetTimerEvent(60);
        setClock();

    }

    timer()
    {
        setClock();
    }


}
```

Most of the work performed by the analog clock is done by the **setClock** function. This function begins by calling the **llGetWallClock** function. The **llGetWallClock** function returns the number of seconds since midnight Pacific Standard Time, which is Second Life Standard Time.

```
setClock()
{
    integer t = llRound(llGetWallclock());
```

The **setClock** function begins by dividing the number of seconds since midnight by 3,600, which is the number of seconds in an hour. The minutes are calculated by determining how many minutes have passed since the last hour.

```
    integer hours = t / 3600;
    integer minutes = (t % 3600) / 60;
```

Ultimately, the hands show time through angles. Each position of the hour and minute hands are specific angles. Use the **setClock** function to determine the angles for each. Each minute is 6 degrees. 180 degrees is the starting position for the hands.

```
    integer minutes_angle = minutes;
    integer hours_angle = hours;

    minutes_angle*=6;
    minutes_angle = 180-minutes_angle;
```

Each hour is 30 degrees. Additionally, the hour hand should move forward, from its hour position, for the number of minutes. This allows the hour hand to be just before the two at 1:59.

```
    hours_angle *= 30;
    hours_angle+= (minutes/12)*6;
    hours_angle =180 - hours_angle;
```

Finally, the textures are rotated to the correct angles for the hour and minute hands.

```
    llSetLinkPrimitiveParams(3,[PRIM_TEXTURE, 0, "hour",
<1,1,1>, <0,0,0>, hours_angle * DEG_TO_RAD ]);
    llSetLinkPrimitiveParams(2,[PRIM_TEXTURE, 0, "minute",
<1,1,1>, <0,0,0>, minutes_angle * DEG_TO_RAD]);
}
```

The clock begins by setting an event timer for every sixty seconds. The **setClock** function is also called to ensure the clock begins at the correct time.

```
state_entry()
{
    llSetTimerEvent(60);
    setClock();
}
```

At each sixty second interval, update the hands.

```
timer()
{
    setClock();
}
```

This produces an analog clock that is updated every minute.

Recipe 7.3: Weather Station

Weather stations are a popular Second Life gadget, even though they serve little use to typical users. Second Life does have a weather system. There are clouds in the sky and wind speed and direction. Normally, this weather simply influences flags, particle streams, and aircraft. However, it is possible to create a weather station that will display the weather conditions.

Though the weather station is of little use to the average user, it can be helpful to a developer. Knowing the current weather conditions can explain how the weather affects air vehicles. The weather station is shown in Figure 7.3.

Figure 7.3: Weather Station

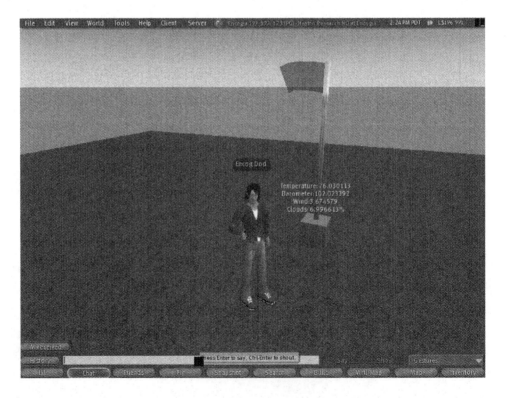

The script necessary to produce the weather station is shown in Listing 7.3.

Listing 7.3: Weather Station (Weather.lsl)

```
float SEALEVEL = 101.32500;

default
{
    state_entry()
    {
        llSetTimerEvent(1);
    }

    timer()
    {
        string result;

        vector sun = llGetSunDirection();
        vector pos = llGetPos();
        float base = llLog10(5- ((pos.z -
            llWater(ZERO_VECTOR))/15500));
        float pascal = (SEALEVEL + base);
        float temperatureF = ((((pascal * (2 * llPow(10,22)))/
        (1.8311*llPow(10,20))/ 8.314472)/19.85553747) + (sun.z
            * 10));
        vector wind = llWind(pos);
        float cloud = llCloud(ZERO_VECTOR);
        cloud = cloud*100.0;

        result = "Temperature: " + (string) temperatureF;
        result+= "\nBarometer:" + (string)pascal;
        result+= "\nWind:" + (string)llVecMag(wind);
        result+= "\nClouds: " + (string)cloud + "%";
        llSetText(result,<0,1,1>,1);

//llSay(0,"Current Temperature is "+ (string)((temperatureF - 32)
* 5/9) +" Degrees Celsius");
    }
}
```

The weather station recipe begins by declaring the barometric pressure at sea-level.

```
float SEALEVEL = 101.32500;
```

The recipe continues by setting a timer to occur every second.

```
state_entry()
{
    llSetTimerEvent(1);
}
```

The **timer** begins by calculating the sun's direction. This is determined by the time of day. The sun's direction will be used to determine the current temperature.

```
timer()
{
     string result;

     vector sun = llGetSunDirection();
     vector pos = llGetPos();
```

Next, the barometric pressure is calculated with the following two lines:

```
     float base = llLog10(5- ((pos.z - llWater(ZERO_VEC-
TOR))/15500));
     float pascal = (SEALEVEL + base);
```

These lines implement the barometric formula. For more information on the barometric formula, refer to this URL:

http://en.wikipedia.org/wiki/Barometric formula

The temperature is calculated next. This temperature calculation makes use of both the sun's position and the barometric pressure. This formula was provided by a Linden Labs example.

```
     float temperatureF = ((((pascal * (2 * llPow(10,22)))/
          (1.8311*llPow(10,20))/ 8.314472)/19.85553747) + (sun.z *
10)));
```

The wind direction and cloud density are also obtained.

```
     vector wind = llWind(pos);
     float cloud = llCloud(ZERO_VECTOR);
     cloud = cloud*100.0;
```

The newly obtained values are linked into a string to be displayed.

```
     result = "Temperature: " + (string) temperatureF;
     result+= "\nBarometer:" + (string)pascal;
     result+= "\nWind:" + (string)llVecMag(wind);
     result+= "\nClouds: " + (string)cloud + "%";
```

The linked string is then displayed.

```
     llSetText(result,<0,1,1>,1);
```

If a Celsius temperature is needed, use the following line to convert to Celsius.

```
//llSay(0,"Current Temperature is "+ (string)((temperatureF - 32)
* 5/9) +" Degrees Celsius");
     }
}
```

The temperature station also includes a small flag, which blows in the direction of the wind.

Recipe 7.4: Slide Show

A slide show in Second Life allows avatars to see images. These images are cycled at regular intervals. All images that should be displayed by the slide show must be stored as textures. These textures must be placed in the object inventory of the slide show object. The slide can be seen in Figure 7.4.

Figure 7.4: Slide Show

The script necessary to produce the slide show is shown in Listing 7.4.

Listing 7.4: Slide Show (SlideShow.lsl)

```
list slides = ["slide1","slide2","slide3","slide4"];
integer index;

newSlide()
{
    string texture = llList2String(slides,index);
    llSetTexture(texture,1);
```

```
        index++;
        if(index>=llGetListLength(slides) )
            index = 0;
}

default
{
    state_entry()
    {
        llSetTimerEvent(30);
        index = 0;
        newSlide();
    }

    touch_start(integer num)
    {
        index = 0;
        newSlide();
        llSay(0,"Starting slide show over");
    }

    timer()
    {
        newSlide();
    }
}
```

The slide show recipe begins with a list containing all slides to be displayed. Additionally, an index variable is declared to hold the current slide being displayed.

```
list slides = ["slide1","slide2","slide3","slide4"];
integer index;
```

The **newSlide** function is called whenever a new slide is to be displayed. The **newSlide** function begins by extracting the current slide from the list. Then, the texture of the slide show object is updated to display that texture. If the end of the slide list has been reached, the index is incremented, and reset to zero. It is important to note that the **newSlide** function displays whichever slide the index is currently on.

```
newSlide()
{
    string texture = llList2String(slides,index);
    llSetTexture(texture,1);
    index++;
    if(index>=llGetListLength(slides) )
        index = 0;
}
```

When the script starts, a new timer is created. This will occur every 30 seconds. The index is reset to the first slide, and that slide is displayed.

```
state_entry()
{
    llSetTimerEvent(30);
    index = 0;
    newSlide();
}
```

If the slide show is touched, the slide show is started over. It may also be desirable to move to the next slide early when touched. If this is the case, replicate the functionality of the timer event handler in the **touch_start** event handler.

```
touch_start(integer num)
{
    index = 0;
    newSlide();
    llSay(0,"Starting slide show over");
}
```

When the **timer** event handler is called, move to the next slide.

```
timer()
{
    newSlide();
}
```

The slide show object cycles endlessly through all the textures. A slide show can also be setup so that the script does not need to be modified to configure the slides. A notecard can be used. The next recipe also shows how to create a slide show that is controlled by a notecard.

Recipe 7.5: Notecard Controlled Slide Show

The slide show script shown in the last section is configured by directly modifying the script. This is not always desirable. When an object is purchased in Second Life, the ability to modify the script is usually restricted. This is done by script creators to protect their software from being copied. Because of this, the purchaser of that script cannot configure the script if they are not allowed to modify the script.

To solve this problem, a notecard can be used. A notecard can be used as a type of configuration file. It is a separate object from the script, and is stored in the object's inventory. The slide show object shown in this recipe looks exactly like the slide show in the previous recipe. However, it works quite differently, as it is controlled by a notecard. This notecard is shown in Listing 7.5.

Listing 7.5: Slide Control Notecard (SlideControl.not)

```
slide1
slide2
slide3
slide4
```

The notecard lists the name of each slide on a separate line. The script needed to produce the slide show is shown in Listing 7.6.

Listing 7.6: A Notecard Controlled Slide Show (NotecardSlideShow.lsl)

```
integer index;

// for loading notecard
string notecardName;
key notecardQuery;
integer notecardIndex;
list notecardList;

newSlide()
{
    string texture = llList2String(notecardList,index);
    llSetTexture(texture,1);
    index++;
    if(index>=llGetListLength(notecardList) )
        index = 0;
}

default
{
    state_entry()
    {
        if( llGetListLength(notecardList)==0 )
        {
            notecardName = "SlideControl";
            state loading;
        }
        else
        {
            llSetTimerEvent(30);
            index = 0;
            newSlide();
        }
    }

    touch_start(integer num)
    {
```

```
            index = 0;
            newSlide();
            llSay(0,"Starting slide show over");
        }

        timer()
        {
            newSlide();
        }
}

state loading
{
    state_entry()
    {
        llSay(0,"Slideshow loading data...");
        notecardIndex = 0;
        notecardQuery = llGetNotecardLine(notecardName,
            notecardIndex++);
    }

    dataserver(key query_id, string data)
    {
        if ( notecardQuery == query_id)
        {
            // this is a line of our notecard
            if (data == EOF)
            {
                llSay(0,"Slideshow loaded...");
                state default;

            } else
            {
                notecardList += [data];
                notecardQuery = llGetNotecardLine(notecardName,
                    notecardIndex++);
            }
        }
    }
}
```

The notecard based slide show begins by loading the list of slides to a list. After the slides are in the list, this recipe works in the same way as the previous recipe that did not use a notecard. This code can be reused anytime a notecard should be read to a list. Several variables are defined to read in the notecard.

```
integer index;
```

```
// for loading notecard
string notecardName;
key notecardQuery;
integer notecardIndex;
list notecardList;
```

The **notecardName** variable holds the name of the notecard. The **notecardQuery** variable holds the name of the query that is taking place to the notecard. The **notecardIndex** contains the index number of the notecard line being read. The **notecardList** variable contains the lines read in from the notecard.

The script begins by checking to see whether the slide list has already been loaded. If the list has not been loaded, then set the name of the script to "SlideControl" and the state switches to loading.

```
state_entry()
{
        if( llGetListLength(notecardList)==0 )
        {
                notecardName = "SlideControl";
                state loading;
        }
```

If the list has been loaded, set a timer to display a new texture every 30 seconds.

```
        else
        {
                llSetTimerEvent(30);
                index = 0;
                newSlide();
        }
}
```

The loading state begins by announcing that the slide show is loading. The query begins by requesting the first line from the notecard. Notecard reading is asynchronous. As lines are read in they are passed to the **dataserver** event handler.

```
state loading
{
    state_entry()
    {
        llSay(0,"Slideshow loading data...");
        notecardIndex = 0;
        notecardQuery = llGetNotecardLine(notecardName,
                notecardIndex++);
    }
```

The **dataserver** event handler is called for each line that is read in. First, the **dataserver** handler checks to see whether the information received relates to the query being processed.

```
dataserver(key query_id, string data)
{
    if ( notecardQuery == query_id)
    {
```

Next, it is determined whether we had reached the end of the notecard. If the end has been reached, then return to the **default** state. There will be items in the list, and the slide show can start.

```
        // this is a line of our notecard
        if (data == EOF)
        {
            llSay(0,"Slideshow loaded...");
            state default;
```

Each line read in from the notecard is stored in the list.

```
        } else
        {
            notecardList += [data];
            notecardQuery = llGetNotecardLine(notecardName,
                notecardIndex++);
        }
    }
}
}
```

The mechanism for displaying the textures is the same as the previous recipe. For more information on how that works, refer to the previous recipe.

Recipe 7.6: Announcer Script

An announcer script is a script that reads text and "says" that text to all avatars near by. These are sometimes more effective than signs because most users will read what is being said around them. The text to be announced is read in from a notecard.

The announcer script presented in this recipe reads a famous speech by Mark Antony. The script is shown in Listing 7.7.

Listing 7.7: An Announcer Script (NotecardReader.lsl)

```
integer index;
key query;
```

```
default
{
    state_entry()
    {
        llSetText(
      "Touch me to\nHear me read from a notecard.",<0,1,1>,1);
    }

    touch_start(integer total_number)
    {
        index = 0;
        query = llGetNotecardLine("MarkAntony",index++);
        llSetTimerEvent(10);
    }

    timer()
    {
        query = llGetNotecardLine("MarkAntony",index++);
    }

    dataserver(key query_id, string data)
    {
        if (query == query_id)
        {
            // this is a line of our notecard
            if (data == EOF)
            {
                llSetTimerEvent(0);

            } else
            {
            // increment line count
                llSay(0, data);
            }
        }
    }
}
```

Unlike the previous recipe, this recipe will not load the notecard into a list. This recipe simply announces the notecard as it is read. The recipe begins by creating an index variable that holds the current line number being announced, and a query variable that holds the current query to the notecard.

```
integer index;
key query;
```

Next, the recipe displays text that tells avatars to touch it to hear it read its notecard.

```
state_entry()
{
      llSetText("Touch me to\nHear me read from a notecard.",
            <0,1,1>,1);
}
```

Once the announcer is touched, a notecard query is begun. Additionally, a timer is set for every ten seconds.

```
touch_start(integer total_number)
{
      index = 0;
      query = llGetNotecardLine("MarkAntony",index++);
      llSetTimerEvent(10);
}
```

The timer is very simple, it requests the next notecard line every ten seconds.

```
timer()
{
      query = llGetNotecardLine("MarkAntony",index++);
}
```

When a requested line is received by the **dataserver** event handler, that text is announced to nearby avatars using the **llSay** function.

```
dataserver(key query_id, string data)
{
      if (query == query_id)
      {
            // this is a line of our notecard
            if (data == EOF)
            {
                  llSetTimerEvent(0);
            } else
            {
            // increment line count
                  llSay(0, data);
            }
      }
}
```

If the end of the notecard has been reached, the timer is killed, and the object stops announcing. Some announcer scripts run continuously. To cause this script to do that, restart the query.

Recipe 7.7: Online Indicator

Most commerce in Second Life is conducted completely automatically. Most commonly, an avatar clicks on something and then pays for it. However, sometimes it is necessary to page an avatar to the business. This is particularly true of the service industry in Second Life.

An online indicator is a small cube that is green if the shop owner is online, red otherwise. It also includes text that explains the online status of the avatar. If an avatar clicks the cube, the shop owner will be paged. The online indicator can be seen in Figure 7.5.

Figure 7.5: Online Indicator

The online indicator script can be seen in Listing 7.8.

Listing 7.8: Online Indicator (OnlineIndicator.lsl)

```
string name = "";
string last_online = "";
key nameKey = NULL_KEY;
integer isAvailable = TRUE;
integer isOnline = FALSE;
```

```
list MONTHS = ["Jan","Feb","Mar","Apr","May","Jun","Jul","Aug",
"Sep","Oct","Nov","Dec"];

string get_date()
{
    integer t = llRound(llGetWallclock());

    integer hours = t / 3600;
    integer minutes = (t % 3600) / 60;
    integer seconds = t % 60;

    string time = (string)hours + ":";
    if(minutes < 10) time += "0" + (string)minutes + ":";
    else time += (string)minutes + ":";
    if(seconds < 10) time += "0" + (string)seconds;
    else time += (string)seconds;

    string DateToday = "";
    string DateUTC = llGetDate();
    list DateList = llParseString2List(DateUTC, ["-", "-"], []);
    integer year = llList2Integer(DateList, 0);
    integer month = llList2Integer(DateList, 1);
    integer day = llList2Integer(DateList, 2);
    month = month - 1;
    if(day < 10) DateToday = "0";
    DateToday += (string)day + "-";

    DateToday += llList2String(MONTHS,month);
    DateToday += " ";
    DateToday += (string)year;

    time = time + " " + DateToday;
    return time;
}


default
{
    on_rez(integer p)
    {
        llResetScript();
    }

    state_entry()
    {
```

```
        llSetText("Online Detector\nTouch to Claim",<1,1,1>,1);
}

touch_start(integer total_number)
{
    if(name == "")
    {
        nameKey = llDetectedKey(0);
        name = llDetectedName(0);
        llSetText(name + "\nSetting up...",<1,1,1>,1);
        llSetTimerEvent(4.0);
        return;
    }

    if(llDetectedName(0) == name)
    {
        if(isAvailable == FALSE)
        {
            isAvailable = TRUE;
            llWhisper(0, "IM's will be sent to you.");
            return;
        }
        else
        {
            isAvailable = FALSE;
            llWhisper(0, "IM's will not be sent to you.");
            return;
        }

    }
    else
    {
        if(isAvailable && isOnline)
        {
            llInstantMessage(nameKey, llDetectedName(0)
              + " is paging you from " + llGetRegionName());
            llWhisper(0,"A message has been sent to " + name);
        }
    }
}
```

```
timer()
{
    if(nameKey)
    {
        llRequestAgentData(nameKey,DATA_ONLINE);
    }
}

dataserver(key query, string data)
{
    string text = "";

    if((integer)data == 1)
    {
        isOnline = TRUE;
        llSetColor(<0,1,0>,ALL_SIDES);
        text = name + " is ONLINE";
        if(isAvailable) text += "\nClick to Send IM";
        llSetText(text, <0.25,1.0,0.25>,1);
        last_online = "";
    }
    else
    {
        isOnline = FALSE;
        llSetColor(<1,0,0>,ALL_SIDES);
        text = name + " is OFFLINE";

        if(last_online == "") last_online = get_date();
        text += "\nLast Online: " + last_online;
        llSetText(text, <1.0,0.25,0.25>,1);
    }
}
}
```

The online indicator begins by defining several variables that will hold the current status. First, the name of the avatar that is being tracked is kept. The **last_online** variable holds the last time that avatar was online. The **isAvailable** variable holds whether the avatar can be paged or not. The **isOnline** variable holds if the avatar is online.

```
string name = "";
string last_online = "";
key nameKey = NULL_KEY;
integer isAvailable = TRUE;
integer isOnline = FALSE;
```

The **MONTHS** list holds all of the months of the year for display purposes.

```
list MONTHS = ["Jan","Feb","Mar","Apr","May","Jun","Jul","Aug","Se
```

```
p","Oct","Nov","Dec"];
```

The **get_date** function is a useful function that returns the time and date as a string. This function was based on a function provided by Linden Labs.

```
string get_date()
{
    integer t = llRound(llGetWallclock());
```

First determine the hours, minutes and seconds.

```
    integer hours = t / 3600;
    integer minutes = (t % 3600) / 60;
    integer seconds = t % 60;
```

If any of the hours minutes or seconds is a single digit, add a zero to make it a two digit number. For example the number "1" becomes "01".

```
    string time = (string)hours + ":";
    if(minutes < 10) time += "0" + (string)minutes + ":";
    else time += (string)minutes + ":";
    if(seconds < 10) time += "0" + (string)seconds;
    else time += (string)seconds;
```

Next, get the date and parse to a string. This will separate the month, day and year.

```
    string DateToday = "";
    string DateUTC = llGetDate();
    list DateList = llParseString2List(
DateUTC, ["-", "-"], []);
```

Break out the month day and year as integers.

```
    integer year = llList2Integer(DateList, 0);
    integer month = llList2Integer(DateList, 1);
    integer day = llList2Integer(DateList, 2);
    month = month - 1;
```

If the day is single digit, make it multidigit.

```
    if(day < 10) DateToday = "0";
    DateToday += (string)day + "-";
```

Add in the month from the list defined earlier.

```
    DateToday += llList2String(MONTHS,month);
    DateToday += " ";
    DateToday += (string)year;
```

Construct the time and date combination and return the result.

```
    time = time + " " + DateToday;
    return time;
}
```

This function can be used anywhere that the time and date needs to be formatted as a string.

The **on_rez** event handler begins by resetting the script. That way, if the object has changed owners, the owner variable will be properly set.

```
on_rez(integer p)
{
  llResetScript();
}
```

Set the text to confirm that the script is unclaimed.

```
  state_entry()
  {
      llSetText("Online Detector\nTouch to Claim",<1,1,1>,1);
  }
```

After someone touches the pager, set up to track that avatar.

```
  touch_start(integer total_number)
  {
      if(name == "")
      {
```

Save the avatar's key and name and indicate that the object is setting up.

```
          nameKey = llDetectedKey(0);
          name = llDetectedName(0);
          llSetText(name + "\nSetting up...",<1,1,1>,1);
          llSetTimerEvent(4.0);
          return;
      }
```

If the object is being touched by the owner, toggle the availability status.

```
      if(llDetectedName(0) == name)
      {
```

The avatar is available to receive pages.

```
          if(isAvailable == FALSE)
          {
              isAvailable = TRUE;
              llWhisper(0, "IM's will be sent to you.");
              return;
          }
          else
          {
```

The avatar is not available to receive pages.

```
                      isAvailable = FALSE;
                      llWhisper(0,
"IM's will not be sent to you.");
                      return;
                 }

            }
```

If the object is not being touched by the one who claimed it and they are available, send an instant message.

```
            else
            {
                 if(isAvailable && isOnline)
                 {
                      llInstantMessage(nameKey,
llDetectedName(0) + " is paging you from "
+ llGetRegionName());
                      llWhisper(0,"A message has been sent to "
+ name);
                 }
            }
        }
```

The **timer** checks the online status of the avatar. Checking the online status is very similar to reading a notecard. A query is sent and the **dataserver** event is called to indicate the online status.

```
    timer()
    {
        if(nameKey)
        {
            llRequestAgentData(nameKey,DATA_ONLINE);
        }
    }

    dataserver(key query, string data)
    {
        string text = "";
```

If the user is online, update the object.

```
        if((integer)data == 1)
        {
            isOnline = TRUE;
            llSetColor(<0,1,0>,ALL_SIDES);
            text = name + " is ONLINE";
            if(isAvailable) text += "\nClick to Send IM";
            llSetText(text, <0.25,1.0,0.25>,1);
```

```
        last_online = "";
    }
    else
```

If the user is not online, indicate when the user was last online.

```
    {
        isOnline = FALSE;
        llSetColor(<1,0,0>,ALL_SIDES);
        text = name + " is OFFLINE";

        if(last_online == "") last_online = get_date();
        text += "\nLast Online: " + last_online;
        llSetText(text, <1.0,0.25,0.25>,1);
    }
  }
}
```

This script can be used to track the online status for both the owner and other avatars. When the owner first creates the object, it is unclaimed. The owner can then claim the online status indicator, or allow someone else to claim it.

Summary

This chapter introduced a variety of recipes that did not fit into the categories established by the other chapters in this book. A variety of useful objects such as clocks, cannons, online indicators and slide shows were demonstrated. Additionally, it was shown how to use note-cards for script configuration.

Commerce is a very important aspect of Second Life. Some people who earn their entire income through Second Life. The next chapter will provide several recipes for scripts that allow money to be exchanged.

CHAPTER 8: COMMERCE

- Drawing Traffic with Camping
- Paying Money
- Receiving Money
- Using a Vendor Object
- Accepting Tips

Commerce occurs in Second Life whenever money exchanges hands. At the most simple level any object can be marked for sale. Then any avatar that encounters that object can purchase that object for the marked price. Many stores in Second Life operate exactly that way. Such a transaction needs no custom scripting.

However, many stores employ custom scripts to enhance the buying experience. Further, sometimes what is being purchased may be a service. For example, an avatar may purchase a ride on a ferris wheel. A script is necessary to collect the money and start the ride.

This chapter presents recipes for some of the most common commerce needs in Second Life. Camping chairs, rental scripts, vendor objects and tip jars will all be discussed. These items will be discussed in the following recipes.

Recipe 8.1: Camping Pad

Camping is a very popular activity in Second Life. By camping I do not mean grabbing a tent and heading for the great outdoors. Camping in Second Life is something entirely different. Before camping is explained, it is important to understand how traffic works in Second Life.

There are many different ways that an avatar will find a particular location in Second Life. One of the most common methods is the search. When something is entered into the "Places Search" a list of places is returned that match the search. However, what order are these results sorted in?

The results of a search are sorted by traffic. The higher the traffic numbers, the higher the search spot. Traffic is a number defined by how much time avatars spend on the specified parcel of land. Only Linden Labs knows the exact formula for how traffic is calculated. Figure 8.1 shows the traffic numbers for a parcel of land.

Figure 8.1: Traffic

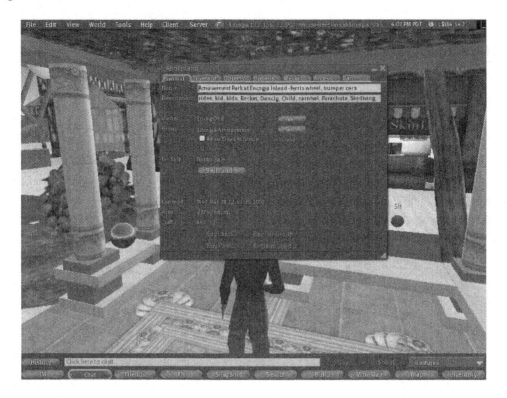

As you can see, the land shown above has a traffic number of 863. Some of the most popular sites in Second Life have traffic numbers around 100,000.

Therefore, if land's traffic number is increased, that land will be placed higher in the search. Therefore, this will likely give the land even more traffic. Because of this, some land owners want to encourage avatars to remain on their land, even if those avatars are not actually doing anything. Even if an avatar is just sitting, or camping, on the land, the traffic number is improved.

This is what camping in Second Life is. To the average user of Second Life, camping is the easiest way to earn money. However, it also the lowest paid job in Second Life. A camping pad is an object that the avatar sits on. The pad is then paid money based on how long the avatar remains on that pad. Pay rates are usually in the range of one Linden dollar per five minutes to one Linden dollar per minute.

From the land owner's perspective, camping is paid advertising for their attraction. Figure 8.2 shows a camping pad.

Figure 8.2: A Camping Pad

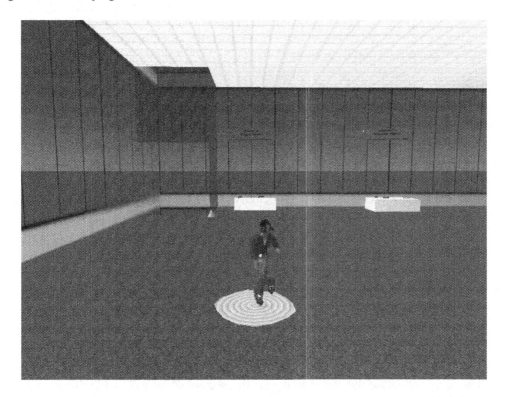

Most camping pads will have the avatar doing something while they are camping. Usually the avatar will be dancing, as seen in Figure 8.2. However, some make it appear as though the avatar is performing a job, such as planting flowers or sweeping the floor.

The camping script in this recipe is controlled by a configuration notecard. This notecard is shown in Listing 8.1.

Listing 8.1: Camping Pad Configuration (CampConfig.not)

```
1
1
2
```

The first line defines how many minutes must pass before the avatar is paid. The second number defines how much money the avatar is paid every time the interval, defined by the first line, elapses. The third line defines after how many intervals the avatar will be stood up. Standing the avatar up causes the avatar to get paid, but no additional payments are made because the avatar is standing. This prevents the avatar from being left endlessly at the camping spot. Many camping pads do not ever stand the avatar up. If this is the desired behavior, use a zero for the third line.

Two scripts are necessary to create this camping object. One single prim can have any number of scripts. If more than one script is contained in a prim, both scripts will execute simultaneously. There are many different reasons for having more than one script. One is simply to organize what would otherwise be a very lengthy single script. However, the camping pad uses two scripts out of necessity.

Chapter 5 introduced the need to request permissions of the avatar. For example, in Chapter 5, the vehicles need to request permission to take the controls. There are other permission requests that can be made. The permission requests are summarized here:

- Permission to take money
- Permission to take the controls
- Permission to animate the avatar
- Permission to attach/detach from the object
- Permission to change links
- Permission to change the agent's camera position
- Permission to control the agent's camera

The camping pad script needs two of these permissions. Firstly, it must animate the avatar so that the avatar will dance. Secondly, it must have permission to take money from its owner to pay the avatar to camp.

However, a single script can only have permissions from one avatar. The camping script needs permission to take money from its owner and it needs animation permission from the avatar using it. These are two separate avatars. As a result, two separate scripts are needed. The first script will cause the avatar to dance; the second script will handle the money and pay the dancing avatar.

Camping Pad Dance Script

The first script causes the avatar to dance. It is independent of the main camping control script. Listing 8.2 shows the dance script.

Listing 8.2: Camping Pad Dancing (CampDance.lsl)

```
key avataronsittarget;

default
{
    state_entry()
    {
        llSetTextureAnim(ANIM_ON | ROTATE | LOOP | SMOOTH,
            ALL_SIDES, 0, 0, 0, 100, 1);
        llSitTarget(<0,0,1>,<0,0,0,1>);
        llSetSitText("Camp");
        llSetTimerEvent(3);
    }
```

```
changed(integer change)
{
    if(change & CHANGED_LINK)
    {
        avataronsittarget = llAvatarOnSitTarget();
        if( avataronsittarget != NULL_KEY )
        {
            if ((llGetPermissions() &
PERMISSION_TRIGGER_ANIMATION) && llGetPermissionsKey() ==
avataronsittarget)
            {
                llStopAnimation("sit");
                llStartAnimation("dance1");
            }
            else
            {
                llRequestPermissions(avataronsittarget,
                    PERMISSION_TRIGGER_ANIMATION);
            }
        }
    }
}

timer()
{
    if ((llGetPermissions() & PERMISSION_TRIGGER_ANIMATION)
        && llGetPermissionsKey() == avataronsittarget)
    {
        llStartAnimation("dance1");
    }
}

run_time_permissions(integer perm)
{
    if(perm)
    {
        llStopAnimation("sit");
        llStartAnimation("stand");
    }
}


}
```

The script begins by declaring a variable that will hold the key to the avatar that has sat on the camping pad.

```
key avataronsittarget;
```

The dance script begins by creating a texture animation that gives the camping pad its "spinning spiral" look. For more information on texture animation, refer to Chapter 3. A sit target is defined, as well as new "sit text". The "sit text" appears on the menu when the user clicks the camping pad.

```
state_entry()
{
    llSetTextureAnim(ANIM_ON | ROTATE | LOOP | SMOOTH,
        ALL_SIDES, 0, 0, 0, 100, 1);
    llSitTarget(<0,0,1>,<0,0,0,1>);
    llSetSitText("Camp");
    llSetTimerEvent(3);
}
```

As seen in previous recipes, the **changed** event handler is called when the avatar sits on the camping script.

```
changed(integer change)
{
    if(change & CHANGED_LINK)
    {
```

The key to the avatar that has sat down is obtained.

```
        avataronsittarget = llAvatarOnSitTarget();
        if( avataronsittarget != NULL_KEY )
        {
```

Permission is obtained to animate the avatar. Animating the avatar allows the avatar to dance. The "dance1" animation is built into Second Life. For a complete list of animations, refer to Appendix B.

```
            if ((llGetPermissions() &
                PERMISSION_TRIGGER_ANIMATION) &&
            llGetPermissionsKey() == avataronsittarget)
            {
                llStopAnimation("sit");
                llStartAnimation("dance1");
            }
            else
            {
                llRequestPermissions(avataronsittarget,
                    PERMISSION_TRIGGER_ANIMATION);
            }
        }
    }
}
```

The dance animation only lasts briefly. It will need to be replayed at regular intervals.

```
timer()
{
    if ((llGetPermissions() &
            PERMISSION_TRIGGER_ANIMATION) &&
            llGetPermissionsKey() == avataronsittarget)
    {
            llStartAnimation("dance1");
    }
}
```

This simple script causes the avatar to dance. The camping pad control script does all the important work of the script.

Camping Pad Control Script

The dance script reviewed in the previous section requested permissions from the avatar using the camping pad. The camping control script covered in this section must request payment permission from the owner of the camping pad. This allows the camping pad to pay the camper.

Listing 8.3: Camping Pad Control (Camp.lsl)

```
integer campmoney = 0;
integer campadd = 2;
integer camptime = 300;
integer campcycle = 2;
integer cyclesLeft = 0;
string reciever;

// for loading notecard
string notecardName;
key notecardQuery;
integer notecardIndex;

displayText()
{
    if( reciever!=NULL_KEY )
    {
        if( campcycle>0 )
        {
            llSetText("Money:"+(string)campmoney +
            "\nCycles Left: " + (string)cyclesLeft,<0,0,0>,1);
        }
        else
        {
            llSetText("Money:"+(string)campmoney,<0,0,0>,1);

        }
```

```
    }
    else
    {
        llSetText("Sit here for free money,\nL$"
            +(string)campadd+" every "
            +(string)(camptime/60)+" minutes.",<0,0,0>,1);
    }


}

default
{
    state_entry()
    {
        llRequestPermissions(llGetOwner(), PERMISSION_DEBIT );
    }

    on_rez(integer s)
    {
        llResetScript();
    }

    run_time_permissions (integer perm)
    {
        if(perm & PERMISSION_DEBIT)
        {
            notecardName = "Config";
            state loading;
        }
    }
}

state ready
{
    state_entry()
    {
        reciever = NULL_KEY;
        displayText();
        llSitTarget(<0, 0, 1>, ZERO_ROTATION);
    }

    touch_start(integer num_detected)
    {
        if( llDetectedKey(0)==llGetOwner() )
        {
```

```
        llSay(0,"Camping pad resetting.");
        llResetScript();
    }
}

changed(integer change)
{
    if (change & CHANGED_LINK)
    {
        if (llAvatarOnSitTarget() != NULL_KEY)
        {
            cyclesLeft = campcycle;
            reciever = llAvatarOnSitTarget();
            displayText();
            llSetTimerEvent(camptime);
        }
        else
        {
            if( campmoney<1 )
            {
                llInstantMessage(reciever,
    "You did not stay long enough to earn any money.");
            }
            else
            {
                llGiveMoney(reciever,campmoney);
            }

            reciever=NULL_KEY;
            campmoney=0;
            displayText();
            llSetTimerEvent(0);
        }
    }
}


timer()
{
    campmoney = campmoney+campadd;
    if( campcycle>0 )
    {
        cyclesLeft--;
        if( cyclesLeft<=0 )
        {
```

```
                    llSay(0,"Standing avatar after " +
(string)campcycle + " cycles.");
                    llUnSit(reciever);
                }
        }
        displayText();
    }
}

state loading
{
    state_entry()
    {
        llSay(0,"Camping pad loading data...");
        notecardIndex = 0;
        notecardQuery = llGetNotecardLine(notecardName,
            notecardIndex++);
    }

    dataserver(key query_id, string data)
    {
        if ( notecardQuery == query_id)
        {
            // this is a line of our notecard
            if (data == EOF)
            {
                llSay(0,"Data loaded...");
                state ready;

            } else
            {
                if( notecardIndex==1 )
                {
                    camptime = ((integer)data)*60;
                }
                else if( notecardIndex==2 )
                {
                    campadd = (integer)data;
                }
                else if( notecardIndex==3 )
                {
                    campcycle = (integer)data;
                }

                notecardQuery = llGetNotecardLine(notecardName,
                    notecardIndex++);
```

```
            }
          }
        }
}
```

The camping control script begins by defining some variables that will hold the state of the camping script. The values here are simply defaults, the real values will be read from the notecard.

```
integer campmoney = 0;
integer campadd = 2;
integer camptime = 300;
integer campcycle = 2;
integer cyclesLeft = 0;
string receiver;
```

The **campmoney** variable holds how much money the camper has been paid. This money will be given to the camper when they stand up. The **camptime** variable holds the amount of time for each camping cycle. The **campadd** variable holds the amount of money to add to **campmoney** for each cycle. The **cyclesLeft** variable holds the amount of cycles left before the avatar will be stood up. The **campcycle** variable holds the starting number of cycles before an avatar is stood up. The **receiver** variable holds the name of the avatar that will receive the money.

Additionally, several variables are defined to read the notecard.

```
// for loading notecard
string notecardName;
key notecardQuery;
integer notecardIndex;
```

The **notecardName** variable holds the name of the notecard. The **notecardQuery** variable holds the query to the notecard. The **notecardIndex** holds the current line being read in the notecard.

The **displayText** function is called each time the descriptive text above the camping pad needs updating.

```
displayText()
{
    if( receiver!=NULL_KEY )
    {
```

If there is someone sitting at the camping pad, display how much money they have obtained. Also, if this camping pad will stand the avatar up after a certain number of cycles, display that as well.

```
        if( campcycle>0 )
        {
```

```
                llSetText("Money:"+(string)campmoney +
                "\nCycles Left: " + (string)cyclesLeft,<0,0,0>,1);
            }
            else
            {
                llSetText("Money:"+(string)campmoney,<0,0,0>,1);


            }
        }
```

If there is no one sitting at the camping pad, display how much money will be paid by the camping pad.

```
    else
    {
        llSetText("Sit here for free money,\nL$"
            +(string)campadd+" every "
            +(string)(camptime/60)+" minutes.",<0,0,0>,1);
    }
}
```

When the camping pad first starts up, the **default** state is entered.

Camping Default State

The **default** state has only one purpose. That is to request permission from the camping pad owner to deduct money. This money will be used to pay campers.

```
state_entry()
{
    llRequestPermissions(llGetOwner(), PERMISSION_DEBIT );
}
```

When this object is rezed make sure to reset. The owner may have changed if it has been transferred to someone else's inventory.

```
on_rez(integer s)
{
    llResetScript();
}
```

Next the **run_time_permission** event handler is presented.

```
run_time_permissions (integer perm)
{
    if(perm & PERMISSION_DEBIT)
    {
        notecardName = "Config";
        state loading;
    }
}
```

After the permission has been obtained, enter the **loading** state.

Camping Loading State

The camping pad obtains all of its configuration information from the configuration notecard. The loading state begins by announcing that the camping pad is loading data. The initial query is sent for the first line of data from the notecard.

```
state_entry()
{
      llSay(0,"Camping pad loading data...");
      notecardIndex = 0;
      notecardQuery =
      llGetNotecardLine(notecardName,notecardIndex++);
}
```

As each line is read in, the **dataserver** event handler is called.

```
dataserver(key query_id, string data)
{
      if ( notecardQuery == query_id)
      {
```

If the last line of the notecard has been read, switch to the ready state. The **ready** state will wait for a camper.

```
            // this is a line of our notecard
            if (data == EOF)
            {
                  llSay(0,"Data loaded...");
                  state ready;
            } else
            {
```

The first line of the configuration card specifies how much time the camper just sits to be paid. This is the length of time for each interval.

```
            if( notecardIndex==1 )
            {
                  camptime = ((integer)data)*60;
            }
```

The second line specifies the amount of money paid for each interval.

```
            else if( notecardIndex==2 )
            {
                  campadd = (integer)data;

            }
```

The third line specifies how many intervals should pass before the camper is stood up.

```
else if( notecardIndex==3 )
{
        campcycle = (integer)data;
}
```

The **dataserver** event handler then reads the next line.

```
notecardQuery =
llGetNotecardLine(notecardName,notecardIndex++);
}
}
}
```

After all of the configuration information has been read, the camping pad enters the **ready** state.

Camping Ready State

When the **ready** state is first entered, the **receiver** is set to **NULL_KEY** and the informational text is displayed. The sit target is set to just above the camping pad.

```
state_entry()
{
    receiver = NULL_KEY;
    displayText();
    llSitTarget(<0, 0, 1>, ZERO_ROTATION);
}
```

If the owner touches the camping pad, it will reset. This is useful for when the configuration notecard changes.

```
touch_start(integer num_detected)
{
    if( llDetectedKey(0)==llGetOwner() )
    {
        llSay(0,"Camping pad resetting.");
        llResetScript();
    }
}
```

The process begins when an avatar sits on the camping pad. The **cyclesLeft** counter is reset and the text is updated to indicate how much money the avatar has earned. In the beginning this will be zero, but it will increase as the avatar remains on the camping pad.

```
changed(integer change)
{
    if (change & CHANGED_LINK)
    {
```

```
if (llAvatarOnSitTarget() != NULL_KEY)
{
        cyclesLeft = campcycle;
        receiver = llAvatarOnSitTarget();
        displayText();
        llSetTimerEvent(camptime);
}
else
{
```

If the avatar is standing and did not earn any money, inform the avatar that they did not remain long enough.

```
if( campmoney<1 )
{
        llInstantMessage(receiver,
"You did not stay long enough to earn any money.");
}
```

If the avatar stayed long enough to earn some money, pay the avatar.

```
else
{
        llGiveMoney(receiver,campmoney);
}
```

Finally, reset the camping pad for the next camper.

```
receiver=NULL_KEY;
campmoney=0;
displayText();
llSetTimerEvent(0);
}
}
}
```

The **timer** event updates the displayed text and also checks to see whether it is time to stand up the avatar. The timer is called once per interval.

```
timer()
{
```

First, the correct amount of money is added to the money already accumulated by the avatar.

```
campmoney = campmoney+campadd;
if( campcycle>0 )
{
        cyclesLeft--;
        if( cyclesLeft<=0 )
        {
```

```
            llSay(0,"Standing avatar after " +
                (string)campcycle + " cycles.");
            llUnSit(receiver);
        }
    }
```

Finally, the display is updated to reflect how much money the avatar has earned so far.

```
    displayText();
}
```

Camping scripts are a good way to build traffic to a parcel of land. This demonstrates a recipe that pays out money. The next recipe will receive money.

Recipe 8.2: Simple Tip Jar

Tip jars are useful to help cover the costs of running an attraction in Second Life. The tip jar presented in this chapter allows money to be paid to the owner of the tip jar. The tip jar tracks how much money has been contributed and displays that value. The tip jar can be seen in Figure 8.3.

Figure 8.3: A Tip Jar

The script needed to produce the tip jar is shown in Listing 8.4.

Listing 8.4: Simple Tip Jar (TipJar.lsl)

```
integer CHANNEL = 55;
integer total;

generalParticleEmitterOn()
{
    llParticleSystem([
        PSYS_PART_FLAGS , 0
    //| PSYS_PART_BOUNCE_MASK
//Bounce on object's z-axis
    //| PSYS_PART_WIND_MASK
//Particles are moved by wind
    | PSYS_PART_INTERP_COLOR_MASK
//Colors fade from start to end
    | PSYS_PART_INTERP_SCALE_MASK
//Scale fades from beginning to end
    | PSYS_PART_FOLLOW_SRC_MASK      //Particles follow the emitter
    //| PSYS_PART_FOLLOW_VELOCITY_MASK//Particles are created at
the velocity of the emitter
    //| PSYS_PART_TARGET_POS_MASK    //Particles follow the target
    | PSYS_PART_EMISSIVE_MASK        //Particles will glow
    //| PSYS_PART_TARGET_LINEAR_MASK
//Undocumented--Sends particles in straight line?
    ,

    //PSYS_SRC_TARGET_KEY , NULL_KEY,
//The particles will head towards the specified key
    //Select one of the following for a pattern:
    //PSYS_SRC_PATTERN_DROP               Particles start at emit-
ter with no velocity
    //PSYS_SRC_PATTERN_EXPLODE            Particles explode from
the emitter
    //PSYS_SRC_PATTERN_ANGLE              Particles are emitted
in a 2-D angle
    //PSYS_SRC_PATTERN_ANGLE_CONE         Particles are emitted
in a 3-D cone
    //PSYS_SRC_PATTERN_ANGLE_CONE_EMPTY   Particles are emitted
everywhere except for a 3-D cone

    PSYS_SRC_PATTERN,                PSYS_SRC_PATTERN_EXPLODE

    ,PSYS_SRC_TEXTURE,               ""
//UUID of the desired particle texture, or inventory name
    ,PSYS_SRC_MAX_AGE,               0.0
```

```
//Time, in seconds, for particles to be emitted. 0 = forever
    ,PSYS_PART_MAX_AGE,          10.0
//Lifetime, in seconds, that a particle lasts
    ,PSYS_SRC_BURST_RATE,        1.0
//How long, in seconds, between each emission
    ,PSYS_SRC_BURST_PART_COUNT,  1
//Number of particles per emission
    ,PSYS_SRC_BURST_RADIUS,      10.0
//Radius of emission
    ,PSYS_SRC_BURST_SPEED_MIN,   0.001
//Minimum speed of an emitted particle
    ,PSYS_SRC_BURST_SPEED_MAX,   0.001
//Maximum speed of an emitted particle
    ,PSYS_SRC_ACCEL,             <0,0,0>
//Acceleration of particles each second
    ,PSYS_PART_START_COLOR,      <1,1,1>
//Starting RGB color
    ,PSYS_PART_END_COLOR,        <1,1,1>
//Ending RGB color, if INTERP_COLOR_MASK is on
    ,PSYS_PART_START_ALPHA,      1.0
//Starting transparency, 1 is opaque, 0 is transparent.
    ,PSYS_PART_END_ALPHA,        1.0
//Ending transparency
    ,PSYS_PART_START_SCALE,      <.25,.25,.25>
//Starting particle size
    ,PSYS_PART_END_SCALE,        <.25,.25,.25>
//Ending particle size, if INTERP_SCALE_MASK is on
    ,PSYS_SRC_ANGLE_BEGIN,       1.54
//Inner angle for ANGLE patterns
    ,PSYS_SRC_ANGLE_END,         1.55
//Outer angle for ANGLE patterns
    ,PSYS_SRC_OMEGA,             <0.0,0.0,0.0>
//Rotation of ANGLE patterns, similar to llTargetOmega()
            ]);
}


generalParticleEmitterOff()
{
    llParticleSystem([]);
}


updateText()
{
    string str = llKey2Name(llGetOwner()) + "'s Tip Jar\n";
    if( total>0 )
        str+= (string)total + " donated so far.";
```

```
        else
            str+= "Empty";

        llSetText(str, <0,1,0>, 1);
    }

default
{
    on_rez(integer s)
    {
        llResetScript();
    }

    state_entry()
    {
        updateText();
        generalParticleEmitterOn();
        llListen(CHANNEL, "", llGetOwner(), "");
    }

    money(key giver, integer amount) {
        llSay(0, "Thanks for the " + (string)amount + "L$, "
      + llKey2Name(giver));
        total+=amount;
        updateText();
    }

    touch_start(integer count)
    {
        if(llDetectedKey(0)==llGetOwner())
        {
            llDialog(llDetectedKey(0), "Clear total amount?",
              ["Yes","No"], CHANNEL);
        }
    }

    listen(integer channel, string name, key id, string message)
    {
        if( message=="Yes" && id==llGetOwner() )
        {
            total = 0;
            updateText();
        }
    }
}
```

The tip jar begins by defining what channel it will listen on. A variable named **total** is created that holds the total amount of money contributed.

```
integer CHANNEL = 55;
integer total;
```

The **updateText** function is used to update the displayed text above the tip jar. The name of the avatar who owns the tip jar, as well as how much money has been collected is displayed.

```
updateText()
{
    string str = llKey2Name(llGetOwner()) + "'s Tip Jar\n";
    if( total>0 )
        str+= (string)total + " donated so far.";
    else
        str+= "Empty";
```

Once the string has been constructed, it can be displayed.

```
    llSetText(str, <0,1,0>, 1);
}
```

The script begins by updating the text and turning on a particle emitter. Particle emitters were covered in Chapter 4. The particle effect is used to make the tip jar glow.

```
state_entry()
{
    updateText();
    generalParticleEmitterOn();
    llListen(CHANNEL, "", llGetOwner(), "");
}
```

The only way that a script can collect money from avatars it encounters is by using the **money** event handler. Once a money event handler is present, the "Pay" menu option becomes available when the object is right-clicked. The **money** event handler presented here will thank the avatar and update the total amount.

```
money(key giver, integer amount)
{
    llSay(0, "Thanks for the " + (string)amount + "L$, "
        + llKey2Name(giver));
    total+=amount;
    updateText();
}
```

When the tip jar is touched by the owner, the owner is given the option to clear the tip jar.

```
touch_start(integer count)
{
    if(llDetectedKey(0)==llGetOwner())
    {
        llDialog(llDetectedKey(0),
        "Clear total amount?", ["Yes","No"], CHANNEL);
    }
}
```

If the owner chooses to clear the tip jar, the listen event handler is called.

```
listen(integer channel, string name, key id, string message)
{
    if( message=="Yes" && id==llGetOwner() )
    {
        total = 0;
        updateText();
    }
}
```

This tip jar only collect tips for the avatar that actually owns it. The next recipe shows how to use a club style tip jar where the profits are split between whoever has claimed the tip jar and the tip jar owner.

Recipe 8.3: Club Tip Jar

Clubs are very common in Second Life. Second Life clubs often employ entertainers. These entertainers are paid entirely with tips. The club owner sometimes takes a portion of those tips.

This recipe shows how to create a club style tip jar. The jar will initially start as un-claimed. However, the next avatar to touch the tip jar will claim the tip jar. They will receive all tips from the jar until they either touch it again, or their claim times out. The club tip jar is configured with a notecard. This notecard can be seen in Listing 8.5.

Listing 8.5: Club Tip Jar (ClubTipJar.not)

```
10,20,30,40
75
60
group
```

The first line specifies the four recommended tip amounts that show up when the user clicks pay. The pay dialog allows predefined numbers to be specified. Figure 8.4 shows such a dialog.

Figure 8.4: A Pay Dialog

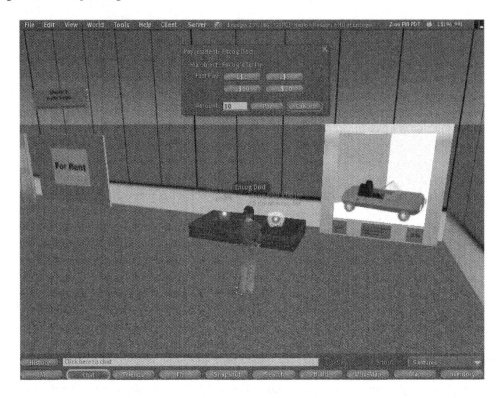

The third line, of Listing 8.5, specifies what percentage the avatar should get. The third line specifies the number of minutes until the tip jar reverts to no-one claiming it. The script needed to produce the tip jar is shown in Listing 8.6.

Listing 8.6: Club Tip Jar (TipJarClub.lsl)

```
integer CHANNEL = 56;
integer total;
key claimed_key = NULL_KEY;
string claimed_name;
integer index;
key query;
float percent;
integer check_group = FALSE;
integer timeout = 0;

generalParticleEmitterOn()
{
    llParticleSystem([
        PSYS_PART_FLAGS , 0
    //| PSYS_PART_BOUNCE_MASK
```

```
//Bounce on object's z-axis
    //| PSYS_PART_WIND_MASK
//Particles are moved by wind
    | PSYS_PART_INTERP_COLOR_MASK
//Colors fade from start to end
    | PSYS_PART_INTERP_SCALE_MASK
//Scale fades from beginning to end
    | PSYS_PART_FOLLOW_SRC_MASK      //Particles follow the emitter
    //| PSYS_PART_FOLLOW_VELOCITY_MASK
//Particles are created at the velocity of the emitter
    //| PSYS_PART_TARGET_POS_MASK    //Particles follow the target
    | PSYS_PART_EMISSIVE_MASK        //Particles will glow
    //| PSYS_PART_TARGET_LINEAR_MASK
//Undocumented--Sends particles in straight line?
    ,

    //PSYS_SRC_TARGET_KEY , NULL_KEY,
//The particles will head towards the specified key
    //Select one of the following for a pattern:
    //PSYS_SRC_PATTERN_DROP                 Particles start at
emitter with no velocity
    //PSYS_SRC_PATTERN_EXPLODE              Particles explode from
the emitter
    //PSYS_SRC_PATTERN_ANGLE                Particles are emitted
in a 2-D angle
    //PSYS_SRC_PATTERN_ANGLE_CONE           Particles are emitted
in a 3-D cone
    //PSYS_SRC_PATTERN_ANGLE_CONE_EMPTY     Particles are emitted
everywhere except for a 3-D cone

    PSYS_SRC_PATTERN,               PSYS_SRC_PATTERN_EXPLODE

    ,PSYS_SRC_TEXTURE,               ""
//UUID of the desired particle texture, or inventory name
    ,PSYS_SRC_MAX_AGE,              0.0
//Time, in seconds, for particles to be emitted. 0 = forever
    ,PSYS_PART_MAX_AGE,             10.0
//Lifetime, in seconds, that a particle lasts
    ,PSYS_SRC_BURST_RATE,           1.0
//How long, in seconds, between each emission
    ,PSYS_SRC_BURST_PART_COUNT,     1
//Number of particles per emission
    ,PSYS_SRC_BURST_RADIUS,         10.0
//Radius of emission
    ,PSYS_SRC_BURST_SPEED_MIN,      0.001
//Minimum speed of an emitted particle
```

```
        ,PSYS_SRC_BURST_SPEED_MAX,    0.001
//Maximum speed of an emitted particle
        ,PSYS_SRC_ACCEL,              <0,0,0>
//Acceleration of particles each second
        ,PSYS_PART_START_COLOR,       <1,1,1>  //Starting RGB color
        ,PSYS_PART_END_COLOR,         <1,1,1>
//Ending RGB color, if INTERP_COLOR_MASK is on
        ,PSYS_PART_START_ALPHA,       1.0
//Starting transparency, 1 is opaque, 0 is transparent.
        ,PSYS_PART_END_ALPHA,         1.0
//Ending transparency
        ,PSYS_PART_START_SCALE,       <.25,.25,.25>
//Starting particle size
        ,PSYS_PART_END_SCALE,         <.25,.25,.25>
//Ending particle size, if INTERP_SCALE_MASK is on
        ,PSYS_SRC_ANGLE_BEGIN,        1.54
//Inner angle for ANGLE patterns
        ,PSYS_SRC_ANGLE_END,          1.55
//Outer angle for ANGLE patterns
        ,PSYS_SRC_OMEGA,              <0.0,0.0,0.0>
//Rotation of ANGLE patterns, similar to llTargetOmega()
            ]);
}

generalParticleEmitterOff()
{
    llParticleSystem([]);
}

updateText()
{
    string str;

     if( claimed_key==NULL_KEY )
        str = "Touch to Claim Tip Jar\n";
    else
        str = claimed_name + "'s Tip Jar\n";

    if( total>0 )
        str+= (string)total + " donated so far.";
    else
        str+= "Empty";

    llSetText(str, <0,1,0>, 1);
}
```

```
default
{
    state_entry()
    {
        llRequestPermissions(llGetOwner(), PERMISSION_DEBIT );
    }

    on_rez(integer s)
    {
        llResetScript();
    }

    run_time_permissions (integer perm)
    {
        if(perm & PERMISSION_DEBIT)
        {
            state unclaimed;
        }
    }
}


state unclaimed
{
    state_entry()
    {
        if( claimed_key!=NULL_KEY )
        {
            llSay(0,"Tip jar switching back to unclaimed.");
        }
        index = 0;
        query = llGetNotecardLine("Config",index++);
        claimed_key = NULL_KEY;
        claimed_name = "";
        total = 0;
        updateText();
    }

    touch_start(integer count)
    {
        integer success = FALSE;

        if( check_group )
        {
```

```
        if( llDetectedGroup(0) )
        {
            success = TRUE;
        }
        else
        {
            llSay(0,"Sorry, you are not in the correct group
to claim this jar.");
        }
    }
    else success = TRUE;


    if( success )
    {
        claimed_key = llDetectedKey(0);
        claimed_name = llDetectedName(0);
        llInstantMessage(claimed_key,"You have claimed the tip
Jar, touch again to uncliam.");
        llInstantMessage(claimed_key,"You will get "
        + (string)(percent*100) + "% of the tips.");
        state claimed;
    }
}

money(key giver, integer amount) {
    llSay(0, "Thanks for the " + (string)amount + "L$, " +
llKey2Name(giver));
    total+=amount;
    updateText();
}

dataserver(key query_id, string data)
{
    if (query == query_id)
    {
        // this is a line of our notecard
        if (data != EOF)
        {
            // process first line, tip price list
            if( index==1 )
            {
                list l = llCSV2List(data);
                list l2 = [];

                integer length = llGetListLength(l);
```

```
            integer i;
            for(i=0;i<length;i++)
            {
                l2+=[llList2Integer(l,i)];
            }


            llSetPayPrice(llList2Integer(l2,0),l2);
        }
        // Line 2: Percent to pay to tip claimer
        else if( index==2 )
        {
            percent = (integer)data;
            percent/= 100;
        }
        else if( index==3 )
        {
            timeout = (integer)data;
        }
        else if( index==4 )
        {
            if( llToLower(data)=="group" )
            {
                check_group = TRUE;
            }
        }
        query = llGetNotecardLine("Config",index++);


            }
        }
    }
}


state claimed
{
    state_entry()
    {
        if( percent>1 )
        {
            llInstantMessage(claimed_key, "Payback it set to more
than 100%, can't claim tip jar.");
            state unclaimed;
        }

        updateText();
```

```
            generalParticleEmitterOn();
            llListen(CHANNEL, "", llGetOwner(), "");
            if( timeout>0 )
                llSetTimerEvent(60*timeout);
        }

    money(key giver, integer amount) {
        llSay(0, "Thanks for the " + (string)amount + "L$, "
            + llKey2Name(giver));
        total+=amount;
        llGiveMoney(claimed_key,(integer)(amount*percent));
        updateText();
    }

    touch_start(integer count)
    {
        if( (llDetectedKey(0)==claimed_key)
            || (llDetectedKey(0)==llGetOwner()) )
        {
            state unclaimed;
        }
    }

    timer()
    {
        state unclaimed;
    }

    touch_start(integer count)
    {
        if( llDetectedKey(0)==claimed_key ||
            llDetectedKey(0)==llGetOwner() )
        state unclaimed;
    }
}
```

The club script jar begins by defining the channel it will use to communicate. The **total** variable holds the total amount donated. The **claimed_key** variable holds the key of the avatar that claimed the tip jar. The **claimed_name** holds the string name of the avatar who claimed the tip jar.

```
integer CHANNEL = 56;
integer total;
key claimed_key = NULL_KEY;
string claimed_name;
```

The variable **index** holds the current line of the configuration notecard being read. The variable **query** holds the current notecard query. The variable **percent** holds the percent of the tip that should be given to the performer. The variable **check_group** is true of the avatar who wishes to claim must be in the same group as the object. The variable **timeout** tracks whether the avatar's claim has timed out.

```
integer index;
key query;
float percent;
integer check_group = FALSE;
integer timeout = 0;
```

The **updateText** function updates the displayed text for the tip jar.

```
updateText()
{
    string str;
```

If no-one has claimed the tip jar, indicate this, otherwise display who has claimed the tip jar. This will be the last avatar to touch the tip jar while it was unclaimed.

```
    if( claimed_key==NULL_KEY )
        str = "Touch to Claim Tip Jar\n";
    else
        str = claimed_name + "'s Tip Jar\n";
```

If money has been donated, that amount is displayed. Otherwise the tip jar reports that it is empty.

```
    if( total>0 )
        str+= (string)total + " donated so far.";
    else
        str+= "Empty";
```

Finally, the string is displayed.

```
    llSetText(str, <0,1,0>, 1);
}
```

The tip jar begins in the **default** state.

Default State for the Club Tip Jar

The **default** state exists only to request permission to take money from the tip jar owner then return to the **unclaimed** state. It is necessary to be able to take money from the tip jar owner so that the avatar who has claimed the tip jar can be paid. For example, consider a tip jar that is owned by Avatar A, the club owner, and which pays 90% of tips to whoever has claimed the tip jar. Avatar B claims the tip jar and is paid L$10. The L$10 is immediately deposited into Avatar A's account. However, the script will now pay $L9 to Avatar B.

```
state_entry()
```

```
{
        llRequestPermissions(llGetOwner(), PERMISSION_DEBIT );
}
```

The **run_time_permissions** event handler processes the result of the permission request.

```
run_time_permissions (integer perm)
{
        if(perm & PERMISSION_DEBIT)
        {
                state unclaimed;
        }
}
```

Once the permission has been obtained, continue to the **unclaimed** state.

Unclaimed State for the Club Tip Jar

When the tip jar enters the **unclaimed** state, it is from either one of two paths. The first scenario is that the tip jar has just started, and the **unclaimed** state is being entered through the **default** state. The second scenario is that the tip jar is being entered through the **claimed** state, as it has just become **unclaimed**.

If the tip jar is being entered through the **claimed** state, then avatars that the tip jar is returning to **unclaimed** state.

```
state_entry()
{
        if( claimed_key!=NULL_KEY )
        {
                llSay(0,"Tip jar switching back to unclaimed.");
        }
```

The tip jar should now begin reading from its configuration notecard.

```
        index = 0;
        query = llGetNotecardLine("Config",index++);
```

All internal variables should be set to their unclaimed states. The text should be updated to reflect this.

```
        claimed_key = NULL_KEY;
        claimed_name = "";
        total = 0;
        updateText();
}
```

When an avatar touches the tip jar, that avatar may claim the tip jar. If the configuration notecard has specified that group access must be checked, the avatar must be in the same group as the group that owns the tip jar. This may be useful to ensure that only club employees can claim the tip jars.

```
touch_start(integer count)
{
     integer success = FALSE;

     if( check_group )
     {
          if( llDetectedGroup(0) )
          {
               success = TRUE;
          }
          else
          {
               llSay(0,
"Sorry, you are not in the correct group to claim this jar.");
          }
     }
     else success = TRUE;
```

If the avatar has successfully claimed the tip jar, update the internal variables to reflect that avatar's claim. It is important to note that the actual ownership of the tip jar does not change. The tip just keeps note of who has claimed it.

```
     if( success )
     {
          claimed_key = llDetectedKey(0);
          claimed_name = llDetectedName(0);
```

Send an instant message to whoever has claimed the tip jar. Update the display text to reflect the new claimant.

```
          llInstantMessage(claimed_key,
"You have claimed the tip Jar, touch again to uncliam.");
          llInstantMessage(claimed_key,
"You will get " + (string)(percent*100) + "% of the tips.");
          state claimed;
     }
}
```

The money event handler is called whenever a donation is made. However, the tip jar is in the **unclaimed** state. In this case, the money is given to the tip jar owner. Nothing is shared with anyone else.

```
money(key giver, integer amount)
```

```
{
        llSay(0, "Thanks for the " + (string)amount + "L$, "
            + llKey2Name(giver));
        total+=amount;
        updateText();
}
```

As each line of the configuration notecard is read in, the data server event handler is called.

```
dataserver(key query_id, string data)
{
        if (query == query_id)
        {
```

Stop reading if the end of file has been reached.

```
                // this is a line of our notecard
                if (data != EOF)
                {
```

Read the first line of the index, this specifies the suggested tip amounts.

```
                        // process first line, tip price list
                        if( index==1 )
                        {
```

The suggested tip amounts are contained in a comma separated value (CSV) list. Use the **llCSV2List** function to parse the CSV list to a regular Linden Scripting Language list. These values are then added to a second list, named **l2**, as integers. This is because the **llSetPayPrice** function requires the suggested payments to be as integers.

```
                            list l = llCSV2List(data);
                            list l2 = [];

                            integer length = llGetListLength(l);
                            integer i;
                            for(i=0;i<length;i++)
                            {
                                l2+=[llList2Integer(l,i)];
                            }
```

Suggested payment prices are specified using the **llSetPayPrice** function. The **llSetPayPrice** accepts two parameters. The first specifies the default pay price. For this recipe, the first pay price is set to be the default pay price. The second parameter is the list of pay prices to be given to the avatar. This is the list of four numbers presented earlier in this section.

```
                            llSetPayPrice(llList2Integer(l2,0),l2);
                    }
```

Line two holds the percent to pay to the one who has claimed the tip jar.

```
else if( index==2 )
{
    percent = (integer)data;
    percent/= 100;
}
```

Line three holds the timeout. Avatars cannot claim the tip jar indefinitely.

```
else if( index==3 )
{
    timeout = (integer)data;
}
```

Line four specifies whether only group members can claim the tip jar.

```
else if( index==4 )
{
    if( llToLower(data)=="group" )
    {
        check_group = TRUE;
    }
}
```

Read the next line from the configuration notecard.

```
            query = llGetNotecardLine("Config",index++);


        }
    }
}
```

The tip jar will remain in the unclaimed state until it is touched. Once touched, the tip jar enters the claimed state.

Claimed State for Club Tip Jar

Once the tip jar has been claimed, all tips must be shared between the tip jar owner and the avatar who claimed the tip jar.

```
state_entry()
{
    if( percent>1 )
    {
        llInstantMessage(claimed_key,
"Payback set to more than 100%, can't claim tip jar.");
        state unclaimed;
    }
```

The text should be updated to reflect that the tip jar is now claimed. Additionally, set a timer for the timeout value.

```
updateText();
llListen(CHANNEL, "", llGetOwner(), "");
if( timeout>0 )
        llSetTimerEvent(60*timeout);
}
```

The **money** event handler is called whenever money is sent to the tip jar.

```
money(key giver, integer amount)
{
        llSay(0, "Thanks for the " + (string)amount + "L$, "
                + llKey2Name(giver));
```

The avatar is thanked, and the total is updated. The **llGiveMoney** function call is then used to give the avatar that claimed the tip jar their portion of the tip.

```
total+=amount;
llGiveMoney(claimed_key, (integer)(amount*percent));
updateText();
}
```

If the claimed tip jar is touched either by its owner or the avatar who claimed the tip jar, return to an **unclaimed** state.

```
touch_start(integer count)
{
        if( (llDetectedKey(0)==claimed_key) ||
            (llDetectedKey(0)==llGetOwner()) )
        {
                state unclaimed;
        }
}
```

The **timer** event handler will be called when the tip jar times out.

```
timer()
{
        state unclaimed;
}
```

The club tip jar is a very useful recipe that can be used for a variety of purposes in Second Life. It allows workers at a club to earn money and optionally contribute money to the club owner as well.

Recipe 8.4: Vendor Script

A major component of Second Life commerce is the sale of objects. For example, many of the objects created in this book could be sold for Linden Dollars. The easiest way to have a store in Second Life is to construct a small region and place the objects for sale there. Then, select each object and mark it for sale. If the "Sell Copy" option is selected, the original item stays for some other avatar to buy. This is a popular means of selling items in Second Life. Figure 8.5 shows a typical Second Life store.

Figure 8.5: A Second Life Store

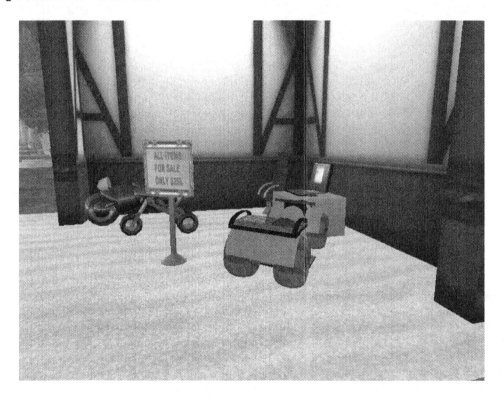

However, if there are a large number of items for sale, it will take a large amount of space to sell all of them. Additionally, many people sell items in malls in Second Life. If selling in a mall, only a limited number of prims will be available for the store. To save on prim usage and take up less space, vendor scripts are often used.

Think of a vendor script as a kiosk. The vendor script shows pictures of each of the items for sale. The avatar usually selects forward and backward buttons to move through the items that are for sale. Figure 8.6 shows a vendor.

Figure 8.6: Using a Vendor Script

The vendor script is controlled by a configuration notecard. This notecard can be seen in Listing 8.7.

Listing 8.7: Vendor Notecard (Vendor.not)

```
buyredcar
Encog's Red Car
25
buyyellowcar
Super Car
30
buyboat
Encog's Boat
35
```

The lines in the configuration file occur in groups of three. The first group of three is:

```
buyredcar
Encog's Red Car
25
```

The first line specifies the name of the texture that should be displayed when this item is the current item. The second line specifies the name of the item. The object being sold must be in the vendor's object inventory. The second line specifies this name. The third line specifies the cost, in Linden Dollars, for that item.

A total of three scripts are used to run the vendor. They consist of the main script and two scripts to control each of the arrows.

Main Vendor Script

The main vendor script does most of the work. There is also a navigational script inside the forward and reverse buttons. However, the navigation scripts simply communicate to the main script that it should navigate. The main vendor script is shown in Listing 8.8.

Listing 8.8: Main Vendor Script (Vendor.not)

```
integer index;

// for loading notecard
string notecardName;
key notecardQuery;
integer notecardIndex;
list notecardList;
integer price;
string itemName;

displayItem()
{
    string textureName = llList2String(notecardList,index*3);
    itemName = llList2String(notecardList,(index*3)+1);
    string p = llList2String(notecardList,(index*3)+2);
    price = (integer)p;
    string display = itemName + "\nL$" + p;
    llMessageLinked(LINK_ALL_OTHERS , 0, ":"+display, NULL_KEY);
    llSetLinkPrimitiveParams(5,[PRIM_TEXTURE, 1, textureName,
            <1,1,1>, <0,0,0>, 0 ]);
    llSetPayPrice(PAY_HIDE, [price, PAY_HIDE, PAY_HIDE,
            PAY_HIDE]);
}

default
{
    state_entry()
    {
        if( llGetListLength(notecardList)==0 )
        {
            notecardName = "Config";
```

```
            state loading;
        }
        else
        {
            index = 0;
            displayItem();
        }
    }

    link_message(integer sender_num, integer num, string str,
      key id)
    {
        if( str=="back" )
        {
            index--;
        }

        if( str=="forward" )
        {
            index++;
        }


        if(index>=(llGetListLength(notecardList)/3) )
            index = 0;

        if(index<0 )
        {
            index = (llGetListLength(notecardList)/3);
            index--;
        }

        displayItem();
    }

    money(key id, integer amount)
    {
        if( amount>=price )
        {
            llGiveInventory(id,itemName);
            llSay(0,"Thanks for your purchase!");
        }
    }


}
```

```
state loading
{
    state_entry()
    {
        llSay(0,"Loading product data...");
        notecardIndex = 0;
        notecardQuery = llGetNotecardLine(notecardName,
            notecardIndex++);
    }

    dataserver(key query_id, string data)
    {
        if ( notecardQuery == query_id)
        {
            // this is a line of our notecard
            if (data == EOF)
            {
                llSay(0,"Products loaded...");
                state default;

            } else
            {
                notecardList += [data];
                notecardQuery =
            llGetNotecardLine(notecardName,notecardIndex++);
            }
        }
    }
}
```

The main vendor script begins by declaring some variables that it needs to perform.

```
integer index;
string notecardName;
key notecardQuery;
integer notecardIndex;
list notecardList;
integer price;
string itemName;
```

The **index** variable holds the index of the currently viewed item. The **noteCardName** variable holds the name of the notecard being read. The **notecardQuery** variable holds the query used to read the configuration notecard. The **notecardList** variable holds the list of items read from the notecard. The **price** variable holds the price of the current item. The **itemName** variable holds the current item's price.

The **displayItem** function updates the vendor object to display the newly selected item. The **displayItem** function begins by obtaining the texture, which is the image of the item, from the list. Three data items are kept for each item. The first three lines of the **displayItem** function read these items.

```
displayItem()
{
    string textureName = llList2String(notecardList,index*3);
    itemName = llList2String(notecardList,(index*3)+1);
    string p = llList2String(notecardList,(index*3)+2);
```

The **price** variable is converted to an integer and stored. Next, the **price** variable is displayed. A message is sent to all linked objects so that the buy button can display this text.

```
    price = (integer)p;
    string display = itemName + "\nL$" + p;
    llMessageLinked(LINK_ALL_OTHERS , 0, ":"+display, NULL_KEY);
```

The texture is displayed, and the pay price is set.

```
    llSetLinkPrimitiveParams(5,[PRIM_TEXTURE, 1, textureName,
        <1,1,1>, <0,0,0>, 0 ]);
    llSetPayPrice(PAY_HIDE, [price, PAY_HIDE, PAY_HIDE, PAY_
HIDE]);
}
```

When the **default** state begins, the script checks to see whether any items are loaded. If there are no items loaded, the script enters the **loading** state.

```
default
{
    state_entry()
    {
        if( llGetListLength(notecardList)==0 )
        {
            notecardName = "Config";
            state loading;
        }
```

If there are items loaded, the first item is displayed.

```
        else
        {
            index = 0;
            displayItem();
        }
    }
```

The navigation buttons will send messages. The **link_message** event handler processes these messages.

```
link_message(integer sender_num, integer num, string str,
  key id)
{
```

The back button moves to the previous item.

```
    if( str=="back" )
    {
        index--;
    }
```

The forward button moves to the next item.

```
    if( str=="forward" )
    {
        index++;
    }
```

If the last item has been passed, wrap around to the first item.

```
    if(index>=(llGetListLength(notecardList)/3) )
        index = 0;
```

If the first item has been passed, wrap around to the last item.

```
    if(index<0 )
    {
        index = (llGetListLength(notecardList)/3);
        index--;
    }
```

Finally, display the item.

```
    displayItem();
}
```

When the user buys the item, the **money** event handler will be called.

```
money(key id, integer amount)
{
    if( amount>=price )
    {
        llGiveInventory(id,itemName);
        llSay(0,"Thanks for your purchase!");
    }
}
}
```

If the user paid enough, give them their item.

The loading state begins by submitting a query to read the notecard.

```
state loading
{
    state_entry()
    {
        llSay(0,"Loading product data...");
        notecardIndex = 0;
        notecardQuery = llGetNotecardLine(notecardName,
            notecardIndex++);
    }
```

As the lines are read from the note card, the **dataserver** event handler is called.

```
    dataserver(key query_id, string data)
    {
        if ( notecardQuery == query_id)
        {
```

Stop reading once the end is reached. Return to the **default** state.

```
            if (data == EOF)
            {
                llSay(0,"Products loaded...");
                state default;
```

Add all of the data read in to the **notecardList** variable.

```
            } else
            {
                notecardList += [data];
                notecardQuery = llGetNotecardLine(notecardName,
                    notecardIndex++);
            }
        }
    }
}
```

There are three other scripts in the vendor object. The others handle navigation and display of the textual information about the item.

Vendor Navigation Scripts

The vendor object has two buttons that allow navigation. Clicking the forward and backward buttons will switch the current object for sale. The forward button's script can be seen in Listing 8.9.

Listing 8.9: The Forward Button (VendorForward.lsl)

```
default
{
    touch_start(integer total_number)
    {
        llMessageLinked(LINK_ALL_OTHERS , 0, "forward", NULL_KEY);
    }
}
```

The forward button sends a forward message that will be picked up by the main vendor script. The vendor object can also go backward. The backward button script is shown in Listing 8.10.

Listing 8.10: The Backward Button (VendorBack.lsl)

```
default
{
    touch_start(integer total_number)
    {
        llMessageLinked(LINK_ALL_OTHERS , 0, "back", NULL_KEY);
    }
}
```

The backward button simply sends a backward message that will be picked up by the main vendor script. The buy button only has instructions on buying. To buy an item, pay the object and the item will be purchased. However, the buy button is useful because it is right under the texture. Adding text to the buy button will display just under the picture of the item. The buy button is shown in Listing 8.11.

Listing 8.11: The Buy Button (VendorBuy.lsl)

```
default
{

    link_message(integer sender_num, integer num, string str,
            key id)
    {
        string prefix = llGetSubString(str,0,0);
        if( prefix==":" )
        {
            string rest = llGetSubString(str,1,-1);
            llSetText(rest,<0,0,0>,1);


        }
    }
}
```

The buy button simply waits for messages, and then displays them.

Summary

Commerce is a very important aspect of Second Life. Some earn a living completely through Second Life. This chapter showed how to create scripts that can pay avatars. An example of such a script is a camping pad. Camping pays avatars to stay on a specific plot of land.

This chapter also showed how to collect money from avatars. The first recipe that collected money was the tip jar. Tip jars allow avatars to contribute money to the specified avatar. This chapter introduced two types of tip jars. The first tip jar simply gives all tips to its owner. The second type of tip jar splits the tips with its owner and the avatar who has claimed the tip jar. This allows employees of clubs to receive tips from customers and give a cut to the club owner.

Another important commerce topic is rental property. Rental property is very common in Second Life and will be covered in the next chapter.

CHAPTER 9: RENTAL PROPERTY

- Renting Property in Second Life
- Creating a Rental Script
- Controlling the Rental Door
- Installing a Second Rental Door

Rental property is very popular in Second Life. Rental property may be a plot of land, or in a large building or a box high in the sky. Figure 9.1 shows an apartment building.

Figure 9.1: An Apartment Building

In Second Life some own many islands composed entirely of rental property. These are often themed communities. Both residential and commercial property can be rented. Commercial property rental is very popular. To make money selling goods in Second Life, multiple stores are often needed. The process of selling in Second Life generally involves renting stores and continually removing under-performing stores and renting new stores.

Second Life is a world where it never rains, never gets cold, and avatars simply disappear when their human user is not logged in. It is logical to wonder why someone would need a "home" in Second Life. Yet residential rentals are very common. There are many reasons for this. One of the most basic is personal expression. The home can be decorated to suit the taste of the owner. This can include elements that would not be feasible in real life.

There are a variety of rental scripts used in Second Life. Some are nothing more than a cube that counts down when the rental period is up. Others control access to the area. This chapter presents a rental script.

Recipe 9.1: Rental Script

The apartment building shown in Figure 9.1 has many units. Each unit has two doors. The primary door is a sliding glass door that opens onto the balcony. The secondary door opens to an interior hallway.

Primary Door

The primary door is the door that the apartment renter interacts with to pay the rent. The primary door is a sliding glass door that will be placed on the balcony. Figure 9.2 shows the primary door.

Figure 9.2: The Primary Door

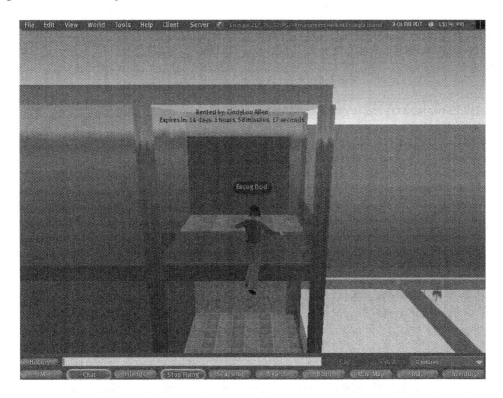

The primary rental script contains many elements from previous scripts in this book. Therefore, its complete listing is not reproduced here. The new components added by the primary rental door will be covered in the following sections.

The primary rental door begins by declaring a number of constants.

```
// constants
float       TIMER_CLOSE = 5.0;
integer     DOOR_OPEN   = 1;
integer     DOOR_CLOSE  = 2;
integer     DAYSEC = 86400;
```

The **TIME_CLOSE** constant defines the number of seconds to wait before closing the door. The **DOOR_OPEN** and **DOOR_CLOSE** constants represent the state of the door. The **DAYSEC** content holds the number of seconds in a day.

There are several configuration constants defined as well. These can be changed to set the rental agreement. These variables are all prefixed with **config_**.

```
// configuration
integer config_rentwarning = 3;
```

```
integer config_graceperiod = 3;
integer config_rate = 43;
integer config_min_days = 7;
```

The **config_rentwarning** specifies the number of days before the rent is due that a warning will be sent. The **config_graceperiod** variable specifies the number of days that rent can be unpaid before the avatar is evicted. The **config_rate** variable specifies the rental rate per day. The **config_min_days** specifies the minimum number of days for which the unit can be rented.

```
// data about renter
string data_rented;
key data_rented_key;
integer data_leased_until;
```

Additionally, other variables are defined for the script to function. The **originalPos** variable tracks the original position of the door. The **text** variable is used to parse text commands sent to the door. The **allow** list specifies which avatars, in addition to the renter, can enter. Additionally, two flags are used to track which notices have been sent. This prevents the notices from being re-sent.

```
// other variables
vector originalPos;
string text;
list allow;
```

The **warningSent** flag tracks if a warning has been sent about the rental due date approaching. The **reminderSent** flag tracks if a rent reminder has been sent.

```
integer warningSent = FALSE;
integer reminderSent = FALSE;
```

The **door** function is called when the state of the door changes.

```
door(integer what)
{
```

First, the current size of the door is obtained.

```
 vector scale = llGetScale();
```

Any **timer** events are cleared.

```
 llSetTimerEvent(0);

 if ( what == DOOR_OPEN )
 {
```

If the door is to be opened, play the door open sound. Then move the door over and resize it to make it very small. This makes it appear to slide into the wall.

```
  llTriggerSound("doorOpen", 1);
```

```
    scale.x = 1;
    vector pos = llGetPos();
    pos.x+=2.5;
    llSetPos(pos);
} else if ( what == DOOR_CLOSE)
{
```

When the door is closed, return to the original size and play the door closing sound.

```
    llTriggerSound("doorClose", 1);
    scale.x = 5;
}

    llSetScale(scale);
}
```

The **validateUser** function is used from two places inside the door script. First, if an avatar touches the door then the user must be validated. Second, when the secondary door requests a validation of a user, this function is also used.

```
integer validateUser(string who)
{
    integer shouldOpen = FALSE;
```

The door should always open for the owner. The owner is usually the landlord.

```
    if( who==llKey2Name(llGetOwner()) )
        shouldOpen = TRUE;
```

The door should always open for the renter.

```
    if( data_rented==who )
        shouldOpen = TRUE;
```

The door should open for anyone in the **allow** list.

```
    string name = llToUpper(who);
    if( llListFindList(allow,[name]) != -1 )
        shouldOpen = TRUE;
```

Return the **shouldOpen** status.

```
    return shouldOpen;
}
```

The text above the rental door displays information regarding the current rental agreement. Any time something happens that might change this text, call the **updateText** function. The **updateText** function updates this text to the correct value.

```
updateText()
{
    string display = "";
```

If the unit is rented by someone, display data about the agreement. Calculate the number of days remaining.

```
if( llStringLength(data_rented)>0 )
{
    display = "Rented by: " + data_rented;
    display+= "\nExpires in: " + timespan(data_leased_until -
llGetUnixTime());
    llSetTexture("rental-rented",3);
}
else
{
```

If the unit is not rented, display the terms.

```
    display = "Not rented\n";
    display+="Rent for " + (string)(config_rate*
        config_min_days) + "L/";
```

The code below causes the script to call a week a week, not 7 days.

```
    if( config_min_days!=7 )
    {
        display+=(string)config_min_days+" day(s).";
    }
    else
    {
        display+="week.";
    }
```

Display the correct texture and update the string.

```
    llSetTexture("rental-forrent",3);
    display+="\nTo rent, right-click and choose pay.";
}
```

Finally, display the text.

```
llSetText(display,<0,0,0>,1.0);
}
```

The **timespan** function formats time as days, hours, minutes and seconds.

```
string timespan(integer time)
{
```

First, break the timespan into days, hours, minutes and seconds.

```
integer days = time / DAYSEC;
integer curtime = (time / DAYSEC) - (time % DAYSEC);
integer hours = curtime / 3600;
integer minutes = (curtime % 3600) / 60;
```

```
integer seconds = curtime % 60;
```

Display the amount of time remaining.

```
return (string)llAbs(days) + " days, " + (string)llAbs(hours)
        + " hours, "
        + (string)llAbs(minutes) + " minutes, "
        + (string)llAbs(seconds) + " seconds";
```

```
}
```

Like many of the other commerce scripts in this book, the only purpose of the **default** state is to request debt permission and move to the ready state.

```
default
{
    state_entry()
    {
```

Request permission to remove money from the avatar. This is necessary to refund over-payments.

```
        llRequestPermissions(llGetOwner(), PERMISSION_DEBIT );
    }
```

```
    run_time_permissions (integer perm)
    {
```

If the permission request was successful, enter the ready state.

```
        if(perm & PERMISSION_DEBIT)
        {
            state ready;
        }
    }
}
```

Once permission is obtained the ready state begins.

```
state ready
{
    state_entry()
    {
```

First, set up the payment prices. Calculate the minimum amount that the avatar would pay to rent. Then set up four multiples of this amount.

```
        integer amount = config_rate * config_min_days;
        llSetPayPrice(PAY_HIDE, [amount, amount*2, amount*3,
            amount*4] );
```

Obtain the original position. This will be used to return the door to its original position after closing.

```
originalPos = llGetPos();
```

The door must listen on channel zero to get commands from the renter. The door must also listen on channel 72 for requests from the secondary door.

```
llListen(0, "", NULL_KEY, "");
llListen(72, "", NULL_KEY, "");
```

Finally, update the text, as described earlier. Also, set a timer for every minute.

```
updateText();
llSetTimerEvent(60);
}
```

The **money** event handler is called whenever an avatar pays an amount to the door. It is up to the money event handler to initially set up the lease, as well as extend it.

```
money(key giver, integer amount)
{
```

First, check to see whether the door has already been rented. If it has already been rented, this is likely an extension of rent. If the door has not been rented, a new lease should be established.

```
if( data_rented == "" )
{
```

If there is no renter, this section will establish a new lease. First, thank the avatar for renting. Then hand them a notecard explaining the terms of the lease. The notecard "Encogia Beach Apartments" should be replaced with whatever notecard makes sense for the rental unit the script is being used with.

```
llSay(0,
"Thanks for renting! You may now open the doors.");
llGiveInventory(giver,"Encogia Beach Apartments");
```

Remember the name and key of the avatar who is renting.

```
data_rented = llKey2Name(giver);
data_rented_key = giver;
```

Reset the allowed list to zero.

```
allow = [];
```

Next, check to see whether the amount paid by the avatar is an even multiple of the minimum lease amount. If it is not, issue a refund for the amount overpaid.

```
if ((amount % config_rate ) != 0)
{
```

```
llSay(0,"You overpaid. Here is a partial refund");
llGiveMoney(giver,(amount % config_rate));
}
```

Calculate the amount of time that the avatar paid for and credit that to their account. This is done by calculating the **data_leased_until** time.

```
integer credit = (amount - (amount % config_rate))
    /config_rate;
data_leased_until = llGetUnixTime() + (credit
    * (24*60*60));
```

Send an instant message to the owner of the apartment to let them know that a new lease has been established.

```
llInstantMessage(llGetOwner(), "NEW LEASE - $"
+  (string)(amount - (amount % config_rate))
+ "L - " + rentalInfo());
```

Reset the reminder and warning flags.

```
reminderSent = FALSE;
warningSent = FALSE;
}
else
{
```

Money has been paid to an apartment that was already rented. First determine whether it was the renter who paid.

```
string who = llKey2Name(giver);

if( who==data_rented )
{
```

If the renter has paid, extend the lease by the correct amount.

```
integer credit = (amount - (amount %
    config_rate))/config_rate;
data_leased_until = data_leased_until +
    (credit * (24*60*60));
llSay(0,"Your lease has been extended.");
```

Reset the warning and reminder flags.

```
reminderSent = FALSE;
warningSent = FALSE;
}
else
{
```

If money was paid by an avatar who is not the renter, refund the money and inform them that this apartment is already rented.

```
                llGiveMoney(giver,amount);
                llSay(0,
"This unit is already rented, please find another to rent.");
                }
            }
```

Finally, update the text to reflect any changes caused by this payment.

```
        updateText();
    }
```

Touching the door is a request to open the door.

```
    touch_start(integer total_number)
    {
```

First determine who has touched the door, and call **validateUser** to see whether the door should open.

```
        key who = llDetectedName(0);
        integer shouldOpen = validateUser(who);
```

If the door should open, say hello to the avatar and enter the **open_state** state.

```
        if( shouldOpen == TRUE )
        {
            llSay(0,"Hello " + llDetectedName(0) );
            door(DOOR_OPEN);
            state open_state;
        }
        else
        {
```

If the door should not open, check to confirm whether the unit is rented or not. If the unit is not rented, give out a notecard that describes the rental unit.

```
            if( data_rented=="" )
            {
                llGiveInventory(llDetectedKey(0),
                   "Encogia Beach Apartments");
            }
            else
            {
```

If the unit is rented, sound the door bell and announce the avatar who is at the door.

```
                llSay(0,llDetectedName(0) + " is at the door." );
                llTriggerSound("doorbell", 0.8);
            }
        }
    }
```

The **timer** event handler is called once per minute. The timer keeps the text above the door up to date, as well as sending out reminders and warnings.

```
timer()
{
```

If the unit is in a **rented** state, check to see whether any action needs to be taken.

```
if( data_rented!="" )
{
```

If it is time to remind the user that their rent is due, send the reminder.

```
if (data_leased_until > llGetUnixTime() &&
    data_leased_until - llGetUnixTime() <
    config_rentwarning * DAYSEC)
{
```

Only send the reminder if the **reminderSent** flag is false. If not for the **reminderSent** flag the rental script would bombard the user with a reminder every minute.

```
if(!reminderSent)
{
    llInstantMessage(data_rented_key,
        "Your rent is due in "+
        (string)config_rentwarning
        +" days! - " + rentalInfo());
    reminderSent = TRUE;
}
}
```

If the lease has expired, send the user a warning, that the rent is now due.

```
else if (data_leased_until < llGetUnixTime()
    && llGetUnixTime() - data_leased_until
    < config_graceperiod * DAYSEC)
{
```

Only send the reminder if the **warningSent** flag is false. If not for the **warningSent** flag the rental script would bombard the user with a reminder every minute.

```
if (!warningSent)
{
    llInstantMessage(data_rented_key,
    "Your rent is due! - " + rentalInfo());
    llInstantMessage(llGetOwner(),
    "RENT DUE - " + rentalInfo());
    warningSent = TRUE;
}
```

```
        llSetTexture("lease-ex",ALL_SIDES);
    }
```

Check to see whether the lease has expired and the grace period is up. If this is the case, evict the avatar. The avatar is sent a message telling them this. Further, the owner is informed that the apartment should be cleaned out.

```
    else if (data_leased_until < llGetUnixTime())
    {
        llInstantMessage(data_rented, "Your lease has
expired. Please clean up the space or contact the space owner.");
        llInstantMessage(llGetOwner(), "LEASE EXPIRED:
CLEANUP! -  " + rentalInfo());
```

The rental script sets up for a new tenant. However, the rental script cannot return the items from the evicted owner. This is the landlord's responsibility.

```
        data_rented = "";
        data_rented_key = "";
        allow = [];
        reminderSent = FALSE;
        warningSent = FALSE;
    }
```

Update the text for changes that may have occurred.

```
        updateText();
    }
  }
```

If the door moves, update the original position.

```
  moving_end()
  {
      originalPos = llGetPos();
  }
```

The primary door is always listening on channels zero and 72. As soon as a message is received, call the listen event handler.

```
  listen(integer channel, string name, key id, string message)
  {
```

Any message on channel 72 is a request from the secondary door to validate a user. Requests from the secondary door will be in this form:

```
[Door Name] [Avatar Name] [Security Code]
```

The door name is the object name of both the primary and secondary door. If there is to be a secondary door, it is vital that it has the same object name as the primary door. This links the primary and secondary doors.

The avatar name is the name of the avatar that is to be validated. The security code is a random number generated by the secondary door. This code must be returned to the secondary door for it to open. This provides a very minimal degree of security from a spoofed command to the secondary door.

```
if( channel==72 )
{
```

The command comes in as a comma separated value (CSV) string. Convert the CSV string to a list and obtain the individual values.

```
list l = llCSV2List(message);
string n = llList2String(l,0); // name
string w = llList2String(l,1); // who
string c = llList2String(l,2); // code
```

If this is a message to this door, attempt to validate the user.

```
if( name==llGetObjectName() )
{
```

If the user is validated successfully, the code is returned to the secondary door. This will cause the secondary door to open.

```
if( validateUser(w)==TRUE )
{
    llSay(72,c);
}
else
{
```

If the user did not validate, tell them to see the balcony door for rental terms.

```
        llSay(0,"To rent an apartment please visit the
door located on the balcony.");
        }
    }

}
```

The rest of the listen event handler is the same as Recipe 3.4, the multi-user lockable door. This allows commands to be spoken to the door by the renter, which in turn allows the list of approved avatars to be maintained. For information on these commands, or how they are processed, refer to Recipe 3.4.

When the door is opened, the **open_state** state is entered.

```
state open_state
{
    state_entry()
    {
```

Begin by setting a **timer** to automatically close the door.

```
        llSetTimerEvent(TIMER_CLOSE);
    }

    touch_start(integer num)
    {
```

Close the door if the user touches the door and does not wait for the timer.

```
        door(DOOR_CLOSE);
        llSetPos(originalPos);
        state ready;
    }

    timer()
    {
```

Close the door if the timer elapses.

```
        door(DOOR_CLOSE);
        llSetPos(originalPos);
        state ready;
    }
```

Close the door if the door is moved while in an open state.

```
    moving_start()
    {
        door(DOOR_CLOSE);
        state ready;
    }
}
```

The script examined in this section processes the primary door. The secondary door is optional.

Secondary Door

The secondary door links to the primary door. All of the secondary door's information is obtained from the primary door. Whenever someone tries to open the secondary door, the secondary door asks the primary door for permission. The secondary door is optional. For the apartment complex shown in Figure 9.1 the secondary door is open to the building's interior hallways. Figure 9.3 shows the secondary door.

Figure 9.3: The Secondary Door

The secondary door is based on Recipe 3.2, the open door. The main difference is that the **touch** event handler seeks permission from the primary door. A **listen** event handler is used to receive permission from the primary door to open. Only those parts that are different to Recipe 3.2 will be discussed. For more information on the mechanics of door opening, refer to Recipe 3.2.

This recipe creates a global variable to hold the last code sent to the server. If a message, with this code, is received, the door opens.

```
string lastCode;
```

When the door starts up the original position is saved. The object name is also displayed. The object name should be similar to "Apartment 8A". It is important that this name be the same as the primary door's name.

```
state_entry()
{
    originalPos = llGetPos();
    llSetText(llGetObjectName(),<0,0,0>,1.0);
    llListen(72, "", NULL_KEY, "");
}
```

When the door is touched, calculate a random number. Build a command based on the object name, avatar name and random code. Refer to the previous section about the master door to view the format of this command. This command is then transmitted on channel 72.

```
touch_start(integer total_number)
{
    lastCode = (string)llRound(llFrand(1000000.));
    list l = [llGetObjectName(),llDetectedName(0),lastCode];
    string str = llList2CSV(l);
    llSay(72,str);
}
```

The **listen** event handler waits for commands from the primary door.

```
listen(integer channel, string name, key id, string message)
{
```

If the primary door has requested the secondary to open, then the **open_date** state.

```
    if( message==lastCode )
    {
        door(DOOR_OPEN);
        state open_state;
    }
}
}
```

The rest of this script is the same as Recipe 3.2, the open door script. Refer to Recipe 3.2 for additional information about this script.

Other Rental Considerations

The rental script automates most of the rental process. However, it cannot perform every task. In particular, it cannot handle objects added by avatars. When an avatar rents a unit, they will likely want to furnish the area. To do this, the landlord needs to set the permissions to allow this. This can be accomplished in two ways.

- Set permissions so that anyone can drop items in the rental units
- Create a group that is allowed to drop items in the rental units

There are pros and cons to both approaches. Additionally, many rental units in Second Life use one method or the other. There does not seem to be a clear choice as to which method.

If the landlord sets the permissions so that anyone can add objects, the new renter can begin using the unit just after it has been rented. They will not have to wait to be added to a group. However, anyone will be able to create objects. As a result, the landlord must keep very close tabs on the objects created, and delete any extras from unauthorized users.

Creating the group is more secure. However, every new renter must be added to the group, as well as every evicted user removed. While this is extra work for the landlord, it also means that there will be fewer unauthorized objects. However, renters must wait to be added to the group. This requires the landlord to keep a close eye on new rental requests. A renter will not be happy if they rent the unit for seven days, and it takes the landlord five days to add them to the correct group.

Another consideration that landlords should be aware of is teleporting. A renter will most likely create a landmark to the inside of the rental unit. However, when the rent is up this allows the avatar to teleport directly back, skipping the doors. This is undesirable. Further, guests of the renter may create such land marks. This allows them to bypass the renter's door.

To protect against direct teleporting, set a landing point. Usually this landing point will be just in front of the rental complex. A landing point is set from the "About Land" window. Select the "Options" tab. This window is shown in Figure 9.4.

Figure 9.4: Setting a Landing Point

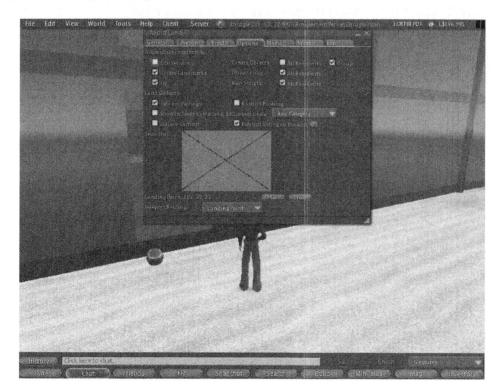

Once set, avatars will only teleport to that point. This helps when avatars attempt to teleport around doors.

Of course doors do not provide absolute security. Many users know how to get around a door. By adjusting the camera angle an avatar can see through a door. Then select something to sit on. The avatar will pass through the locked door. Despite this, doors add a basic level of security. They keep out inexperienced users, as well as make it slightly more difficult for advanced users.

Summary

The chapter expanded on the commerce scripts, introduced in Chapter 8, to include a rental script. Rental property is very popular in Second Life. The rental script automates much of the rental process. The script collects rent from avatars, handles rent extensions and sends warnings and notices when the lease is due to expire.

However, it is up to the landlord to remove objects left by the avatar after the lease expires. The landlord must keep an eye on objects left by other non-renters, if the security is set such that anyone can leave objects. A group can be created to limit who can create objects.

Second Life shares many attributes with video games. An avatar can have a health indicator between zero and 100%, just like a shootout style video game. This health is decreased by weapons. Chapter 10 shows how to create weapons in Second Life.

CHAPTER 10: WEAPONS

- Creating a Basic Gun
- Creating a Multi Bullet Gun
- Damage Bullets
- Push Bullets
- Explosion Bullets

It is possible to be hurt in Second Life. However, this may only occur in certain areas. When a user is in one of those areas they will notice a heart, and percentage number at the top of their screen. This percentage number indicates the health of the avatar. If this percentage becomes zero, the avatar dies.

Death is not all that bad in Second Life. When an avatar dies, they are warped back to wherever the home position is set. Dying is exactly the same as selecting the World menu and then "Teleport Home". Nothing more than that! When an avatar dies it loses nothing, it is simply teleported home.

Figure 10.1 shows an avatar in an area where damage can be inflicted. Notice the heart symbol at the top of the screen.

Figure 10.1: An Area that Allows Damage

This chapter will focus on guns, which are the most common type of weapon in Second Life. Bullets are just as important as the gun that fires them. This chapter presents recipes for several different bullet types.

Recipe 10.1: Basic Gun

The first gun presented in this chapter is a basic single-bullet gun. This gun should be worn on the avatar and mouselook used to fire it. Mouselook is a special mode of Second Life where the mouse controls what the avatar is looking at. In mouselook mode a small cross-hair can be seen at the center of the screen. Figure 10.2 shows mouselook mode.

Figure 10.2: Mouselook Mode

When the mouse button is clicked, the weapon will be fired. Movement works a little differently in mouselook mode. However, it is still controlled by the cursor keys. It is best to experiment with moving in mouselook mode to understand how it works.

While using the basic gun, the avatar holds the gun ready to be fired. Figure 10.3 shows an avatar holding the basic gun.

Figure 10.3: Holding a Gun

Two scripts make up the basic gun. The first script handles the gun itself. The second script is for the bullet. The effect produced by the gun is more a function of the bullet than the gun.

Basic Gun Script

First, a basic single-bullet gun script is examined. The script for the basic gun can be seen in Listing 10.1.

Listing 10.1: Basic Gun (BasicGun.lsl)

```
float SPEED         = 80.0;
integer LIFETIME    = 7;

float DELAY         = 0.2;
vector vel;
vector pos;
rotation rot;
integer have_permissions = FALSE;

integer armed = TRUE;
```

```
string bulletName = "bullet";


fire()
{
    if (armed)
    {
        armed = FALSE;
        rot = llGetRot();
        vel = llRot2Fwd(rot);
        pos = llGetPos();
        pos = pos + vel;
        pos.z += 0.75;

        vel = vel * SPEED;

        llTriggerSound("shoot", 1.0);
        llRezObject(bulletName, pos, vel, rot, LIFETIME);

        llSetTimerEvent(DELAY);
    }
}

default
{
    state_entry()
    {
        if (!have_permissions)
        {
            llRequestPermissions(llGetOwner(),
                PERMISSION_TRIGGER_ANIMATION|
                    PERMISSION_TAKE_CONTROLS);
        }
    }
    on_rez(integer param)
    {
        llPreloadSound("shoot");
    }

     run_time_permissions(integer permissions)
    {
        if (permissions == PERMISSION_TRIGGER_ANIMATION|
            PERMISSION_TAKE_CONTROLS)
        {
            llTakeControls(CONTROL_ML_LBUTTON, TRUE, FALSE);
```

```
            llStartAnimation("hold_R_handgun");
            have_permissions = TRUE;
        }
    }

    attach(key attachedAgent)
    {
        if (attachedAgent != NULL_KEY)
        {
            llRequestPermissions(llGetOwner(),
                PERMISSION_TRIGGER_ANIMATION|
                    PERMISSION_TAKE_CONTROLS);
        }
        else
        {
            if (have_permissions)
            {
                llStopAnimation("hold_R_handgun");
                llStopAnimation("aim_R_handgun");
                llReleaseControls();
                llSetRot(<0,0,0,1>);
                have_permissions = FALSE;
            }
        }
    }

    control(key name, integer levels, integer edges)
    {
        if (  ((edges & CONTROL_ML_LBUTTON) == CONTROL_ML_LBUTTON)
           &&((levels & CONTROL_ML_LBUTTON) ==
                CONTROL_ML_LBUTTON)  )
        {
            fire();
        }
    }

    timer()
    {
        llSetTimerEvent(0.0);
        armed = TRUE;
    }

}
```

The basic gun begins by defining some variables.

```
float SPEED          = 80.0;
```

```
integer LIFETIME     = 7;

float DELAY          = 0.2;
vector vel;
vector pos;
rotation rot;
integer have_permissions = FALSE;

integer armed = TRUE;
string bulletName = "bullet";
```

The **SPEED** variable defines how fast the bullet will be traveling when fired from the gun. The **LIFETIME** variable defines how many sections the bullet will last. The **DELAY** variable specifies how much time must elapse between each firing of the gun.

The **vel** and **pos** variables hold the initial velocity and position of the bullet. The **rot** variable holds the bullet's initial rotation. The **have_permissions** flag tracks whether the gun has permission to animate the avatar. These animations cause the avatar to hold the gun in a realistic manner. The armed variable is true if the gun is ready to fire. The **bulletName** variable holds the name of the bullet to be fired.

The **fire** function is called whenever the gun is to be fired.

```
fire()
{
```

First, the **fire** function checks to see whether the gun is armed.

```
    if (armed)
    {
```

The position and initial velocity are calculated for the bullet.

```
        armed = FALSE;
        rot = llGetRot();
        vel = llRot2Fwd(rot);
        pos = llGetPos();
        pos = pos + vel;
        pos.z += 0.75;

        vel = vel * SPEED;
```

A shooting sound is made and the bullet is rezzed. It is rezzed with the previously determined velocity. This causes the bullet to immediately begin heading towards its target.

```
        llTriggerSound("shoot", 1.0);
        llRezObject(bulletName, pos, vel, rot, LIFETIME);
```

A timer is set to indicate when the gun should rearm itself.

```
            llSetTimerEvent(DELAY);
    }
}
```

The **default** state begins by requesting permissions.

```
default
{
    state_entry()
    {
        if (!have_permissions)
        {
```

Two permissions are required for the gun script. The first is the animation permission. This allows the script to animate how the avatar holds the gun. The second is the permission to take the controls. This allows the avatar to fire the gun by clicking when in mouselook mode.

```
            llRequestPermissions(llGetOwner(),
                PERMISSION_TRIGGER_ANIMATION| PERMISSION_TAKE_CON-
TROLS);
        }
    }
```

Preload the shooting sound when the object is rezzed.

```
    on_rez(integer param)
    {
        llPreloadSound("shoot");
    }
```

Once permission is obtained, animate the avatar with the "hold_R_handgun" built in animation. Also take the controls for the left mouse button. The "hold_R_handgun" is a built in animation. For a complete list of built in animations, refer to Appendix B.

```
    run_time_permissions(integer permissions)
    {
        if (permissions == PERMISSION_TRIGGER_ANIMATION|
            PERMISSION_TAKE_CONTROLS)
        {
            llTakeControls(CONTROL_ML_LBUTTON, TRUE, FALSE);
            llStartAnimation("hold_R_handgun");
            have_permissions = TRUE;
        }
    }
```

The **attach** function is called whenever the avatar wears or removes the gun.

```
    attach(key attachedAgent)
    {
```

If the gun is being attached, request the appropriate controls.

```
if (attachedAgent != NULL_KEY)
{
    llRequestPermissions(llGetOwner(),
        PERMISSION_TRIGGER_ANIMATION|
            PERMISSION_TAKE_CONTROLS);
}
else
{
```

If the gun is being detached, stop the animations and release controls.

```
    if (have_permissions)
    {
        llStopAnimation("hold_R_handgun");
        llStopAnimation("aim_R_handgun");
        llReleaseControls();
        llSetRot(<0,0,0,1>);
        have_permissions = FALSE;
    }
    }
}
```

The **control** event handler is called when the avatar clicks the mouse button in mouseview mode.

```
control(key name, integer levels, integer edges)
{
    if (  ((edges & CONTROL_ML_LBUTTON) == CONTROL_ML_LBUTTON)
        &&((levels & CONTROL_ML_LBUTTON) ==
            CONTROL_ML_LBUTTON) )
    {
```

If the button has been clicked, fire the bullet.

```
        fire();
    }
}
```

The **timer** event sets armed back to true. This causes a delay between rounds fired.

```
timer()
{
    llSetTimerEvent(0.0);
    armed = TRUE;
}
}
```

Of course the gun is only half of the gun object. The bullet must also be considered.

Basic Bullet Script

The bullets are bigger than real life bullets. This makes it easier to see the bullet. Figure 10.4 shows a typical bullet next to the gun. The bullet is fairly large, relative to the size of the gun.

Figure 10.4: Basic Bullet

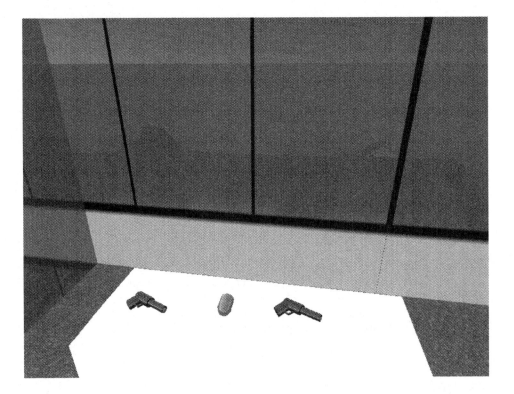

The script for the basic bullet is shown in Listing 10.2.

Listing 10.2: Basic Bullet (BulletBasic.lsl)

```
default
{
    state_entry()
    {
        llSetStatus( STATUS_DIE_AT_EDGE, TRUE);
        llSetTimerEvent(7);
        llSetDamage(20);
    }

    on_rez(integer i)
```

```
    {
        llSetBuoyancy(1.0);//  Make bullet float and not fall
        llCollisionSound("", 1.0);//  Disable collision sounds
    }

    collision_start(integer total_number)
    {
        llDie();
    }

    land_collision_start(vector pos)
    {
        llDie();
    }

    timer()
    {
        llDie();
    }
}
```

The bullet is a basic 20% damage bullet. When an avatar is touched by this bullet, 20% damage is inflicted.

```
default
{
```

The bullet is set up so that it dies at the edge of a sim. A timer is set for 7 seconds, the bullet will vanish at that point. Finally, the damage value is set.

```
    state_entry()
    {
        llSetStatus( STATUS_DIE_AT_EDGE, TRUE);
        llSetTimerEvent(7);
        llSetDamage(20);
    }

    on_rez(integer i)
    {
        llSetBuoyancy(1.0);
        llCollisionSound("", 1.0);
    }
```

The bullet should vanish if it hits something.

```
    collision_start(integer total_number)
    {
        llDie();
    }
```

The bullet should vanish if it hits land.

```
land_collision_start(vector pos)
{
    llDie();
}
```

The bullet should die when the timer is up.

```
timer()
{
    llDie();
}
}
```

The basic gun fires only one type of bullet. The next recipe shows how to create a gun that can fire a number of different bullet types.

Recipe 10.2: Multi Bullet Gun

The recipe in this chapter shows how to produce a multi-bullet gun. Six different bullet types are supported. These bullets are summarized in Table 10.1.

Table 10.1: Bullet Types

Bullet Name	Purpose
Explode	This bullet explodes when it hits something. It does no damage but produces a nice effect.
Kill	This bullet inflicts 100% damage and will instantly kill any avatar it hits.
Push	The push bullet pushes the avatar about 300 meters into the air. No damage is inflicted.
20%	The 20% bullet inflicts 20% of damage on the avatar.
Blank	The blank bullet creates no damage. It hits objects, so it could be used to shoot a can off a fence.
Cage	The cage bullet does not cause any damage, but it places a cage around the avatar it hits. The cage vanishes after one minute.

To switch between bullets simply say "load". This presents the avatar with the menu seen in Figure 10.5.

Figure 10.5: Load the Gun

The gun script for the multi-bullet gun is shown in Listing 10.3.

Listing 10.3: Multi Bullet Gun (MultiGun.lsl)

```
integer CHANNEL = 44;
float SPEED       = 80.0;

float DELAY       = 0.2;
vector vel;
vector pos;
rotation rot;
integer have_permissions = FALSE;

integer armed = TRUE;

string bulletName = "bullet:Blank";


fire()
{
```

```
    if (armed)
    {
        armed = FALSE;
        rot = llGetRot();
        vel = llRot2Fwd(rot);
        pos = llGetPos();
        pos = pos + vel;
        pos.z += 0.75;

        vel = vel * SPEED;

        llTriggerSound("shoot", 1.0);
        llRezObject(bulletName, pos, vel, rot, 10);

        llSetTimerEvent(DELAY);
    }
}

load()
{
    list bulletList = [];
    string bullet = "";
    integer i = 0;
    do
    {
        bullet = llGetInventoryName(INVENTORY_OBJECT,i);

        if( bullet!="" )
        {
            list cmd = llParseString2List(bullet,[":"],[]);

            if( llList2String(cmd,0)=="bullet" )
                bulletList+=llList2String(cmd,1);
        }
        i++;
    } while( bullet!="" );
    llDialog(llGetOwner(),"Choose a bullet type:",bulletList,
            CHANNEL);
}

default
{
    state_entry()
    {
        if (!have_permissions)
        {
```

```
            llRequestPermissions(llGetOwner(),
                PERMISSION_TRIGGER_ANIMATION|
                  PERMISSION_TAKE_CONTROLS);
        }
    llListen(0,"",llGetOwner(),"");
    llListen(CHANNEL,"",llGetOwner(),"");
    llOwnerSay("Say 'load' to change bullet type");
}
on_rez(integer param)
{
    llPreloadSound("shoot");
}


 run_time_permissions(integer permissions)
{
    if (permissions == PERMISSION_TRIGGER_ANIMATION|
        PERMISSION_TAKE_CONTROLS)
    {
        llTakeControls(CONTROL_ML_LBUTTON, TRUE, FALSE);
        llStartAnimation("hold_R_handgun");
        have_permissions = TRUE;
    }
}

listen(integer channel, string name, key id, string message)
{
    if( id==llGetOwner() && channel ==0  )
    {
        if( llToLower(message) == "load" )
        {
            load();
        }
    }
    else if( channel==CHANNEL )
    {
        bulletName = "bullet:" + message;
        llOwnerSay(message + " now loaded");
    }
}



attach(key attachedAgent)
{
    if (attachedAgent != NULL_KEY)
    {
        llRequestPermissions(llGetOwner(),
```

```
                        PERMISSION_TRIGGER_ANIMATION|
                        PERMISSION_TAKE_CONTROLS);
        }
        else
        {
            if (have_permissions)
            {
                llStopAnimation("hold_R_handgun");
                llStopAnimation("aim_R_handgun");
                llReleaseControls();
                llSetRot(<0,0,0,1>);
                have_permissions = FALSE;
            }
        }
    }

    control(key name, integer levels, integer edges)
    {
        if (  ((edges & CONTROL_ML_LBUTTON) == CONTROL_ML_LBUTTON)
            &&((levels & CONTROL_ML_LBUTTON) ==
                    CONTROL_ML_LBUTTON) )
        {
            fire();
        }
    }

    timer()
    {
        llSetTimerEvent(0.0);
        armed = TRUE;
    }

}
```

Much of the script for the multi-bullet gun is the same as the basic gun. Only the new parts will be discussed. For more information on the mechanics of firing a bullet, refer to Recipe 10.1.

Because of the menu used to load a round, the script must listen on a specific channel for menu choices. The channel chosen is 44. The multi-bullet gun uses the string **bulletName** to hold the current bullet. Notice how the bullet name is prefixed with "bullet:"? Any bullet added to the inventory of the gun object shows up in the menu if it is prefixed in this way. This allows the gun to be expanded easily with even more bullet types.

```
integer CHANNEL = 44;
string bulletName = "bullet:Blank";
```

The **load** function is called when the user has selected to load bullets into the gun.

```
load()
{
```

The script begins by creating variables to hold the list of bullets.

```
list bulletList = [];
string bullet = "";
integer i = 0;
```

Next, the **load** function loops across every inventory object. This is done using the **llGetInventoryName** function.

```
do
{
    bullet = llGetInventoryName(INVENTORY_OBJECT,i);
```

Next, the bullet name is checked to see whether it is prefixed with "bullet:". If this is the case, the bullet name is added to the list.

```
if( bullet!="" )
{
    list cmd = llParseString2List(bullet,[":"],[]);

    if( llList2String(cmd,0)=="bullet" )
        bulletList+=llList2String(cmd,1);
}
i++;
} while( bullet!="" );
```

Once an empty string is returned, the end of the script has been reached. The menu is then displayed and the user allowed to pick one.

```
llDialog(llGetOwner(),"Choose a bullet type:",bulletList,
    CHANNEL);
}
```

The **listen** event handler is called when the user either says something or loads a new bullet.

```
listen(integer channel, string name, key id, string message)
{
```

If something has been said by the owner, check to see whether the user said "load". If the user said "load", call the **load** function. The **load** function prompts the user for a bullet type.

```
if( id==llGetOwner() && channel ==0  )
{
    if( llToLower(message) == "load" )
    {
```

```
                    load();
            }
    }
```

If the message is from the menu, load the correct bullet type.

```
    else if( channel==CHANNEL )
    {
            bulletName = "bullet:" + message;
            llOwnerSay(message + " now loaded");
    }
}
```

The next section will explain how the different bullets were created.

Bullets for the Multi Bullet Gun

There is a total of six bullets that the multi-bullet gun comes preloaded with, as summarized in Table 10.1. These bullet types can be broken down into the following groups.

- Damage Bullets
- Explosion Bullets
- Push Bullets
- Cage Bullets

Each of these group types will be covered in the next sections.

Damage Bullets

Three different damage bullets are included with the gun. The blank bullet does not cause any damage. The 20% bullet inflicts 20% damage. The kill bullet inflicts 100% damage and kills an avatar instantly on impact. The script for the blank bullet is shown in Listing 10.4.

Listing 10.4: Blank Bullet (BulletBlank.lsl)

```
default
{
    on_rez(integer delay)
    {
        llSetStatus( STATUS_DIE_AT_EDGE, TRUE);
        llSetDamage(0);
        llSetBuoyancy(1.0);//  Make bullet float and not fall
        llCollisionSound("", 1.0);//  Disable collision sounds

        if (delay >0 )
        {
            llSetTimerEvent(delay);
        }
```

```
    }

    collision_start(integer total_number)
    {
    }

    land_collision_start(vector pos)
    {
    }

    timer()
    {
        llDie();
    }

}
```

The blank bullet causes no damage because of the following line:

```
llSetDamage(0);
```

While zero damage is the default behavior, the above line emphasizes that for demonstration purposes.

The gun also includes a 20% damage bullet. The 20% damage bullet is shown in Listing 10.5.

Listing 10.5: 20% Bullet (Bullet20.lsl)

```
default
{
    on_rez(integer delay)
    {
        llSetStatus( STATUS_DIE_AT_EDGE, TRUE);
        llSetDamage(20);
        llSetBuoyancy(1.0);//  Make bullet float and not fall
        llCollisionSound("", 1.0);//  Disable collision sounds

        if (delay >0 )
        {
            llSetTimerEvent(delay);
        }
    }

    collision_start(integer total_number)
    {
    }
```

```
    land_collision_start(vector pos)
    {
    }

    timer()
    {
        llDie();
    }

}
```

The 20% bullet specifies 20% damage with the following line.

```
llSetDamage(20);
```

The final damage bullet provided is a kill bullet. The kill bullet can be seen in Listing 10.6.

Listing 10.6: Kill Bullet (BulletKill.lsl)

```
default
{
    on_rez(integer delay)
    {
        llSetStatus( STATUS_DIE_AT_EDGE, TRUE);
        llSetDamage(100);
        llSetBuoyancy(1.0);//  Make bullet float and not fall
        llCollisionSound("", 1.0);//  Disable collision sounds

        if (delay >0 )
        {
            llSetTimerEvent(delay);
        }
    }

    collision_start(integer total_number)
    {
    }

    land_collision_start(vector pos)
    {
    }

    timer()
    {
        llDie();
```

```
    }

}
```

The kill bullet specifies 100% damage, an instant kill, with the following line.

```
llSetDamage(100);
```

The damage bullets are all the same, except for the amount of damage they inflict.

Explosion Bullets

The explosion bullet causes a small explosion on impact with either an agent, an object or the ground. The explosion bullet can be seen in Listing 10.7.

Listing 10.7: Explosion Bullet (BulletExplode.lsl)

```
fakeMakeExplosion(integer particle_count, float particle_scale,
float particle_speed,
                float particle_lifetime, float source_cone,
string source_texture_id,
                vector local_offset)
{
    //local_offset is ignored
    llParticleSystem([
        PSYS_PART_FLAGS,PSYS_PART_INTERP_COLOR_MASK|
            PSYS_PART_INTERP_SCALE_MASK|
            PSYS_PART_EMISSIVE_MASK|PSYS_PART_WIND_MASK,
        PSYS_SRC_PATTERN,              PSYS_SRC_PATTERN_ANGLE_CONE,
        PSYS_PART_START_COLOR,         <1.0, 1.0, 1.0>,
        PSYS_PART_END_COLOR,           <1.0, 1.0, 1.0>,
        PSYS_PART_START_ALPHA,         0.50,
        PSYS_PART_END_ALPHA,           0.25,
        PSYS_PART_START_SCALE,         <particle_scale,
            particle_scale, 0.0>,
        PSYS_PART_END_SCALE,           <particle_scale * 2 +
            particle_lifetime, particle_scale * 2 +
            particle_lifetime, 0.0>,
        PSYS_PART_MAX_AGE,             particle_lifetime,
        PSYS_SRC_ACCEL,                <0.0, 0.0, 0.0>,
        PSYS_SRC_TEXTURE,              source_texture_id,
        PSYS_SRC_BURST_RATE,           1.0,
        PSYS_SRC_ANGLE_BEGIN,          0.0,
        PSYS_SRC_ANGLE_END,            source_cone * PI,
        PSYS_SRC_BURST_PART_COUNT,     particle_count / 2,
        PSYS_SRC_BURST_RADIUS,         0.0,
        PSYS_SRC_BURST_SPEED_MIN,      particle_speed / 3,
```

```
                PSYS_SRC_BURST_SPEED_MAX,     particle_speed * 2/3,
                PSYS_SRC_MAX_AGE,            particle_lifetime / 2,
                PSYS_SRC_OMEGA,             <0.0, 0.0, 0.0>
                ]);
}

explode()
{
        fakeMakeExplosion(80, 1.0, 13.0, 2.2, 1.0, "fire",
            <0.0, 0.0, 0.0>);
        llSleep(.5);
        fakeMakeExplosion(80, 1.0, 13.0, 2.2, 1.0, "smoke",
            <0.0, 0.0, 0.0>);
        llSleep(1);
        llParticleSystem([]);
}

default
{
    on_rez(integer delay)
    {
        llSetStatus( STATUS_DIE_AT_EDGE, TRUE);
        llSetDamage(0);
        llSetBuoyancy(1.0);     //  Make bullet float and not fall
        llCollisionSound("", 1.0); //  Disable collision sounds

        if (delay >0 )
        {
            llSetTimerEvent(delay);
        }
    }

    collision_start(integer total_number)
    {
        explode();
    }

    land_collision_start(vector pos)
    {
        explode();
    }

    timer()
    {
        llDie();
    }
```

```
}
```

The explosion bullet uses the explosion script from Recipe 4.5. The following two event handlers cause the explosion.

```
collision_start(integer total_number)
{
    explode();
}

land_collision_start(vector pos)
{
    explode();
}
```

When the bullet collides with either an object, avatar or land the explosion function is called. For more information on how the explosion is created see recipe 4.5.

Push Bullets

The push bullet applies a large push to any avatar it hits. The avatar is sent high into the sky. No damage is caused. The push bullet can be seen in Listing 10.8.

Listing 10.8: Push Bullet (BulletPush.lsl)

```
default
{
    on_rez(integer delay)
    {
        llSetStatus( STATUS_DIE_AT_EDGE, TRUE);
        llSetDamage(0);
        llSetBuoyancy(1.0);//  Make bullet float and not fall
        llCollisionSound("", 1.0);//  Disable collision sounds

        if (delay >0 )
        {
            llSetTimerEvent(delay);
        }
    }

    collision_start(integer total_number)
    {
        if (llDetectedType(0) & AGENT)
        {
            llPushObject(llDetectedKey(0), <0,0,2147483647>,
                ZERO_VECTOR, FALSE);
```

```
        }
        llDie();
    }

    timer()
    {
        llDie();
    }

}
```

The push bullet detects a collision using the **collision_start** event handler.

```
collision_start(integer total_number)
{
```

Once a collision is detected, it is checked to see whether it collided with an avatar.

```
        if (llDetectedType(0) & AGENT)
        {
```

If the collision was with an avatar, push the avatar up with maximum force.

```
            llPushObject(llDetectedKey(0), <0,0,2147483647>, ZERO_
VECTOR, FALSE);
        }
        llDie();
}
```

Once the push has been applied, the bullet is no longer needed and is destroyed with a call to **llDie**.

Cage Bullets

The cage bullet places a cage around the avatar it hits. The cage disappears in a minute. While the cage is blocking the avatar's path, the avatar can still teleport away. An avatar in a cage can be seen in Figure 10.6.

Figure 10.6: An Avatar in a Cage

The cage bullet can be seen in Listing 10.9.

Listing 10.9: Cage Bullet (BulletCage.lsl)

```
default
{
    on_rez(integer delay)
    {
        llSetStatus( STATUS_DIE_AT_EDGE, TRUE);
        llSetDamage(0);
        llSetBuoyancy(1.0);//  Make bullet float and not fall
        llCollisionSound("", 1.0);//  Disable collision sounds

        if (delay >0 )
        {
            llSetTimerEvent(delay);
        }
    }

    collision_start(integer total_number)
    {
```

```
        if (llDetectedType(0) & AGENT)
        {
            llRezObject("Cage", llDetectedPos(0), ZERO_VECTOR,
ZERO_ROTATION, 0);
        }
    }

    timer()
    {
        llDie();
    }

}
```

The cage bullet detects a collision using the **collision_start** event handler.

```
collision_start(integer total_number)
{
    if (llDetectedType(0) & AGENT)
    {
        llRezObject("Cage", llDetectedPos(0), ZERO_VECTOR,
            ZERO_ROTATION, 0);
    }
}
```

The cage object, which is in the bullet's object inventory, is rezzed over the avatar.

Summary

Weapons are one of the more video game like elements of Second Life. Avatars have a health number which is slowly decreased as the avatar takes more damage. This is similar in concept to a video game. This chapter showed how to create a gun and several bullet types.

The gun primarily fires a bullet in a specific direction. The nature of damage inflicted is completely determined by the bullet. This chapter provided six bullet types. The blank causes no damage. The 20% bullet inflicts 20% damage. The kill bullet kills instantly. The cage bullet puts a cage around an avatar. The push bullet pushes the avatar high into the air. The explosion bullet causes a small explosion.

Wearable items are not just limited to clothes. Often wearable objects contain scripts that provide a wide array of tasks. The next chapter will discuss wearable scripted objects.

CHAPTER 11: WEARABLE OBJECTS

- Creating a Parachute
- Understanding Heads Up Display (HUD)
- Flying with a Jet Pack
- Creating an Anti Push Bracelet

For many people, wearable objects are one of the biggest elements of the Second Life experience. There is a wide array of items for sale that attach to avatars. This includes clothing, jewelry, shoes, hair, and many other items. Considerable money in the Second Life world is spent on avatar attachments, or wearable objects.

Usually these wearable objects do not contain scripts. However, some very interesting wearable objects can be created when scripts are used. This chapter explains how wearable objects are constructed.

Recipe 11.1: Parachute

Parachuting is another example of a real world activity that has found its way into Second Life. This is in spite of the fact that parachutes are completely unneeded in Second Life. In Second Life, avatars can fly. Even when they do fall, they can hit the ground as hard as they like and suffer no damage. After a particularly bad fall, an avatar just gets up and dusts himself off.

However, parachuting is still popular in Second Life. A parachute is worn on the back of an avatar. Figure 11.1 shows an avatar wearing a parachute.

Figure 11.1: Wearing a Parachute

Figure 11.2 shows an avatar parachuting.

Figure 11.2: Parachuting in Second Life

The parachute in this recipe is fairly easy for the avatar to operate. Simply get high in the air. There are many ways to do that. Then start falling. Once the avatar starts falling the parachute begins operating. Once the parachute detects that it is within 150 meters of the ground it will deploy. The parachute script can be seen in Listing 11.1.

Listing 11.1: Parachute (Parachute.lsl)

```
displayChute(float alpha)
{
    llSetLinkPrimitiveParams(2,[PRIM_COLOR, ALL_SIDES,<1,1,1>,
            alpha ]);
    llSetLinkPrimitiveParams(3,[PRIM_COLOR, ALL_SIDES,<1,1,1>,
            alpha ]);
    llSetLinkPrimitiveParams(4,[PRIM_COLOR, ALL_SIDES,<1,1,1>,
            alpha ]);
    llSetLinkPrimitiveParams(5,[PRIM_COLOR, ALL_SIDES,<1,1,1>,
            alpha ]);
    llSetLinkPrimitiveParams(6,[PRIM_COLOR, ALL_SIDES,<1,1,1>,
            alpha ]);
}
```

```
integer calculateGroundDistance()
{
    vector pos = llGetPos();
    float ground = llGround(pos);
    float distance = llRound(pos.z-ground);
    return (integer)distance;
}

displayGroundDistance()
{
    llSetText("Distance to Ground: " +
            (string)calculateGroundDistance(),<0,1,0>,1);
}



default
{
    attach(key id)
    {
        if(id)
        {
            state attached;
        }
    }
}


state attached
{
    state_entry()
    {
        displayChute(0);
        llSetTimerEvent(1);
        llRequestPermissions(llGetOwner(),
            PERMISSION_TRIGGER_ANIMATION);
        llPreloadSound( "parachute" );

    }

    attach(key id)
    {
        if(id==NULL_KEY)
        {
            state default;
        }
    }
```

```
    }

    timer()
    {
        if(  (llGetAgentInfo(llGetOwner()) & AGENT_IN_AIR) &&
            !(llGetAgentInfo(llGetOwner()) & AGENT_FLYING) )
        {
            state falling;
        }
        displayGroundDistance();
    }
}

state falling
{
    state_entry()
    {
        llSetTimerEvent(1);
    }

    timer()
    {
        integer dist = calculateGroundDistance();

        if( (dist<150) && (dist>20) )
            state deployed;
        displayGroundDistance();
    }

    attach(key id)
    {
        if(id==NULL_KEY)
        {
            state default;
        }
    }
}

state deployed
{
    state_entry()
    {
        llTriggerSound("parachute",1);
        displayChute(1);
        llSetTimerEvent(0.1);
        llStopAnimation("falldown");
```

```
        llStartAnimation("hover");
    }

    timer()
    {
        // on the ground
        if (    !(llGetAgentInfo(llGetOwner()) & AGENT_IN_AIR) &&
            !(llGetAgentInfo(llGetOwner()) & AGENT_FLYING) )
        {
            llStopAnimation("hover");
            state attached;
        }

        // started flying
        if( llGetAgentInfo(llGetOwner()) & AGENT_FLYING)
        {
            llStopAnimation("hover");
            state attached;
        }

        vector v = llGetVel();
        if( v.z < -7 )
        {
            llPushObject(llGetOwner(), <0,0,7>,
                ZERO_VECTOR, FALSE);
        }

        displayGroundDistance();
    }

    attach(key id)
    {
        if(id==NULL_KEY)
        {
            llStopAnimation("hover");
            state default;
        }
    }
}
```

The parachute script begins by defining some useful functions that it will use for its operation. The **displayChute** function is used to either display or hide the chute. This is done by passing it an alpha value. This alpha value will be applied to all of the components of the chute, but not the backpack. An alpha is basically a transparency. A value of zero is invisible and a value of one is solid. The display chute function uses the **llSetLinkPrimitiveParms** function to set each of the components to the specified alpha.

```
displayChute(float alpha)
{
    llSetLinkPrimitiveParams(2,[PRIM_COLOR, ALL_SIDES,<1,1,1>,
            alpha ]);
    llSetLinkPrimitiveParams(3,[PRIM_COLOR, ALL_SIDES,<1,1,1>,
            alpha ]);
    llSetLinkPrimitiveParams(4,[PRIM_COLOR, ALL_SIDES,<1,1,1>,
            alpha ]);
    llSetLinkPrimitiveParams(5,[PRIM_COLOR, ALL_SIDES,<1,1,1>,
            alpha ]);
    llSetLinkPrimitiveParams(6,[PRIM_COLOR, ALL_SIDES,<1,1,1>,
            alpha ]);
}
```

It is easy to determine the altitude that an avatar is at. Figure 11.3 shows an avatar standing on the beach, notice the altitude.

Figure 11.3: Avatar on the Ground at Low Altitude

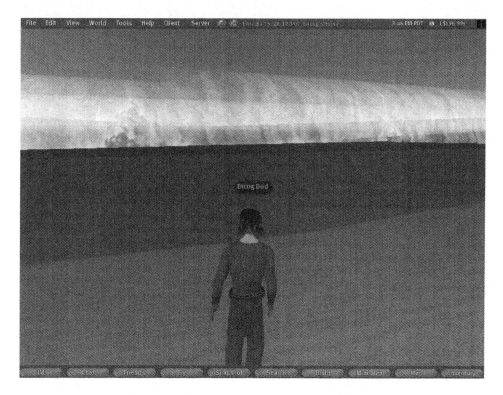

The altitude is the third number on the same line as the menu bar. This is the z-coordinate, or altitude. Because the avatar is standing on the beach it is almost zero. Zero means that the avatar is near sea level, not that they are on the ground. Figure 11.4 shows the avatar standing on the ground again.

Figure 11.4: Avatar on the Ground at High Altitude

However, this time the z-coordinate is much hither. The avatar is much further inland and on higher ground. The parachute wants to deploy at around 150 meters above the ground. This must be calculated, the z-coordinate alone will not show the height above the ground. The **calculateGroundDistance** function is used to calculate how far above the ground the avatar is.

```
integer calculateGroundDistance()
{
```

First, obtain the current position of the avatar. Then query Second Life to determine the height of the ground at that point.

```
vector pos = llGetPos();
float ground = llGround(pos);
```

The distance above the ground is the difference between the z-coordinate and the ground height.

```
float distance = llRound(pos.z-ground);
return (integer)distance;
}
```

The parachute constantly displays the current distance from the ground. This display is updated by the **displayGroundDistance** function.

```
displayGroundDistance()
{
    llSetText("Distance to Ground: " +
            (string)calculateGroundDistance(),<0,1,0>,1);
}
```

The **default** state of the parachute does nothing more than wait for the parachute to be attached. Once the parachute is attached, the parachute moves on to the **attached** state.

```
default
{
    attach(key id)
    {
        if(id)
        {
            state attached;
        }
    }
}
```

The **attached** state begins by hiding the chute, in case it was not hidden already.

```
state attached
{
    state_entry()
    {
        displayChute(0);
```

The parachute sets one second timer events. These control when the chute deploys. The parachute deploy sound is preloaded.

```
        llSetTimerEvent(1);
        llRequestPermissions(llGetOwner(),
            PERMISSION_TRIGGER_ANIMATION);
        llPreloadSound( "parachute" );

    }
```

If the parachute is detached, return to the **default** state.

```
attach(key id)
{
    if(id==NULL_KEY)
    {
        state default;
    }
}
```

The **timer** event handler checks to see whether the avatar starts to fall. This check is made by calling **llGetAgentInfo**. If the agent is in the air, but they are not flying, then they are falling. The following lines check this.

```
timer()
{
    if(   (llGetAgentInfo(llGetOwner()) & AGENT_IN_AIR) &&
        !(llGetAgentInfo(llGetOwner()) & AGENT_FLYING) )
    {
```

If the agent is falling, enter the **falling** state.

```
        state falling;
    }
```

Update the ground distance display as part of the timer event.

```
        displayGroundDistance();
    }
}
```

The **falling** state waits until it is time to deploy the parachute. It is necessary to have a **falling** state so that the parachute does not deploy during regular flight.

```
state falling
{
```

As soon as the **falling** state begins, set a **timer** event for one second.

```
    state_entry()
    {
        llSetTimerEvent(1);
    }
```

The **timer** event will be called each second.

```
    timer()
    {
```

During the **timer**, calculate the ground distance.

```
        integer dist = calculateGroundDistance();
```

If the distance is between 20 and 150 meters, deploy the chute. If the avatar is below 20 meters, there is no longer time to deploy the chute.

```
    if( (dist<150) && (dist>20) )
        state deployed;
    displayGroundDistance();
}
```

If the avatar detaches the parachute then return to the **default** state.

```
attach(key id)
{
    if(id==NULL_KEY)
    {
        state default;
    }
}
}
```

The **deployed** state occurs while the avatar is falling to the ground with the chute on.

```
state deployed
{
    state_entry()
    {
```

First, the parachute sound is played and the chute displayed. A **timer** is setup to occur ten times a second. The hover animation is begun.

```
        llTriggerSound("parachute",1);
        displayChute(1);
        llSetTimerEvent(0.1);
        llStopAnimation("falldown");
        llStartAnimation("hover");
    }
```

The avatar is now falling. The fall needs to be slowed to make the parachute seem realistic. The timer, which is called ten times per second, applies a force to slow the fall.

```
    timer()
    {
```

If the avatar has touched down on the ground, return to the **attached** state. This hides the chute.

```
        if (    !(llGetAgentInfo(llGetOwner()) & AGENT_IN_AIR) &&
            !(llGetAgentInfo(llGetOwner()) & AGENT_FLYING) )
        {
            llStopAnimation("hover");
            state attached;
```

```
        }
```

The avatar may also start flying in the middle of a drop. If this is the case, return to the **attached** state. This hides the chute.

```
        // started flying
        if( llGetAgentInfo(llGetOwner()) & AGENT_FLYING)
        {
            llStopAnimation("hover");
            state attached;
        }
```

Check to see how fast the avatar is falling. Do not allow the avatar to fall faster than -7.

```
        vector v = llGetVel();
        if( v.z < -7 )
        {
```

If the avatar is falling too fast, apply upward force to slow the avatar.

```
        llPushObject(llGetOwner(), <0,0,7>, ZERO_VECTOR,
FALSE);
        }
        displayGroundDistance();
    }
```

As a part of the **timer** event, display the ground distance.

Recipe 11.2: HUD Parachute

Heads Up Displays or HUDs, are a common feature of many Second Life objects. Perhaps more control over the object is needed than is available with the motion keys. A HUD allows a control panel to be attached to the screen. The user can click on the control panel to determine what the object does. A HUD display is shown in Figure 11.5.

Figure 11.5: A HUD Display

This recipe presents a manual parachute. Rather than deploying automatically, this recipe uses a HUD to allow that avatar to specify when to deploy and when to hide. The parachute script is shown in Listing 11.2.

Listing 11.2: HUD Parachute (ParachuteHUD.lsl)

```
integer CHANNEL = 155;

displayChute(float alpha)
{
    llSetLinkPrimitiveParams(2,[PRIM_COLOR, ALL_SIDES,<1,1,1>,
      alpha ]);
    llSetLinkPrimitiveParams(3,[PRIM_COLOR, ALL_SIDES,<1,1,1>,
      alpha ]);
    llSetLinkPrimitiveParams(4,[PRIM_COLOR, ALL_SIDES,<1,1,1>,
      alpha ]);
    llSetLinkPrimitiveParams(5,[PRIM_COLOR, ALL_SIDES,<1,1,1>,
      alpha ]);
    llSetLinkPrimitiveParams(6,[PRIM_COLOR, ALL_SIDES,<1,1,1>,
      alpha ]);
}
```

```
integer calculateGroundDistance()
{
    vector pos = llGetPos();
    float ground = llGround(pos);
    float distance = llRound(pos.z-ground);
    return (integer)distance;
}

displayGroundDistance()
{
    llSetText("Distance to Ground: " +
      (string)calculateGroundDistance(),<0,1,0>,1);
}


default
{
    attach(key id)
    {
        if(id)
        {
            state attached;
        }
    }
}


state attached
{
    state_entry()
    {
        displayChute(0);
        llSetTimerEvent(1);
        llRequestPermissions(llGetOwner(),
            PERMISSION_TRIGGER_ANIMATION);
        llPreloadSound( "parachute" );
        llListen( CHANNEL, "", NULL_KEY, "" );

    }

    attach(key id)
    {
        if(id==NULL_KEY)
        {
            state default;
```

```
        }
    }

    listen(integer channel, string name, key id, string message)
    {
        llSay(0,message);
        if( message=="open" )
            state deployed;
    }

    timer()
    {
        displayGroundDistance();
    }
}

state falling
{
    state_entry()
    {
        llSetTimerEvent(1);
        llListen( CHANNEL, "", NULL_KEY, "" );
    }


    timer()
    {
        integer dist = calculateGroundDistance();
        displayGroundDistance();
    }

    attach(key id)
    {
        if(id==NULL_KEY)
        {
            state default;
        }
    }
}

state deployed
{
    state_entry()
    {
        llTriggerSound("parachute",1);
```

```
        displayChute(1);
        llSetTimerEvent(0.1);
        llStopAnimation("falldown");
        llStartAnimation("hover");
        llListen( CHANNEL, "", NULL_KEY, "" );
    }

    listen(integer channel, string name, key id, string message)
    {
        if( message=="close" )
            state attached;
    }

    timer()
    {
        vector v = llGetVel();
        if( v.z < -7 )
        {
            llPushObject(llGetOwner(), <0,0,7>,
                    ZERO_VECTOR, FALSE);
        }

        displayGroundDistance();
    }


    attach(key id)
    {
        if(id==NULL_KEY)
        {
            llStopAnimation("hover");
            state default;
        }
    }
}
```

Much of the HUD parachute is the same as Recipe 11.1. Only the parts of Recipe 11.2 that are different from 11.1 will be explained. For more information on how the parachute actually deploys, refer to Recipe 11.1.

The HUD parachute needs to listen on a channel for instructions from the HUD. Channel 155 was selected.

```
integer CHANNEL = 155;
```

The **listen** event handler listens on channel 155. Once an open command is received from the HUD, the chute is deployed.

```
listen(integer channel, string name, key id, string message)
{
     if( message=="open" )
          state deployed;
}
```

There is a similar **listen** event handler in the deployed state. This event handler waits for a close message. When the close message is received, the chute closes and returns to the **attached** state.

```
listen(integer channel, string name, key id, string message)
{
     if( message=="close" )
          state attached;
}
```

The HUD for the parachute is very simple. A single block forms the control panel backing for the HUD. Additionally, two blocks form the "Open" and "Close" buttons. The script for close is shown in Listing 11.3.

Listing 11.3: Close Parachute (ParaClose.lsl)

```
integer CHANNEL = 155;

default
{

    touch_start(integer total_number)
    {
        llSay(CHANNEL,"close");
    }
}
```

The parachute also includes an open button. The open button's script is shown in Listing 11.4.

Listing 11.4: Open Parachute (ParaOpen.lsl)

```
integer CHANNEL = 155;

default
{

    touch_start(integer total_number)
    {
        llSay(CHANNEL,"open");
    }
```

```
}
```

Both buttons use **llSay** to either send the "open" or "close" commands.

Recipe 11.3: Jet Pack

Jet packs can be very helpful in Second Life. While an avatar does not need a jet pack to fly, a jet pack allows an avatar to fly much higher than is normally allowed. Without assistance, an avatar cannot fly higher than 200 meters.

Using the jet pack is easy, simply attach it to the avatar. Once attached, fly normally. The jet pack will take over and allow the avatar to fly very high. Figure 11.6 shows an avatar wearing a jet pack.

Figure 11.6: A Jet Pack

Listing 11.5 shows the jet pack script.

Listing 11.5: Jet Pack (JetPack.lsl)

```
default
{
```

```
    state_entry()
    {
        llReleaseControls();
    }

    attach(key id)
    {
        if(id)
        {
            state attached;
        }
    }
}

state attached
{
    state_entry()
    {
        llSetTimerEvent(1);
    }

    attach(key id)
    {
        if(id==NULL_KEY)
        {
            state default;
        }
    }

    timer()
    {
        if (llGetAgentInfo(llGetOwner()) & AGENT_FLYING)
        {
            state flying;
        }
    }
}

state flying
{
    state_entry()
    {
        llRequestPermissions(llGetOwner(),
            PERMISSION_TAKE_CONTROLS);
        llSetTimerEvent(1);
    }
```

```
run_time_permissions(integer perm)
{
    if (perm & PERMISSION_TAKE_CONTROLS) {
        llTakeControls(CONTROL_UP|CONTROL_FWD|
            CONTROL_BACK, TRUE, FALSE);
    }
}

attach(key id)
{
    if(id==NULL_KEY)
    {
        state default;
    }
}

timer()
{
    vector pos = llGetPos();
    llSetText("Altitude: " + (string)pos.z, <0,1,0>, 1 );

    if (!(llGetAgentInfo(llGetOwner()) & AGENT_FLYING)  )
    {
        llReleaseControls();
        state attached;
    }
}

control(key id, integer held, integer change)
{
    if (held & CONTROL_UP)
    {
        llPushObject(llGetOwner(), <0,0,2>,
            ZERO_VECTOR, FALSE);
    }
    else if (held & CONTROL_FWD)
    {
        rotation rot = llGetRot();
        vector vel = llRot2Fwd(rot);

        if( llGetAgentInfo(llGetOwner()) & AGENT_FLYING )
            vel*=4;
        else
            vel/=2;
```

```
        llPushObject(llGetOwner(), vel, ZERO_VECTOR, FALSE);
        }
    }
}
```

The jet pack starts in a **default** state. This state serves only to wait to be attached.

```
default
{
    state_entry()
    {
```

The script releases controls when the **default** state is either entered or re-entered.

```
        llReleaseControls();
    }

    attach(key id)
    {
        if(id)
        {
```

Once the jet pack has been attached, enter the **attached** state.

```
            state attached;
        }
    }
}
```

The primary purpose of the **attached** state is to wait for the avatar to start to fly. Once the avatar is in flight, the jet pack kicks in.

```
state attached
{
    state_entry()
    {
```

Set a one second timer to begin waiting for the avatar to take flight.

```
        llSetTimerEvent(1);
    }
```

If the jet pack is detached, return to the **default** state.

```
    attach(key id)
    {
        if(id==NULL_KEY)
        {
            state default;
        }
    }
```

Once per second, check to see whether the avatar is in flight. Once the avatar is in flight begin the **flying** state.

```
timer()
{
    if (llGetAgentInfo(llGetOwner()) & AGENT_FLYING)
    {
        state flying;
    }
}
}
```

If the avatar is in a **flying** state, take the controls. This is how the jet pack works. The controls are taken over and forces are applied when the avatar hits each of the controls.

```
state flying
{
    state_entry()
    {
```

First, request to take the controls. Then set a time for one second intervals.

```
        llRequestPermissions(llGetOwner(),
            PERMISSION_TAKE_CONTROLS);
        llSetTimerEvent(1);
    }
```

If permission is granted, take control of the up, forward and backward controls.

```
    run_time_permissions(integer perm)
    {
        if (perm & PERMISSION_TAKE_CONTROLS) {
            llTakeControls(CONTROL_UP|CONTROL_FWD|
                CONTROL_BACK, TRUE, FALSE);
        }
    }
```

If the jet pack is detached, while in the **flying** state, return to the **default** state.

```
    attach(key id)
    {
        if(id==NULL_KEY)
        {
            state default;
        }
    }
```

The **timer** event handler is called every second.

```
    timer()
    {
```

First, display the altitude, which is the z-coordinate.

```
vector pos = llGetPos();
llSetText("Altitude: " + (string)pos.z, <0,1,0>, 1 );
```

Check to see whether the agent is not flying.

```
if (!(llGetAgentInfo(llGetOwner()) & AGENT_FLYING)  )
{
```

If the agent is no longer flying, release the controls and enter the **attached** state.

```
    llReleaseControls();
    state attached;
}
}
```

The **control** event handler is called whenever the avatar pushes one of the control keys that the script has taken control of.

```
control(key id, integer held, integer change)
{
```

If the upward control is pressed, apply an upward push to the avatar.

```
if (held & CONTROL_UP)
{
    llPushObject(llGetOwner(), <0,0,2>, ZERO_VECTOR,
        FALSE);
}
```

If the user presses forward, apply a forward push.

```
else if (held & CONTROL_FWD)
{
```

Determine which direction the avatar is facing and obtain a single unit velocity to propel the avatar in that direction.

```
rotation rot = llGetRot();
vector vel = llRot2Fwd(rot);
```

Next determine whether the avatar is flying. If they are flying, multiply **vel** by 4, otherwise divide **vel** by 2.

```
if( llGetAgentInfo(llGetOwner()) & AGENT_FLYING )
    vel*=4;
else
    vel/=2;

llPushObject(llGetOwner(), vel, ZERO_VECTOR, FALSE);
}
```

```
    }
}
```

Finally, the object is pushed in the direction that was determined as forward.

Recipe 11.4: Anti-Push Bracelet

Second Life has developed its own culture and rules. The notion of what is rude in Second Life often mirrors real life. One action that is considered very rude in Second Life is pushing. Avatars will often push each other simply to "grief" other players. Griefing is common term heard in the online game world. Wikipedia defines a griefer as: "A griefer is a slang term used to describe a player in an online video game who plays the game simply to cause grief to other players through harassment."

Pushing is one of the most common forms of griefing in Second Life. However, it is easy enough to stop pushing. Anti-push bracelets are somewhat common in Second Life. An anti-push bracelet is not hard to create. Listing 11.6 contains the script for an anti-push script.

Listing 11.6: Anti Push Script (NoPush.lsl)

```
integer locked;
float LOCKTIME = 1.0;

default
{
    state_entry()
    {
    }


    on_rez(integer start_param)
    {
        llRequestPermissions(llGetOwner(),
            PERMISSION_TAKE_CONTROLS);
        locked = FALSE;
    }


    run_time_permissions(integer perm)
    {
        if(perm & (PERMISSION_TAKE_CONTROLS))
        {
            llTakeControls(CONTROL_FWD|
                CONTROL_BACK|
                CONTROL_RIGHT|
                CONTROL_LEFT|
                CONTROL_ROT_RIGHT|
```

```
                    CONTROL_ROT_LEFT|
                    CONTROL_UP|
                    CONTROL_DOWN,
                    TRUE, TRUE);

            llSetTimerEvent(1);
        }
    }

    control(key id, integer level, integer edge)
    {
        if (locked)
        {
            llMoveToTarget(llGetPos(), 0);
            locked = FALSE;
        }
        llResetTime();
    }

    timer()
    {
        if ((!locked) && (llGetTime() > LOCKTIME))
        {
            llMoveToTarget(llGetPos(), 0.2);
            locked = TRUE;
        }
    }
}
```

The anti-push script begins by declaring two variables.

```
integer locked;
float LOCKTIME = 1.0;
```

The **locked** variable determines whether the avatar is locked in its current position, and cannot be pushed. The **LOCKTIME** specifies the number of seconds the avatar must stand still before it will lock and be unpushable.

```
on_rez(integer start_param)
{
    llRequestPermissions(llGetOwner(),
        PERMISSION_TAKE_CONTROLS);
    locked = FALSE;
}
```

The runtime permissions attempts to take control of all movement controls.

```
run_time_permissions(integer perm)
{
```

```
if(perm & (PERMISSION_TAKE_CONTROLS))
{
        llTakeControls(CONTROL_FWD|
            CONTROL_BACK|
            CONTROL_RIGHT|
            CONTROL_LEFT|
            CONTROL_ROT_RIGHT|
            CONTROL_ROT_LEFT|
            CONTROL_UP|
            CONTROL_DOWN,
            TRUE, TRUE);
```

Cause a **timer** event to occur every second. The **timer** will move the avatar back to its locked position every second.

```
        llSetTimerEvent(1);
    }
}
```

When the avatar moves, unlock the position. The locking is not to interfere with regular movement.

```
control(key id, integer level, integer edge)
{
    if (locked)
    {
```

Unlock the target. The value of zero removes the damping set up by the timer event handler.

```
        llMoveToTarget(llGetPos(), 0);
        locked = FALSE;
    }
    llResetTime();
}
```

If the avatar has been in the same location for more than the **LOCKTIME**, lock the avatar in place. The **llMoveToTarget** function call places a damper on the avatar's movement. This locks the avatar in place.

```
timer()
{
    if ((!locked) && (llGetTime() > LOCKTIME))
    {
        llMoveToTarget(llGetPos(), 0.2);
        locked = TRUE;
    }
}
```

With the damping effect created by **llMoveToTarget**, no motion can occur.

Summary

This chapter explained how to create scripts for items that an avatar wears. Recipes were provided for parachutes, HUDs, jet packs and no-push bracelets. Wearable items are very popular in Second Life. Scripts only enhance their appeal.

This is the final chapter of this book. There will likely be future editions as Second Life evolves. We are always looking for suggestions for additional examples for future books. If you have any suggestions or comments on this book feel free to contact us at support@heatonresearch.com.

Heaton Research occasionally schedules classes in the Second Life world. These are almost always free of charge. To keep up to date on our Second Life events, consider joining the Second Life Group:

```
Heaton Research Courses
```

Simply search for it under groups! We hope you find these examples useful. Happy scripting!

Stop by and visit Heaton Research in Second Life. We own the island of Encogia, which can be found at the following URL:

```
http://slurl.com/secondlife/Encogia/197/191/23
```

Happy scripting!

APPENDIX A: DOWNLOADING EXAMPLES

This book contains many source code examples. You do not need to retype any of these examples; they all can be downloaded from the Internet.

Simply go to the site:

`http://www.heatonresearch.com/download/`

This site will give you more information on how to download the example programs.

All examples in this book can also be obtained as actual Second Life objects. This is done inside of Second Life itself. The examples can be found at the Heaton Research HQ. Stop by and visit Heaton Research in Second Life. We own the island of Encogia, which can be found at the following URL:

`http://slurl.com/secondlife/Encogia/197/191/23`

APPENDIX B: BUILT IN ANIMATIONS

Second Life includes many built in animations that can be used with the **llStartAnimation** function. These animations are listed here.

```
aim_l_bow
aim_r_bazooka
aim_r_handgun
aim_r_rifle
angry_fingerwag
angry_tantrum
away
backflip
blowkiss
bow
brush
busy
clap
courtbow
crouch
crouchwalk
dance1
dance2
dance3
dance4
dance5
dance6
dance7
dance8
dead
drink
express_afraid
express_afraid_emote
express_anger
express_anger_emote
express_bored
express_bored_emote
express_cry
express_cry_emote
express_disdain
express_embarrassed
express_embarrassed_emote
```

```
express_frown
express_kiss
express_laugh
express_laugh_emote
express_open_mouth
express_repulsed
express_repulsed_emote
express_sad
express_sad_emote
express_shrug
express_shrug_emote
express_smile
express_surprise
express_surprise_emote
express_tongue_out
express_toothsmile
express_wink
express_wink_emote
express_worry
express_worry_emote
falldown
female_walk
fist_pump
fly
flyslow
hello
hold_l_bow
hold_r_bazooka
hold_r_handgun
hold_r_rifle
hold_throw_r
hover
hover_down
hover_up
impatient
jump
jumpforjoy
kick_roundhouse_r
kissmybutt
land
laugh_short
motorcycle_sit
musclebeach
no_head
no_unhappy
nyanya
```

```
peace
point_me
point_you
prejump
punch_l
punch_onetwo
punch_r
rps_countdown
rps_paper
rps_rock
rps_scissors
run
salute
shoot_l_bow
shout
sit
sit_female
sit_generic
sit_ground
sit_to_stand
sleep
smoke_idle
smoke_inhale
smoke_throw_down
snapshot
soft_land
stand
stand_1
stand_2
stand_3
stand_4
standup
stretch
stride
surf
sword_strike_r
talk
throw_r
tryon_shirt
turn_180
turnback_180
turnleft
turnright
type
walk
whisper
```

```
whistle
wink_hollywood
yes_happy
yes_head
yoga_float
```

Appendix C: Event Functions

Second Life includes many events that a script can register to process. These events are listed here.

```
at_rot_target( integer tnum, rotation targetrot, rotation ourrot )

at_target( integer tnum, vector targetpos, vector ourpos )

attach( key id )

changed( integer change )

collision( integer num_detected )

collision_end( integer num_detected )

collision_start( integer num_detected )

control( key id, integer level, integer edge )

dataserver( key queryid, string data )

email( string time, string address, string subj, string
      message, integer num_left )

http_response( key request_id, integer status, list
      metadata, string body )

land_collision( vector pos )

land_collision_end( vector pos )

land_collision_start( vector pos )

link_message( integer sender_num, integer num, string str,
      key id )

listen( integer channel, string name, key id,
      string message )

money( key id, integer amount )
```

```
moving_end( )

moving_start( )

no_sensor( )

not_at_rot_target( )

not_at_target( )

object_rez( key id )

on_rez( integer start_param )

remote_data( integer event_type, key channel, key
      message_id, string sender, integer idata,
      string sdata )

run_time_permissions( integer perm )

sensor( integer num_detected )

state_entry( )

state_exit( )

timer( )

touch( integer num_detected )

touch_end( integer num_detected )

touch_start( integer num_detected )
```

INDEX

A

Acceleration of particles   101, 108, 112, 116, 154, 240, 246

age   101, 105-6, 108, 112, 114, 116-7, 119, 154, 239-40, 245, 309-10

agent   129, 131-2, 141-2, 146, 159-60, 171, 177-80, 182-3, 186-7, 197-8, 226, 321-2, 326-8, 335-6, 338-9

air   123, 143, 157, 163, 174, 195, 198, 300, 314, 319, 321-2, 326-7

airplane   135, 149, 158, 162, 169

alpha   101-2, 105, 109, 113, 117, 119, 154, 240, 246, 309, 319, 322-3, 329

altitude   68, 96, 323-4, 336, 339

analog clocks   193, 195, 199-202

angle   74, 101-2, 104, 106, 108-10, 112-4, 116-7, 119, 153-4, 200-1, 239-40, 245-6, 309

  particles   104

  patterns   102, 106, 109, 113, 117, 154, 240, 246

  specified   134, 152

angular   128, 130, 134, 136-9, 145, 147-50, 152, 158-9, 161-3, 165-6, 168-70, 173

  deflection   135-6, 138, 150, 162

    efficiency   138, 162

  friction   149, 163

  motor velocity   136-7

animate   96, 129, 132, 146, 160, 167, 171, 226-9, 293-7, 303-4, 320, 325, 330

animation permission   226, 296

anti-push bracelets   340

apartment   277-8, 280-3

attach   226, 294, 296, 303, 317, 320-2, 325-7, 330-2, 334-8

automatic door   177, 184-5

automatically giving notecards   177

avatar   37-41, 131-2, 180-4, 190-3, 197-8, 223-9, 236-8, 250-7, 275-8, 284-6, 289-91, 311-4, 323-4, 326-9, 337-42

  attachments   317

  cannon   195-6

  detaches   327

  name   192, 280-1, 284

  standing   323-4

  touching   44

  wears   296, 343

avataronsittarget   227-9

B

bank, smooth controlled   151

banking   135-6, 145, 149, 151, 159, 163-4, 168-70

barometric formula   204

basic

  emitter script   107

  particle emitter   99, 100, 103

beach   323-4

Beach Front Land in Second Life   68

boat   121, 123, 133, 139, 143-6, 148-53, 155-6, 167-8, 171, 174

  banks   151

  controls   152

  functions   148

  sets   148-9

  shares   143

  wake   153

BOAT Hovers   135

boat script   144, 156

Boat in Second Life   144

Boat.lsl   144

BoatWake.lsl   153

Bounce   100, 103, 107, 111, 115, 135, 153, 239, 244-5

bouncy   136-7

bracelets   114

buildings   35, 67, 69, 71, 73, 75-7, 79, 81, 83, 85, 87-91, 93, 95-7, 106, 282

  apartment   269-70

bullet   290, 292-3, 295, 297-309, 312, 314

  basic   298

  blank   300, 306-7

  cage   300, 306, 312-4

  collides   311

  Explode   289, 306, 309, 314

  explodes   300

  float   299, 306-8, 310-1, 313

  Kill   308

  load   305

  push   289, 300, 306, 311-2, 314

  real life   298

types 290, 300, 302, 304-6, 314
BulletBasic.lsl 298
BulletBlank.lsl 306
BulletCage.lsl 313
BulletExplode.lsl 309
BulletKill.lsl 308
BulletPush.lsl 311
BUOYANCY 145, 150, 159, 163, 168, 170
BUOYANCY Value 136

C

cage 300, 312-4
calculateGroundDistance 320-1, 325-6, 330-1
camera 134, 148-9, 226
camper 229, 233-7
camping 223-5, 266
  control script 226, 229, 233
  object 226
  pad 223-5, 227-9, 231, 233-7, 266
  scripts 225-6, 228, 233, 238
  in Second Life 223
Camping Default State 234
camping pad
  owner 234
  script 226
Camping Pad Control 229
camping pad control script 229
Camping Pad Dance Script 226
Camping Ready State 236
cannon 193, 195-8, 221
  recipe 195, 197
capital 60
Car 123-4, 133-4, 140
Car Script 127
Car in Second Life 125
CAR Vehicle 135
changed
  event handler 131, 141, 156, 166, 174, 197, 228
  owners 219
channel 39, 40, 43, 96, 242, 250, 276, 280-1, 284,
    303-6, 332-3
characters, length of 52, 54
CHILDREN 129, 146, 156, 160, 166
chimney 99, 106-7, 110, 121
  object 110
  script 106-7, 110, 121
    completed 107
chute 322, 325, 327-8, 333
clock 199, 201, 221
cloud 202-4

Club Tip Jar 243-4, 251-2, 255-6
collision 69, 70, 299, 300, 307-8, 310-4
color 40-2, 46
COLOR 100-1, 103, 105-8, 110-3, 115-9, 153-4,
    239-40, 245-6, 309, 319, 323, 329
color component 41
COLOR Specifi 105
color value 41
Colors fade 100, 107, 111, 115, 153, 239, 245
Commerce 221, 223, 225, 227, 229, 231, 233, 235,
    237, 239, 241, 243, 245, 247, 265-7
commerce scripts 275, 286
Communication Function Distance 40
communication functions 39, 40
compare 46, 49, 51-2, 54-6, 58
  function 54
  Function 54
  strings 49, 64
compareLen 51-2, 54-5, 57
  Function 52
  method 54-5
compareNoCase 51, 55-6, 58
  Function 54
  function works 54
compareNoCaseLen 51, 54, 57
  Function 54
Comparing Strings 49
cone 101, 104, 108, 112, 116, 118-9, 154, 239, 245,
    309
CONE 101, 104, 108, 112, 116, 119, 153-4, 239,
    245, 309
CONE Particles 104
config 230, 234, 247, 249, 252, 255, 259, 262, 271-
    2, 274-7, 279
configuration
  information 195, 235-6
  notecard 225, 235, 251-5, 258, 261
configure 207
constants 39, 73, 271
CONTROL 130-1, 133-4, 147-8, 152, 160-2, 164-6,
    172-3, 293-4, 296-7, 303-4, 336, 338-42
  access 270
  event handler 133-4, 151, 153, 164-5, 174, 297,
    339
  keys 133, 339
  panel 328, 333
  system 166
controls 129-33, 138, 146-8, 151-3, 160, 162-4,
    171-2, 174, 226, 259, 293-4, 296-7, 303-4,
    335-6, 338-42
  backward 164, 338
  external 135

mouse 290
   movement 341
   release 297
   take 338, 341
   upward 339
conversations 38, 80, 86
coordinate
   planes 133, 149
   system 74, 163, 165
count 99, 118-9, 309
CSV
   list 254
   string 281
cube 70, 214, 270
   rectangular 70
cursor 76
   keys 131, 133, 291

D

damage 289-90, 299, 300, 306-9, 311, 314, 317
   bullets 289, 299, 306-7, 309
      final 308
      value 299
dance 226-9
dataserver 209, 211-3, 217, 220, 232, 235, 248,
      254, 261, 264
date 215, 217-9, 221, 272, 279, 284, 343
DAYSEC 188, 192, 271, 274, 279
Deflection 128, 135-8, 145, 149-50, 158-9, 162,
      168-70
degrees 70, 72, 74, 77, 81, 110, 114, 152, 186, 201
Degrees Celsius 203-4
delay 293, 295-7, 302, 306-8, 310-1, 313
delimited
   substring 62
   word 86
delta 72, 74, 77, 81, 186
descriptive text 233
Detecting Avatars 191
dialog 41-3, 46, 94, 243
   answers 92, 94
Digital clocks 199
digits 58-60, 218
direction 71-4, 77, 80-1, 130, 133-4, 137, 142, 145,
      147-9, 151-2, 161-6, 172-3, 185-6, 204-5,
      339-40
   opposite 74, 133, 152
   variable 73
Disable collision sounds 299, 306-8, 310-1, 313
doorbell 78-9, 82, 86, 278

sound 79, 86
doors 64, 67, 70-1, 73, 76, 85, 97, 270, 276, 285-6
drive 127, 131-2, 139-40, 144, 156-7, 171, 174

E

elevator 64, 67, 88, 90-7
   call 91, 93-4, 96
emitted particle 101, 108, 112, 116, 154, 240, 245-6
emitter 100-1, 103-4, 107-8, 111-2, 115-6, 153,
      239, 245
   angle, narrow 117
Encog Dod 61, 64, 258
Encogia 90, 276, 278, 343
ending
   particle size 102, 106, 109, 113, 117, 154, 240,
      246
   RGB color 101, 108, 113, 117, 154, 240, 246
   transparency 102, 105, 109, 113, 117, 154, 240,
      246
entertainers 243
entry event handler initializes 134
environment 174, 177, 193
EOF 209, 211-3, 232, 235, 248, 254, 261, 264
Euler form 72, 77, 81, 186
event 37, 94, 131, 180, 326, 342
   handler 37-9, 43, 75, 79, 85-6, 131, 167, 174,
      178, 180, 192, 283, 312, 333
      dataserver 210-1, 213, 235-6, 264
      entry 38-9, 140, 148, 162
      message 156, 167
      money 234, 242, 253, 256, 263, 276
      permissions 131
      sensor 178, 184, 191
      touch 85, 283
      timer 201
explode 118-9, 300, 310-1
explosion 101, 104, 108, 112, 116, 118-21, 153,
      239, 245, 309, 311, 314
   recipe 120
exponential timescale 137

F

fakeMakeExplosion function 118-20, 309-10
fall 121, 139, 299, 306-8, 310-1, 313, 317, 326-8
   leafs 111, 114
flashes 117
flight 337-8
floor 67, 91, 93-7, 225

fly   123, 171, 174, 317, 326, 334, 337, 339
flying, started   322, 328
friction   125-6, 135, 139, 149, 163
function call   70, 141

G

generalParticleEmitterOff   102, 109, 113, 117, 154-
        6, 240, 246
generalParticleEmitterOn   100, 102-3, 107, 109,
        111, 113, 115, 117, 153, 155, 157, 239, 241-
        2, 244, 250
glass   125-6
glitter   114, 121
glow   101, 103, 108, 112, 116, 153, 239, 245
grief   340
griefer   340
ground   126, 135, 149, 158, 163-4, 309, 317, 319-
        20, 322-5, 327, 330
    distance   326, 328
group   43-6, 243-4, 247, 249, 251, 253, 255, 284-6,
        306, 343
gun   290-2, 294-8, 300-1, 303-7, 314
    basic single-bullet   289-92, 294, 304
    multi-bullet   289, 300-1, 304, 306
    object   297, 304
    script   296, 301

H

health   286, 289
Heaton Research   90, 343
    in Second Life   343
helicopter   123, 133, 139, 157-8, 160, 162-7
    controls   164-6
hovering   135-6, 143, 145, 148-50, 163, 168, 322,
        327-8, 332
HUD   317, 328-9, 332-3, 343
    parachute   328-9, 332

I

images   114, 205, 262
informational text   236
inner angle   102, 109, 113, 117, 154, 240, 246
instant messages   38, 40, 46, 187, 216, 219-20, 253,
        277
instructional text   197
inventory   70, 101, 105, 108, 112, 116, 154, 184,
        207, 234, 239, 245, 302, 304-5

isAlpha   60-1
isAlphanumeric   60-1
isNumeric   59-61, 64
isOnline   216-7, 220-1

J

jet pack   317, 334, 337-8, 343
jewelry   97, 99, 114-5, 121, 317
    particle emitter   115
    script   115, 117
job   224-5

L

land   76, 99, 123, 143, 166, 174, 190, 193, 224, 299,
        300, 307-8, 310-1
    owners   224
    parcel of   223, 238, 266, 269
landing point   285
landlord   273, 280, 284-6
language   35
leaf generator   110-1
leafs   112, 114
lease   276-7, 279-80, 286
    new   276-7
Linden Dollars   224, 257, 259
Linden Scripting Language   35-7, 39-41, 46, 49, 85,
        90, 121, 254
Linden Scripting Language Wiki   120
linear
    deflection   138, 150, 162
    motor velocity   137
    velocity   137-8, 162
link   89, 90, 127, 129, 131, 141, 146, 155-6, 159-60,
        166-7, 171, 197-8, 227-8, 259-60, 262-3, 265
linked
    message   156
    objects   262
list   42-3, 80, 85-7, 103, 181-4, 190-2, 206, 209-12,
        217-8, 248, 254, 261-2, 272-3, 281, 305
listen event handler   39, 85-6, 94, 174, 243, 280-1,
        284, 305, 333
llAbs   275
llAvatarOnSitTarget   89, 90, 92, 94, 129, 131, 141,
        146, 159, 171, 197-8, 227-8, 231, 237
llCloud   203-4
llCollisionSound   299, 306-8, 310-1, 313
llCSV2List   248, 254, 281
llDeleteSubList   183-4

llDetectedKey 42, 44, 78-9, 82, 85, 180-1, 183-4, 189, 192, 216, 241, 243, 250, 256, 311-2

llDetectedName 44-5, 78-9, 82, 85-6, 189, 191, 216, 219-20, 248, 253, 278, 284

llDetectedPos 180-1, 314

llDetectedType 311-2, 314

llDetectGroup 46

llDialog 42-3, 92, 94, 241, 243, 302, 305

llDie 299, 300, 307-8, 310, 312, 314

llEuler2Rot 72, 74, 77, 81, 92, 94, 186

llGetAgentInfo 321-2, 326-8, 335-6, 338-9

llGetInventoryName 302, 305

llGetListLength 83, 87, 180-1, 183-4, 189-90, 192, 206, 208, 210, 248, 254, 259-60, 262-3

llGetNotecardLine 209-13, 232, 235-6, 247, 249, 252, 255, 261, 264

llGetObjectName 281, 283-4

llGetOwner 78-9, 82, 85-6, 171, 189-90, 192-3, 230, 240-3, 250, 256, 279-80, 302-3, 320-2, 325-8, 335-41

llGetParcelDetails 189, 191

llGetPermissions 227-9

llGetPermissionsKey 227-9

llGetPos 72, 75, 78, 82, 92, 95, 180-1, 186, 189, 191, 203-4, 273, 276, 280, 341-2

llGetRegionName 216, 220

llGetRot 72, 74, 77, 81, 88-90, 158, 186, 293, 295, 302, 336, 339

llGetSubString 50, 52, 56, 59, 61, 63, 81, 265

llGetSunDirection 203-4

llGetTime 341-2

llGetUnixTime 274, 277, 279-80

llGetVel 130, 133, 142-3, 147, 152, 172, 322, 328, 332

llGetWallclock 188, 192, 200-1, 215, 218

llGiveInventory 183-4, 260, 263, 276, 278

llGiveMoney 231, 237, 250, 256, 277-8

llGround 320, 324, 330

llInstantMessage 40, 190, 193, 216, 220, 231, 237, 248-9, 253, 255, 277, 279-80

llKey2Name 40, 180-1, 240-2, 248, 250, 254, 256, 273, 276-7

llList2CSV 190, 192, 284

llList2Integer 180-1, 215, 218, 249, 254

llList2String 84, 87, 180-1, 205-6, 208, 215, 218, 259, 262, 281, 302, 305

llListen 38, 40, 42, 82, 92, 94, 170, 241-2, 250, 256, 276, 283, 303, 330-2

  function 39

llListFindList 82, 85, 92, 94, 183-4, 189, 191, 273

llListSort 180-1

llLog10 203-4

llLoopSound 129, 132, 146, 160, 171

llMoveToTarget 341-2

llOwnerSay 40, 303, 306

llParseString2List 64, 215, 218, 302, 305

llParticleSystem 100, 102-3, 106-7, 109, 111, 113, 115, 117-8, 120-1, 153, 155, 239-40, 244, 246, 309-10

llPow 203-4

llPreloadSound 119, 128, 135, 145, 148, 158, 170, 293, 296, 303, 320, 325, 330

llPushObject 129, 132, 146, 159, 171, 197-8, 311-2, 322, 328, 332, 336-7, 339

llRegionSay 40, 96

llReleaseControls 129, 132, 147, 160, 172, 294, 297, 304, 335-7, 339

llRemoveVehicleFlags 148, 168

llRequestAgentData 217, 220

llRequestPermissions 129, 132, 146, 160, 171, 227-8, 230, 234, 247, 252, 275, 293-4, 296-7, 303, 340-1

llResetScript 72, 75, 77, 82, 129, 132, 147, 160, 172, 186, 189-90, 215, 219, 230-1, 234

llResetTime 341-2

llRezObject 293, 295, 302, 314

llRot2Fwd 293, 295, 302, 336, 339

llRound 200-1, 215, 218, 284, 320, 325, 330

llSay 35-40, 44-5, 51, 55, 58, 60, 78-9, 82-9, 92-5, 189-92, 209-13, 231-2, 235-6, 247-8, 276-8

llSensor 177

llSensorRepeat 178-80, 182-3, 186-7, 189, 191

llSetBuoyancy 299, 306-8, 310-1, 313

llSetCameraAtOffset 128, 135, 145, 148, 158, 170

llSetCameraEyeOffset 128, 135, 145, 148, 158, 170

llSetColor 41, 43, 217, 220-1

  function 41

llSetDamage 298-9, 306-11, 313

llSetLinkPrimitiveParams 200-1, 259, 262, 319, 323, 329

llSetPayPrice 249, 254, 259, 262, 275

llSetPos 73, 76, 78, 84, 93, 95, 187, 273, 282

llSetRot 72, 74, 77, 81, 158, 186, 294, 297, 304

llSetSitText 89, 90, 128, 134, 144, 148, 158, 170, 226, 228

llSetStatus 127, 129, 132, 146, 160, 171-2, 298-9, 306-8, 310-1, 313

llSetText 88, 90, 92, 94, 96, 119, 180-1, 196-7, 203-4, 212-3, 216-7, 219-21, 229-30, 234, 241-2

llSetTexture 205-6, 208, 274, 280

llSetTextureAnim 69, 70, 142-3, 166-7, 226, 228

llSetTimerEvent 37-8, 73-5, 77-8, 92-3, 95, 197-8, 200-1, 203, 206-8, 212-3, 296-9, 306-8, 320-1, 325-7, 330-2 llSetVehicleFlags 145, 148, 168

llSetVehicleFloatParam 128, 135, 138-9, 145, 149-51, 158-9, 162-4, 168-70

llSetVehicleRotationParam 135, 137, 145, 151, 169

llSetVehicleType 128, 135, 138, 145, 148, 158, 162, 168-9

llSetVehicleVectorParam 128, 130, 133-5, 137, 139, 145, 147-9, 152, 159, 161-6, 168-70, 172-3

llSitTarget 88-90, 92, 94, 128, 134, 140-1, 144, 148, 158, 170, 196-7, 226, 228, 230, 236

llSleep 89, 90, 119-21, 129, 132, 146, 160, 171-2, 190, 192, 310

llStartAnimation 227-9, 294, 296, 303, 322, 327, 332

llStopAnimation 227-8, 294, 297, 304, 321-2, 327-8, 332

llStopSound 129, 132, 146, 160, 172

llStringLength 51, 54-5, 57, 59, 83, 87, 274

llStringTrim 62-3, 81

llSubStringIndex 50, 52, 56, 59, 61-2, 81

llTakeControls 130-1, 147, 160, 172, 293, 296, 303, 336, 338, 340, 342

llTargetOmega 102, 109, 113, 117, 129, 132, 147, 154, 160, 172, 240, 246

llToLower 39, 41, 43, 50-1, 54-5, 57, 83, 86, 249, 255, 303, 305

llToUpper 82-3, 85, 87, 273

llTriggerSound 69, 70, 72, 74, 77-9, 81-2, 86, 119-20, 129, 132, 146, 171, 186, 272-3, 278, 293

llUnSit 89, 90, 129, 132, 141-2, 146, 159, 171, 197-8, 232, 238

llVecDist 180-1

llVecMag 130, 133, 142-3, 147, 152, 172, 203-4

llVolumeDetect 69, 70

llWater 203-4

llWhisper 40, 216, 219-20

llWind 203-4

locks 341-2

lowercase 55, 60

M

malls 257

MarkAntony 212-3

materials 125-6

maximum
  burst 105
  strength 136

MENU, dialog channel list 91-4

meters 67, 88, 93, 105, 143, 177, 180, 300, 319, 324, 327, 334

midnight 187, 190-3, 201

minimum burst 105

money 221, 223-6, 229, 231, 233-4, 236-8, 241-2, 248, 250-1, 253, 256, 260, 263, 266, 275-8
  amount of 233, 235
  collected 266
  free 230, 234

motor 127-8, 130, 133-9, 145, 147-52, 159, 161-6, 168-70, 172-3
  angular 123, 133-4, 136, 138, 150-2, 163, 165-6, 174
  linear 133, 137-8, 149-50, 152, 163-6

Mouselook 149, 290

mouselook mode 290-1, 296

Multi-floor buildings 67

Multi-User Lockable Door 79, 80

N

named
  name 39
  value 36

non-scripted objects 96

notecard 182-4, 195, 207, 209-13, 220, 232-3, 235, 243, 248, 254, 258, 261, 264, 276, 278
  giver 182-3
  line 210, 213
  loading 208, 210, 229, 233, 259
  query 213, 251

Notecard Controlled Slide 207-8

NotecardGiver.lsl 182

NotecardReader.lsl 211

NotecardSlideShow.lsl 208

numeric 49, 56, 59

O

object 35-41, 43-6, 56, 61, 64, 70, 127, 131, 177-8, 205-7, 219-21, 223-4, 257, 284, 286
  communication 46
  cycles 207
  inventory 110, 114, 183, 205, 259, 314
  name 280, 283-4
  stops 213
  window 125

objects
  listen 38
  owner 40

OFFLINE 217, 221

offset, horizontal texture 70

OMEGA 102, 109, 113, 117, 119, 154, 240, 246, 310
online 214, 217, 220-1
Online Detector 214, 216-7, 219-21
onlyContains 58-9
opaque 101, 105, 109, 113, 117, 154, 240, 246
open door 67, 70-1
owner
  club 243, 251, 256, 266
  evicted 280
  locked door 67, 76-7
ownership 253

P

pairs, name-value 103-4
parachute 195, 317-21, 324-7, 330-3, 343
  recipe 195
parachuting 317
Parachuting in Second Life 319
parameters 38-9, 41, 52, 54, 58, 62, 120-1, 177-8, 254
parcel 189-91
parcelName 189-91, 193
parse 63-4, 218, 254
particle
  emission 105
  emitter scripts 106, 121, 153
    basic 99, 106, 110, 121, 153
  emitters 99, 103, 105, 111, 114-5, 121, 242
    leaf 111
  scripts 121, 157
    basic 106, 111, 114-5, 118, 121
  streams 202
  system 103, 106, 121
  texture 101, 105, 108, 110, 112, 116, 154, 239, 245
Particle Effects 99, 101, 103, 105, 107, 109, 111, 113, 115, 117, 119, 121, 242
particles 97, 99-101, 103, 105-8, 111-2, 114-6, 119-21, 153-4, 239-40, 245-6, 309-10
  emit 99, 105-6
  emitting 121
  explode 101, 108, 112, 116, 153, 239, 245
  explosion 120
  follow 100, 107-8, 111-2, 115-6, 153, 239, 245
  producing 106
  red 99, 106, 121
Particles start 101, 104, 106, 108, 112, 116, 153, 239, 245
passenger seat 140-1

passengers 139-40
Paying Money 223
Permission 129, 132, 146, 160, 171, 226-30, 234, 247, 252, 275, 293-4, 296-7, 303-4, 335-6, 340-2
  obtaining 131
  requests 226, 252, 275
permissions 130-1, 147, 160, 172, 226-7, 230, 234-5, 247, 252, 275, 282-4, 292-7, 301-4, 338, 340-1
  event handler processes 252
person 79
Physical objects 127, 132, 177
physics 126, 129, 132, 146, 160, 171-2
PI 119, 129, 132, 147, 160, 172, 177-80, 182-3, 186-7, 189, 191, 309
pool, swimming 68-9
pop 62-3, 83, 86-7
  Function 62
  function works 86
pressure, barometric 203-4
Primary Door 270-1
primitives 99, 106, 121, 125-7, 140-1, 143, 199, 226, 257
purchase 223, 260, 263
pushing 340

Q

quaternions 74

R

RAD 72, 74, 77, 81, 102, 109, 113, 154, 186, 200-1
radar 177-81, 193
radians 74, 106, 177
  rotation 72, 74, 77, 81, 186
RADIUS 101, 108, 112, 116, 119, 154, 240, 245, 309
Radius of emission 101, 108, 112, 116, 154, 240, 245
ramps 88, 97
receiver 233, 236-8
Receiving Money 223
reciever 229-32
refund 276, 278
  partial 277
region 40, 88, 96, 257
rent 270, 272, 274-6, 278-9, 281, 285-6
rental 272-3, 285

primary 271
process 284, 286
property 266, 269, 271, 273, 275, 277, 279, 281,
    283, 285-7
script 223, 269-70, 279-80, 286
  automates 284, 286
  primary 271
  sets 280
units 276, 278, 284-5
Rental Door 269
rentalInfo 277, 279-80
rented state 279
renter 272-3, 276-8, 281, 284-5
renting 269, 276
request permission 226, 229, 234, 251, 275
rez 72, 75, 77, 82, 186, 189-90, 215, 219, 230, 234,
    241, 298-9, 306-8, 310-1, 340-1
RGB color 105
roll 143, 149, 152, 157, 165, 168
Roof 91, 93
root prim 127, 138, 140-1, 144, 151, 156, 158, 167
rotate 69, 70, 74, 76, 88-90, 128, 132-4, 138-41,
    144, 146, 148-9, 151-2, 167, 169-70, 196-7,
    314
rotation
  delta 71, 74, 77, 80, 185
  patterns 106
Rotation of ANGLE patterns 102, 109, 113, 117,
    154, 240, 246
Rotation Point Vehicle Parameters 138
rotation rot 71, 74, 77, 80, 158, 185, 292, 295, 301,
    336, 339
rotors 157, 166
rubber 125-6
rude 340
runtime permissions 341

S

sale 223, 257, 264, 317
sample objects 70
scan 177-8, 180, 190
  llSensor function 177
  llSensorRepeat function 177
scanners 174, 177, 179, 181, 183, 185, 187, 189-91,
    193
scanning frequency 180, 183
screen 289-90, 328
script
  active 177
  announcer 211, 213

anti-push 340-1
cannon 197
changed 133
complex 91
configuration 221
creators 207
custom 223
dance 226, 228-9
default 35
explosion 118, 311
file 195
following 36, 38, 42-5
helicopter 158, 162, 166
navigation 259
navigational 259
parachute 319, 322, 329
programmer 49
releases controls 337
rotor 167
single 226
teleport 89
traffic 191-2
vehicle 127
wake 153, 156
scripted object 97, 177
sea level 68, 203-4
seat 127, 140-1, 144
Second Life Standard Time 201
Second Life Store 257
Second Life Vehicles 124
Second life water 67
Second Life world 64, 67, 70, 90, 317, 343
Secondary Door 269, 280, 282-3
security 79, 85, 281, 286
  code 280-1
  owner 43
sensor 177-80, 183-4, 186-7, 189, 191
  repeating 180, 183, 190
set 56, 60, 62-3, 70, 75-6, 106, 134-5, 137-8, 151-2,
    190-3, 198, 219, 275-6, 284-6, 299
  empty 106
  functions 58
  membership functions 59
  permissions 284
  vehicle parameters 173
shoot 198, 293, 295-6, 300, 302-3
shooting 195, 198
shouldOpen 82, 85, 273, 278
SlideControl 208, 210
SlideControl.not 208
Slideshow 195, 209, 211
  loading data 209-10

Smart Door 67, 80

smoke 97, 99, 106, 108, 110, 118-21, 310
  puffs of 110, 121

sounds 70, 132-3, 135, 143, 148, 158, 273, 278
  open 74, 272
  shooting 295-6
  splash 69, 70, 96

splash 67, 69, 70

Splashing Water 67, 69

stairs 88, 97

Starting
  slide 206-7, 209
  transparency 101, 105, 109, 113, 117, 154, 240,
    246

Starting particle size 102, 106, 109, 113, 117, 154,
    240, 246

Starting RGB color 101, 108, 112, 116, 154, 240,
    246

state
  command 37
  engines 37
  machines 35, 37

stores 223, 269

string parsing 49, 61, 63

strings, parsing 49, 64

substrings 61

success 248, 253

sun 203-4

Super Car 123, 167, 258

support user 36

T

take money 226, 251

teleport 89, 90, 123, 193, 285, 312
  pad 67, 88-90, 97

temperature 203-4

text files 195

textual information 264

texture 70, 96, 101, 106, 108, 110, 112, 114, 116-
    20, 199-201, 205-8, 210-1, 259, 262, 309
  animation 70, 228
  correct 274
  key 104

textured object 121

time 38-40, 62-4, 105-6, 130-2, 135-6, 192, 199,
    215, 217-9, 233-5, 252, 273-5, 277, 295-6,
    326-7

timer 37-8, 73, 75-8, 94-5, 190-3, 198, 202-4, 206-
    7, 212-3, 282, 299, 300, 307-8, 326-7, 335-8,
    341-2

call 38

event 37-8, 76, 198, 272, 325-6, 328
  handler 38, 95, 192, 207, 256, 279, 326, 338,
    342
  sets 297
  updates 237
  interval 198

timescales 137

timespan 274

tip
  jar 223, 238-40, 242-4, 246-8, 250-3, 255-6, 266
  claim 249, 255
  claimed 256
  club style 243
  owner 243, 251, 253, 255
  price list 248, 254

tips 243, 248, 251, 253, 255-6, 266
  suggested 254

tires 126

touch 36-8, 42-5, 72-3, 75-6, 78-9, 84-6, 96, 102,
    109, 113, 118-9, 206-8, 212-3, 243, 250-1
  events 41

traffic 223-4, 238
  scanner 187-8, 190, 192

trees 110, 121

U

unauthorized objects 285

Understanding State Machines 35

unit 270, 272, 274, 278-9, 284-5

unlock 342

user 39, 40, 42-3, 61, 64, 67, 75-6, 79, 80, 85-90,
    133, 152, 164-6, 195, 220-1, 279-82, 305
  advanced 286
  approaches 184
  authorized 86
  average 202, 224
  evicted 285
  functions 46

User names in Second Life 87

user, unauthorized 284

users, inexperienced 76, 286

Using Notecards for Configuration 195

UUID 101, 105, 108, 112, 116, 154, 239, 245

V

vehicle
  parameters 135, 138, 148, 167

type   123, 134-5, 138, 162, 174
z-axis   137
vehicle engine   143
Vehicle Materials   125
vehicles   43, 97, 99, 121, 123-9, 131, 133-45, 147,
     149, 151, 153, 157-9, 161-3, 167-9, 173-5
  air   123, 143, 166, 202
  air-based   162
  flying   157
  ground   123, 149
  hover   149
  sea   166, 174
velocity   100-1, 103-4, 107-8, 111-2, 115-6, 120,
     137, 153, 239, 245
  initial   295
vendor   257, 259
  object   223, 262, 264-5
  script   257-8
    main   259, 261, 265
Vendor Navigation Scripts   264
Vendor Notecard   258
Vendor.not   258-9
video games   286, 314
visitors   187, 190, 192-3
  unique   188-90, 192
visitorsYesterday   190, 192-3

WheelScript.lsl   142
wiki.secondlife.com   120
wind   100, 103, 107, 111, 115, 119, 121, 153, 202-5,
     239, 245, 309
  direction   204
window, object properties   44
wood   125

W, X, Y, Z

wake   143, 153-6
warnings   272, 277, 279, 286
warningSent   277, 279-80
  flag   279
water   67-70, 96, 121, 135, 143, 145, 148-50, 168
  artificial   143
  texture   68
  vehicles   123
waves   121, 143, 153
weapons   286, 289-91
Weapons   289, 291, 293, 295, 297, 299, 301, 303,
     305, 307, 309, 311, 313-5
wearable
  objects   314, 317, 319, 321, 323, 325, 327, 329,
     331, 333, 335, 337, 339, 341, 343
  scripted objects   314
weather   193, 195, 202
  conditions   202
  monitoring Second Life   195
  station   202-3
    recipe   203
wheels   129, 142-3, 158